THE ROMANCE OF INTERPRETATION

THE ROMANCE
OF
INTERPRETATION

Visionary Criticism from Pater to de Man

DANIEL T. O'HARA

New York   Columbia University Press   *1985*

Library of Congress Cataloging in Publication Data

O'Hara, Daniel T., 1948–
The romance of interpretation

Bibliography: p.
Includes index.
1. Criticism—History—20th century.   2. Criticism—
History—19th century.   I. Title.
PN94.045   1985   801'.95   85-477
ISBN 0-231-06068-8

Columbia University Press
New York   Guildford, Surrey
Copyright © 1985 Columbia University Press
All rights reserved

Printed in the United States of America

Clothbound editions of Columbia University Press books are
Smyth-sewn and printed on permanent and durable acid-free paper.

7-29-92

for Alan Wilde—
mentor, colleague, friend

Contents

Acknowledgments

THIS STUDY, composed over a six-year period, owes much to many, not least of all to family and friends, of course, and in particular to my wife and daughter, Joanne and Jessica O'Hara, and to Paul Bové, my comrade in theory. Each has provided great support, intellectual and otherwise, during the process.

I also and especially want to thank Alan Wilde, to whom the book is dedicated. I began a decade ago as his student, soon became his colleague, and will always remain his friend. I could not have done without his generosity of spirit, good sense, penetrating intelligence, and wisdom, all of which one can see at work in his impeccably original and moving explorations of the ironic imagination in modern and postmodern literature. Intellectually and professionally, and I aspire to feel, imaginatively as well, he is my progenitor. I hope my dedication of this book to him conveys even a small measure of my filial gratitude for all he has done for me.

"The Temptations of the Scholar: Walter Pater's Imaginary Portraits" and "The Genius of Irony: Nietzsche in Bloom" originally appeared in somewhat different forms in two collections of essays in contemporary critical theory. These are, respectively: *De-Structing the Novel*, Leonard B. Orr, ed. (Troy, N.Y.: Whitston, 1982) and *The Yale Critics: Deconstruction in America*, Jonathan Arac et al., eds. (Minneapolis: University of Minnesota Press, 1983). These essays were composed originally in summer 1978 and fall 1980. The Pater essay was made possible in part by the Taylor Summer Fellowship from the English Department of

Princeton University, among whose ranks I was then counted. The Bloom essay was first presented as a talk at a *boundary 2* Symposium on Critical Theory/Critical History at the University of Pittsburgh sponsored by the English Department. The Hartman essay, although composed in spring and summer 1981 for a special issue on critical theory of *Sun and Moon*, has not been published until now, as that journal ceased operations. Work on this essay was made possible by a Summer Grant for Research from the English Department of Temple University. Finally, the Frye and de Man essays were composed in the fall 1982 and spring 1983 semesters spent at the University of Pittsburgh, when I was a Visiting Andrew Mellon Fellow in the English Department. To all the institutions involved, and to Mary Briscoe, chairperson of the English Department there, and her many fine colleagues, I am deeply appreciative of the aid received.

Finally, to Mary Korman Tiryak of Temple University, I owe many thanks for that professional rarity: a critical friendship.

To translate man back into nature; to become master over the many vain and overly enthusiastic interpretations and connotations that have so far been scrawled and painted over that eternal basic text of *homo natura:* to see to it that man henceforth stands before man as even today, hardened in the discipline of science, he stands before the *rest* of nature . . . deaf to the siren songs . . . "you are more, you are higher, you are of a different origin!"—that may be a strange and insane task, but it is a *task*—who would deny that? Why did we choose this insane task? Or, putting it differently: "why have knowledge at all?"

Nietzsche, *Beyond Good and Evil*

The rhetoric of crisis states its own truth in the mode of error.

de Man, *Blindness and Insight*

CHAPTER ONE
VISIONARY CRITICISM:
AN INTRODUCTION

VISIONARY PERSPECTIVES shape the influential works and careers of the five major critical theorists of the Romantic imagination studied here. The most significant of these perspectives, for my purposes, is often expressed as a pervasive conviction, Romantic and *Symboliste* in its immediate literary origins, that the "natural," however ultimately determined, must be ruthlessly and rigorously—one could even say, *ritualistically*—sacrificed or even annihilated, no matter what the personal or collective costs. This sacrifice is necessary if it is to be successfully transformed into a truly alien "second nature" or separate textual world, a "supernature," apocalyptic in intention and intensity and radically at odds with, even as such a conviction is finally related to, other such conceptions of "second nature" that animate the religious, philosophical, and literary traditions of Western culture. For only in this manner, it is assumed, can a modern writer, working in a nihilistic age of unbelief and institutionalized terror, perfect a representative style of sublimity and thereby achieve symbolic immortality for himself among the other classics of our literature.

These five critics—Pater, Bloom, Hartman, Frye, and de Man—define the "natural" in a variety of ways. For Pater, it is, practically speaking, indistinguishable from the customary, from the common immemorial round of human experiences in nature and society, for which (pace Woodsworth) no strict philosophical rationale or even aesthetic justification—short of the tragic spectacle of a fatal, Romantic passion—can effectively be given. Ironically enough, for Bloom and Hartman, the "natural" is primarily the cultural. It is, more specifically, the literary past, individuated by Bloom into a few monumental precursors, or taken more impersonally and patiently by Hartman as a "wounding" sublime "otherness," the greatness of "primary" literature which contemporary criticism attempts to emulate by "accommodating" such greatness (and our inferiority complexes in relationship to it) within the "original" confines of imaginative textual inventions (as opposed to Bloom's "strong" "transumptive" "mis-readings"). Of those studied here, Hartman is, appropriately enough, the most Wordsworthian and humane of visionaries.

For Frye, however, the most systematic and schematic, the most Blakean, of these literary theorists, the "natural" is quite simply and reductively any and all blocking agents in the physical universe, in society, or in the writer's own psyche, that inhibit the quest for sublimity and that he therefore subsumes under the visionary emblem for *Natura* drawn from Blake's Prophetic Books: Vala or the Female Will. In this sense, Frye and not Bloom, despite the latter's antithetical claims, is the most Emersonian, Romantic, and I must add, "gnostic" of modern critics, since, like Emerson in the ironically named *Nature* (actually it would be more fitting to call his first volume *Vision*), Frye subsumes all the diversity of existence to the antithesis between the present creative self and its materials for imaginative revision. Neither Valentinus nor Schopenhauer would find this particularly strange. One can only escape both the death-in-life of the "natural" and the Spenglerian gloom of any civilization that venerates nature, Frye seductively counsels in Arnoldian tones of "sweetness and light," by visionary influxes of imaginative power. Such sublime moments would transcend time and human nature and lead a writer to compose his own separate world or "self-culture." Such a visionary "heterocosm" is not, however, a windowless monad; it does interpenetrate with others of its kind—but it does so, for example, as Eliot's *The Waste Land* is said to do by Frye: at the sublime impersonal level of archetypes alone.

Finally, de Man, writing primarily out of the German Romantic and *Symboliste* traditions in literature and the radically existential *and* deconstructionist traditions in philosophy, envisions
the "natural" entirely in this antithetical fashion, as a *figure* of
unmediated presence or extratextual "reality." All such
"presences" as Nature, Society, the Self, Being, etc. are produced, one can contend after de Man, as dreams are produced in
the psychoanalytic session—by a work of interpretation or
"reading," a reading of that ceaseless, insight-provoking interplay of verbal signs which occurs especially at the logically
"abysmal" junctures along the diverse intertextual networks of
one's life. The "natural," then, is for de Man essentially the
"rhetorical," metaphorically (and erroneously) identified as its
opposite. De Man's ironic project, like Derrida's in a different
context, is therefore compatible with Frye's or Bloom's, or even
Pater's and Hartman's to a certain extent. For he is surely Frye's
"negative inversion," as it were, and he can rightly be seen as the
"nihilistic" essence of all their visionary idealisms.

For de Man repeatedly deconstructs all antitheses, all oppositions between the customary and the new and strange, between
earlier and later, between "primary" literature and "secondary"
criticism or between self and language, since all such antinomies,
making for painfully perplexing "aporias" (or dilemmas) derive,
as de Man exhaustively demonstrates, from the fundamental (if
still "fictional") opposition between the "natural" and the
"rhetorical," or, if we conceive this axiomatic opposition even
more broadly and conventionally, between "nature" and "culture." If Frye in a famous conclusion to an essay on the Greek
epics can declare that Homer and Nature are truly "one," that is,
equally productions of the verbal universe; then de Man, one can
imagine, would agree—provided that he could make one strategic revision: the addition of an ironic uncapitalized "n" to supplement—by annihilation—the keyword in Frye's Popean
allusion.

My subject is thus the various "anti-natural" aesthetics informing literary history for the last century or so in the Anglo-
American tradition of critical theory, from Pater's "decadent"

impressionism to de Man's demanding post-structuralism, his programmatically "anti-aesthetic" "allegories of reading." Confronting this critical history of a self-destroying theoretical tradition,[1] a reader may legitimately raise several initial questions, such as: What, specifically, do I mean by my title and subtitle? Why have I included just *these* critics and no others? Similarly, why are the chapters arranged as they are? Finally, does Nietzsche's insistent but unsystematic appearance here as virtually a sixth figure for my revisionary circle—its elusive, eccentric center—have anything to do with the larger significance of this tradition of critical theory in cultural history?[2]

First of all, I mean to suggest by my main title, "the romance of interpretation," that aesthetic idea of imaginative "reader-response," first announced in the Anglo-American tradition by Pater and originally if erratically promoted by his disciple, Oscar Wilde, that criticism can be as creative or even more creative than creation.[3] This post-romantic and post-*Symboliste* notion of "critical creation," often consciously disdained even as it was so unwittingly demonstrated by the schools of criticism sanctioned by Arnold's exemplary tone and the brilliant and lively critical writings of Eliot, Richards, Empson, Leavis and the New Critics, has become a leading principle of critical theory in our own day, as once it nurtured the aspiration of the men of letters associated with the aesthetes and decadents.[4] (This idea of "critical creation" is of a piece with but far from exhausts the anti-natural aesthetics of my chosen writers).

Pater reduced all the great antinomies of Western thinking— the One and the Many, the Necessary and the Free, Good and Evil, Being and Nothingness, etc.—to a question of style, merely, to a question of the expressive and the inexpressive. Later literary critics and theorists, bearing ironic witness to such nihilistic prospects by exposing the simple-minded scholarly moralism of the genteel tradition and subverting the reductive pseudoscientific "positivism" of "close reading," have repeatedly espoused "the romance of interpretation," even as some of them, like Hartman, have attempted to "purify" romance and "accom-

modate" nature, the human kind or otherwise. More often than
not now a demonic parody of such enlightened and purifying
acts, the romance of interpretation is a revisionary way for a
critic to imagine his relationship to society, tradition, "primary"
literature, history, or language—whatever is being strongly misread as "natural" but is in fact a distorted representation of the
means and forces of critical production effective at the time. The
romance of interpretation is thus a deliberately perverse ideology
of literary study, which does little positive to make reforms in the
institution, unless one understands institutional reformation to
consist solely in the securing of a few new positions in critical
theory here and there around the country.

The focus of this theoretical practice or professional ideology
is the single individual who seeks to preserve and develop his
"creative" potential, at any cost, by subverting and/or overcoming all obstacles to the achievement of an original influential style
of critical thinking. The expressions of this personalized and
impossible-seeming desire for academic sublimity both masks
and ironically discloses as it does so the inhumane conditions of
mental production, the bitter psychology of resentment, as a
Nietzsche would say, currently abroad in the profession. The
"visionary criticism" of my subtitle thus does not simply refer to
literary theory possessed by creative or prophetic pretentions. It
refers as well to a form of critical writing that betrays the would-
be sublime critic caught in the act, as it were, of generating or
revising his ironically self-reflecting and all-too-often representa-
tive-sounding phantasmagoria. The work and careers of my
(re-)visionary company of romantic theorists best demonstrate
(and, especially in Hartman's case, help the most critically to
evaluate as well) the rhetorical operations of this ideology of
romance in modern and postmodern literary theory. Of course,
limitations of space—and of interest—also prohibit the inclusion
of full-scale analyses of other cases in point.[5]

By arranging these chapters in the order of their original composition, rather than in a speciously "necessary" historical or
systematic order, I hope to signal thereby not merely the fact that

such a possibility of applying my analysis to other figures exists, but also to highlight my opposition to the two, still dominant conventions of textual organization coercing the structures of critical writing today, namely, the thematic orientation of "the history of ideas" and the philosophical method of argumentation of the treatise in aesthetics. In these pages, my "readings" of the romance of interpretation and its underlying visionary assumptions emerge instead, I hope, as essays of their theoretical occasions, all of which have arisen for me in various personal and academic contexts in the years from 1978 to 1983, the period in recent American culture of the first great wave in the institutionalization of critical theory.

Finally, the question remains concerning Nietzsche's presence in this text. If Pater is often the (unacknowledged) ironic muse for the cult of theory, then Nietzsche is its most comprehensively creative innovator and critic. He experimentally lived and worked through, as my periodic reflections on his influence are intended to suggest, most if not all of the visionary and nihilistic perspectives elaborated and refined by other writers and thinkers and, in the Anglo-American critical context, expecially by these theorists of the Romantic imagination.[6] I have excluded, however, any separate, systematic consideration of Nietzsche as not being exactly germane to my selective focus, which is intended to reveal in part how the Anglo-American strain of visionary criticism, like any such discursive practice, predictably handles all alien and potentially renovating influences—namely, it affiliates them to long established and already familiar categories of thought, such as, in Nietzsche's case the tragic, the aesthetic, the ironic, and so on.[7]

I would like to suggest by my use of Nietzsche here that he should be affiliated most fruitfully now not with any revisionary nature, equally the product of the heroic ideal and the will to nothingness, but rather with what Nietzsche himself characterizes as "the innocence of becoming"—that radical indetermination of meaning, inexorable in its evasions of all merely human categories, such as the sublime, the deconstructive, or the genealogical—which, for Nietzsche at least, approaches that condition of being "beyond" (or "before") "good and evil" so remarkably like that of Nature—or Life—Herself:

> *Vita femina.*—For seeing the ultimate beauties of a work, no knowledge or good will is sufficient; this requires the rarest of lucky accidents: The clouds that veil these peaks have to lift for once so that we see them glowing in the sun. Not only do we have to stand in precisely the right spot in order to see this, but the unveiling must have been accomplished by our own soul because it needed some external expression and parable, as if it were a matter of having something to hold on to and retain control of itself. But it is so rare for all of this to coincide that I am inclined to believe that the highest peaks of everything good, whether it be a work, a deed, humanity, or nature, have so far remained concealed and veiled from the great majority and even from the best human beings. But what does unveil itself for us, *unveils itself for us once only.*
> The Greeks, to be sure, prayed: "Everything beautiful twice and even three times!" They implored the gods with good reason, for ungodly reality gives us the beautiful either not at all or once only. I mean to say that the world is overfull of beautiful things but nevertheless poor, very poor when it comes to beautiful moments and unveilings of these things. But perhaps this is the most powerful magic of life: it is covered by a veil interwoven with gold, a veil of beautiful possibilities, sparkling with promise, resistance, bashfulness, mockery, pity, and seduction. Yes, life is a woman.[8]

Walter Pater, of course, Yeats' prophetic educator in the aesthetic philosophy, has most poignantly and ironically envisioned just such an "innocence of becoming" and its likely effects, in a later, unfortunatly neglected "imaginary portrait": "Apollo in Picardy." Pater writes there of his favorite cultural theme, the return of the pagan deities of nature, exiled by Christianity, in a later, less exalted time. Inevitably, they always return as Apollo does in this tale, as a "veritable 'solar storm' " enflaming and haunting that benighted and self-trivializing age with the passionate knowledge of Dionysian mysteries, to which even they, even clear-eyed Apollo, must occasionally fall victim. Such knowledge, it seems, is tragically destructive and enraging to all cultists of counter-nature, however conceived, but becomes a self-affirming joy to those few who love life enough to want it, if it were possible, all once more.

The manuscript of this legend presented a strange example of a cold and very reasonable spirit disturbed suddenly, thrown off its balance, as by a violent beam, a blaze of new light, revealing, as it glanced here and there, a hundred truths unguessed at before, yet a curse, as it turned out, to its receiver, in dividing hopelessly against itself the well-ordered kingdom of his thought.[9]

"Nietzsche" can thus be said to be, I suppose, my representation of such an apocalyptically ironic nature subversive of the very idea of a "second nature" of any kind. In this light, perhaps I am really recommending, under the guise of Nietzsche's authoritative name these days, that we return to a poetic conception of nature and our relations to and with her which is in fact akin to an often overlooked strain in her one great English prophet: "Strange fits of passion have I known," indeed.

CHAPTER TWO

THE TEMPTATIONS OF THE SCHOLAR: WALTER PATER'S IMAGINARY PORTRAITS

One longs to penetrate into the lives of the men who have given expression to so much power and sweetness. . . . For the way to perfection is through a series of disgusts.

Pater, *The Renaissance*

The Pater Problem

RECENTLY, after many years of disdainful neglect, Walter Pater has emerged once again as a figure of significance in literary history. What precipitated this minor renaissance in Pater appreciation is not completely clear, but some suggestive surmises can be made. First of all, there is the accident of current critical polemics. Pater is a figure much reviled by modernist writers of the school of Eliot, and the latest generation of critics, out of sheer youthful exuberance if nothing else, has taken a provocatively antithetical line on this late Victorian prophet of aestheticism, celebrating him precisely for the thing their critical fathers found so enticingly offensive: his self-referential critical writing. Quite clearly, Pater provides the contemporary critic, anxious for figures he can see as congenial precursors, with a ready-made model of playful intimacy and impersonal yet highly subjective style. Pater's delicately shifting balance of systematic scepticism and insightful self-regard makes him a natural choice for the contemporary critic caught between the exhausted varieties of traditional criticism (formalist and historical) and the fashionable modes of avant garde deconstruction.

But most importantly of all, Pater is a strangely fascinating figure in his own right. His shy retiring manner, his austere life-style, his florid imagination and tireless quest for lucidity, his ritual hesitancy, his long good-bye looks cast in the direction of the great monuments of Western culture: all these things and more—his casual reticence, as if he possessed in reserve some great secret that would allow us to share his enigmatic smile if only we could divine it—give Pater a seductive charm over most of today's readers that is too powerful to resist—except at the cost of the devastating self-caricature that would result if one were desperate enough to stoop to resistance. For as Yeats recognizes (thanks to Oscar Wilde's absurd gestures in the right direction) Pater's charm is that of tragic irony. Pater is the first figure in English literature to reduce the great dualities of Western repre-sentational thinking—the One and the Many, Self and World, Good and Evil—purely to a question of style: "all reducible ulti-mately to terms of *art*, as the *expressive* and *inexpressive*." No wonder Yeats concludes that Pater's "aesthetic philosophy" did but teach one "to walk upon a rope, tightly stretched through serene air," only to be left suspended there "upon a swaying rope in a storm."[1]

The difference between modernist and contemporary views of Pater can best be seen by contrasting the most influential critical styles of each period, and then by showing how the assumptions underlying each style affect the different orientations of the ma-jor Pater critics. In this way, one begins to follow the master of "historical studies" out along the high wire.

In such essays as "Tradition and the Individual Talent" (1919), "The Perfect Critic" (1920), and "The Function of Criticism" (1923), written immediately after the First World War, T. S. Eliot, the premier poet-critic of modernism, argues for the ne-cessity of the critic's being, above all else, a scholar: a careful researcher of the historical, biographical, and textual genesis of the work of literature. Whatever the "truth" of this work might be, Eliot assumes that it could only emerge within the "scheme" of scrupulously objective critical analyses produced by the scholar's research. The purpose of this severe self-effacement of the critic is to allow the great monuments of the tradition to take shape in the modern mind with all their original formal integrity intact, so that they might become once more a creative influence in an otherwise chaotic world. Only in this way can the critic prepare the world for the emergence of both the new literary monument and, perhaps, the new social order.[2]

For Eliot, that great new work walked briskly through the early morning mists into Dublin to be born, in the form of James Joyce's *Ulysses* (1922). Eliot praises *Ulysses* in his famous 1923 review, "*Ulysses*, Order, and Myth," for its material "way of controlling, of ordering, of giving a shape and a significance" to "the immense panorama of futility and anarchy" which is, for Eliot, modern history. Joyce's *Ulysses* does all this by means of "the mythical method," that is, by means of its ironic structure of Homeric parallels and other literary allusions and archetypes—what has come to be called its "spatial form."[3] To Eliot, Joyce's ultimate novel is the perfect model of a literary classic, since it meets the dialectical criterion for originality that he lays down in his 1919 essay, "Tradition and the Individual Talent":

> What happens when a new work of art is created is something that happens simultaneously to all works of art which preceded it. The existing monuments form an ideal order among themselves which is modified by the introduction of the new (the really new) work of art among them. The existing order is complete before the new work arrives; for order to persist after the supervention of novelty, the *whole* existing order must be, if ever so slightly, altered, and so the relations, proportions, values of each work of art toward the whole are readjusted; and this is conformity between the old and the new. Whoever has approved this idea of order, of the form of European, of English literature will not find it preposterous that the past should be altered by the present as much as the present is directed by the past.[4]

Eliot's point is simply this: that a really new work of art like Joyce's *Ulysses* creates a dynamic interpenetration of past and present ways of seeing, of imagining, and of valuing reality. We cannot read Homer today except through the lens of Joyce's work, just as we cannot read Joyce except in light of Homer's epic. Past and present, father and son, meet and engage in a creative dialogue, become like brothers as it were, as Bloom and Stephen seem for a moment to do in the Ithaca chapter of *Ulysses*. And the critic? Ideally conceived by Eliot, one might say he must be content with being the gossip of pregnant situations.

The most pervasive critical influence on our own time is the French thinker, Jacques Derrida. It is appropriate that Derrida is neither a poet nor a literary critic, nor someone who is deeply interested in Pater's work (unlike Eliot or Harold Bloom—but more of them later). For ours is an age of highly revisionist and reductive thinkers who tend to view the cultural past abstractly as a single monumental entity that should be undermined and overturned. All idols rest on shifting sands, and all writers are golden moles. Derrida is a deconstructive writer who delights in pointing out how the language of past thinkers, how the play of metaphor and simile, of literary and mythic examples in the texts of "philosophers" from Plato to Lévi-Strauss, controls, directs, and determines their thought, so much so that one can say that it is language itself, conceived of as a secret and inescapable "archewriting," which "unconsciously" produces philosophy and the ideas of good and evil, nature and culture, self and other, being and nothing: even the idea of man as a rational animal. As with the figure of Socrates in Hegels's dialectical understanding of the history of philosophy, the ruling metaphor of the philosophical text "dies," hollowing out and effacing itself, until one forgets its figurative dimension, all so that the philosophical idea, the ruling obsession at play in a particular philosopher's text might "live" once more. This is the essential "tragedy" of all textual creation as seen by the comedian as the letter "D."

Derrida's immense influence among contemporary critics both here and on the Continent stems from his elaboration of a new method of reading texts—of figurative resurrection, as it were—which seeks to trace in the text to be read all those "blind-spots" or "dead" metaphors which secretly inform the author's apparently rational project. By an act of radical suspicion, Derrida interrogates an author's intended meaning or abstract thought, in pursuit of its figurative genealogy. Derrida thus "deconstructs" the rational significance of a text to uncover the purely formal play of linguistic signs at the basis of all textual or written production. Just as Derrida finds Rousseau's idea of nature to rest on autoerotic fantasies generated by the act of inscription, so all the "ideas" of philosophy are, for Derrida, empty of any rational significance, since the idea of reason itself bears the marks of structural differentiation, as is required by the operation of the linguistic system. Such a requirement, however, has nothing to do with the "laws of nature," but everything to do with the free play of writing, or "différance."

> The writer writes *in* a language and *in* a logic whose proper system, laws, and life has discourse by definition cannot dominate absolutely. He uses them only by letting himself, after a fashion and up to a point, be governed by the system. And the reading of any text must always aim at a certain relationship unperceived by the writer, between what he commands and what he does not command of the patterns he uses. This relationship is not a certain quantitative distribution of shadow and light, of weakness or of force, but a signifying structure that critical reading should produce.[5]

Although both Eliot and Derrida see the same phenomenon, the intricate interweaving in any text of figures from past texts and the present commentary on them, Eliot wants this romance of interpretation to be governed by the larger rules and outlines of the tradition as a whole, as if there were such a thing as what he calls "the mind of Europe," which develops in sophistication and self-consciousness—if in nothing else—as cultural history goes on from the cave paintings of the Magdalenian draftsmen to Shakespeare's plays and Eliot's criticism.

Derrida sees this situation of the writer as an opportunity for showing that there is no such thing as the "mind of Europe," but only the indeterminant interplay of texts from different periods of the history of Western metaphysics that produces an absurd dream of such a mind in which all the traces of writing would body themselves forth as images of full presence in a final and perfect fulfillment of narcissistic desire—a malady constituted not by the fecund weakness of men but by the coy strength of writing. "All metaphor, Malachi," as Yeats would say. Finally, where Eliot reserves the right of participation in the romance of interpretation to creative writers, restricting the critic's role to that of enlightened booster or perhaps merry drudge, Derrida suggests that all writing inevitably involves deconstructive interpretation, revisionism. For Derrida this means the dramatic production in the critic's text of the structure of signification informing a past text, a production which more and more resembles the baroque and violent commentaries of Mallarmé and Artaud on the traditional forms of poetry and theatre.

There should be little surprise that Eliot writes so harshly of Pater. Eliot sees him as a critical impressionist, whose essays mix scholarship, personal opinion, and undisciplined speculation in strings of purple passages that suggest what Eliot calls "spilt creation." Where the truly creative writer is inspired by a past work of art to make his own independent work that incorporates even as it superscedes, in some way, the past work, Pater is overwhelmed by his own impressions of the potentially tragic interplay that exists between the life of the artist and the work of art. Pater writes "studies in the history" of the Renaissance that are neither scholarly essays nor short stories, but are prose poems celebrating the continuing creativity of their author in the face of such past greatness. As if unable to create his own unique voice and impersonal style and independent characters, due to an inherent imaginative weakness, Pater merely refines upon the inherited styles and protagonists, the conventional Romantic models of the artist, those ready-made ciphers for the self-indulgent inscriber to trace on his whimsical palimpsest: "As always in his imaginary portraits, so frequently in his choice of other writers as the subjects of critical studies, Pater is inclined to emphasize whatever is morbid or associated with physical malady. . . . But it is not that he treats people 'in the spirit of art,' exactly; for when we read him on Leonardo or Giorgione, we feel that there is the same preoccupation coming betwen him and the object as it really is." Even Pater's most substantial work, *Marius the Epicurean* (1884), is for Eliot "incoherent; its method is a number of fresh starts; its content a hodgepodge of the learning of the classical don, the impressions of the sensitive holiday visitor to Italy, and a prolonged flirtation with the liturgy."[6] This last item in Eliot's indictment is the key to his condemnation of Pater. Eliot perceives Pater's aesthetic ideal as an imaginative kind of flirtation with ideas and values, forms of belief and practices, that one must choose between, accepting or rejecting one set or another on their own terms, since one cannot choose them all. This ideal embraces all that the tradition serves up, except that by never really choosing at all, or by choosing so abstractly, the man who suffers is clearly visible behind the veil of protective images that the artist creates. For Eliot, Pater and his problems do not deserve the scholar's serious attention. No more than a footnote in the history of the developing religious sensibility of England—this is Pater's lot.

Ironically enough, contemporary critics heap praise upon the very qualities of Pater that raise Eliot's hackles. Harold Bloom, though no disciple of Derrida, does possess an ironic vision of the intertextual relationships that shape literary and cultural history. But where Derrida delights in playing between his touchstones, dancing lightly from one exposed emperor to another, Bloom broods poignantly on the "anxiety of influence," which makes one imagine that precisely at the moment when one seems to be having a sublime vision of one's own absolute originality, one must only be recalling the distorted and ravaged features of some sovereign ghost, perhaps even several at once: Eliot's "familiar cmpound ghost." So Bloom agrees with Eliot that "the most individual parts of a poet's work may be those in which the dead poets, his ancestors, assert their immortality most vigorously," but differs over the possibilities of authentic response such a situation permits. This is why Bloom commends the honesty of Pater's avowal of critical impressionism in opposition to Arnold's (and Eliot's) self-deluding ideal of impersonal objectivity. One can never see the object "as in itself it really is," one must always see it through the eyes the influences of the stars have created, not to mention those of the preceding generations of poets and artists. Similarly, Bloom admires Pater's obfuscation of "the supposed distinction between criticism and creation," for one must create as best one can, in whatever mode is still viable and not exhausted. Finally, Bloom delights in Pater's "hesitant and skeptical emphasis upon a peculiar kind of vision, with which he identifies all aesthetic experience."[7] Flirting with infinity is fine sport to Bloom. Thus Bloom's answer to Eliot essentially is why worry over "spilt creation."

Bloom identifies this vision of Pater's as a form of the sublime, in which the individual self of the poet or critic realizes its own implication in the network of natural, historical, and literary influences, and yet still feels exalted to the point where it can see itself at one with the first star:

> The self still knows that it reduces to "sensations and ideas" (the subtitle of *Marius the Epicurean*), still knows the brevity of its expectation, knows even more strongly it is joined to no immortal soul, yet now believes also that its own integrity can be at one with the system of forces outside it.[8]

In "The Will as Vision" (from *Marius*), Pater expresses this vision in terms of a sublime experience of the presence of a divine spirit, a creative Logos, pervading nature. But Bloom extends the implications of this essentially Wordsworthian vision to cover the experience of the literary sublime—Longinus as well as Edmund Burke is intended by Pater, at least as Bloom sees it. One feels exalted even as one recognizes the shaping spirit of other imaginations, over which one has little control, operative in one's life and works, because in the moment of vision one sees in the terrible beauty of nature, or that of past poetry, reflections of one's own imagined grandeur, echoes of that alienated majesty which intimates one's own divinity. One always puts the best face on the abyss.

Yet, finally, Bloom is dissatisfied with Pater, too. Not for Eliot's reason, Pater's distortions, but precisely because of his too great honesty. Unlike Nietzsche's and Emerson's splendid lies against time and mortality, or Yeats' celebration of the "antithetical" self of the poet as poet, the poet as "daemon," Pater does not deny the anxiety of influence strongly enough, by enforcing upon himself an original forgetting, by living fully the "innocence of becoming." Rather, Pater is always seeking out sources, influences, continuities, admitting along the way that he is "a latecomer longing for a renaissance, a rebirth into imaginative earliness."⁹ If Eliot, despite the costs, would have the tradition absorb the individual critical talent in the interests of an impersonal cultural order; and Bloom, despite the impossibility, would have the individual digest the tradition for reasons of creative self-aggrandizement; then Pater, like Derrida in this one respect at least, would seem to have the good taste not to act as imperial host for such unspeakable rites, such vulgar feasts of the self-conscious modern imagination.

Consider how Pater handles the traditional form of the *bildungs-roman* as inherited from Goethe, Wordsworth, and Hegel. In the 1878 "imaginary portrait," "The Child in the House," Pater employs the form only to subvert its comforting visionary ends. The portrait deals with Florian Deleal who, out walking one day, meets an old man carrying a burden. After helping the old man, Florian begins to reflect on the man's destination, a district of a city in which Florian had spent his earliest, happiest years. As if being rewarded for his pity, Florian has a dream that night in which he recalls all the details of his "old home" with such a "fair light" that it is as if there were "a smile upon it." This dream vision is just the thinking Florian needs to begin his recently projected "design" which is to trace "the story of his spirit . . . that process of brainbuilding by which we are, each one of us, what we are."

What happens to this figure of the smile in "The Chld in the House" is most instructive. Beginning as an inspiration to the effort at autobiographical self-creation, it becomes in turn the image that haunts the interplay of sunlight and factory smog which delights the innocent young boy. Next, it becomes the expression that plays upon the lips of Florian's dead father, originally a figure of benevolent protection abroad in the world increasingly associated with the ghoulist idea of unappeaseable *revenants*. Finally, it appears as "the dark space on the brilliant grass" made by the open grave of a newly dead child. The portrait concludes with "the aspect of . . . the face of one dead" hanging over the ghostly pale, shrouded house, from which in happiness Florian had vainly hoped to leave: "And so with . . . himself in a agony of homesickness, thus capriciously sprung up within him, he was driven quickly away, far into the rural distance, so fondly speculated on, of that favourite country-road."[10] Can there be any doubt that "the aspect of . . . the face of one dead" hanging over this scene is a kind of smile?

This is something more than just a dream turning into a nightmare. Pater begins by accepting the essentially optimistic vision of the autobiographical form as handed down by the Romantics: that survivor's record. Pater seriously puts into question the belief, found most brilliantly expressed in Wordsworth's *The Prelude* (1850), that there is an underlying dialectical pattern to one's life: that despite innumerable shipwrecks, the loss of imaginative power and innocence is truly compensated for by the growth of imaginative sympathy with others and thus of authentic creativity. Pater symbolizes this vision in the initial smile of the dream, when Florian seems to have recovered from its secret hiding place one source of his present self. But then Pater progressively hollows out the figure by retracing its original appearances in his life as it develops in tragic insight. The final result, however, is not a fortuitous balance of light and dark, innocence and experience, nor the aurora borealis of imaginative synthesis. Instead, we witness the full disclosure of the inherited Romantic vision's essence as an empty Cheshire form glittering momentarily with a spectral light. Thus Pater neither engages in a dialectical recuperation of the tradition since he exposes its vacancy, nor does he revise the tradition according to his favorite misreading of a percursor. Rather he projects an "imaginary portrait," an experiment in "negative capability," in which one fictional history of the Romantic vision is played out. But unlike with Derrida, there is no joyful dancing in the resultant void.

Pater takes advantage of the emergence of "the relative spirit," that scientific and historical habit of mind which seeks to analyze present phenomena into their original constituent parts, to examine and ironically to test out one inherited form of his culture. Like some medieval author who writes his quest-romances as endless commentary on some traditional moral view of chivalric love, Pater writes his "imaginative portraits" as part of that modern "dialogue of the mind with itself" which has for the topic of conversation the aesthetic significance of essentially bankrupt but still inescapable cultural forms.[11]

How, then, can Pater be most usefully approached now? What questions should we ask of him? Why must we ask them of him? And whose interests are served by the adventure of such interrogation?

I think that the most useful approach to Pater today is that provided by the hermeneutic phenomenology of Paul Ricoeur. For a number of years now Ricoeur has been developing an interpretive mdoel that avoids both the self-serving idealizations of Eliot and the blatant opportunism of Bloom. Characteristically, Ricoeur begins any act of interpretation by redefining a particular problem in interpretation in terms of an aporia. Unlike Derrida, however, who repeatedly ends there, Ricoeur then attempts in various ways to mediate between the horns of the dilemma by means of an elaborate dialectical exploration. But all synthesis, even the idea of such synthesis, is postponed by Ricoeur as he returns in his interpretation again and again to a poetic, mythological, or symbolic level of discourse, in which a ruling metaphor or set of metaphors reinstates in all its original power for provocation some traditional expression of the essential ambivalence of the human imagination. ("The Minotaur, he is us," one might say speculatively.)

Notice, for example, how Ricoeur "mediates," in a radically paradoxical way, the conflict between two different interpretations of the history of philosophy, the one emphasizing its implicitly systematic order or logic, and the other emphasizing its ironic juxtaposition of sublime personalities: "The encounter with history is never a dialogue; for the first condition of dialogue is that the other *answer*. History is that sector of communication without reciprocity. But, granting this limitation, it is a kind of unilateral friendship, like unrequited love."[12] By invoking the idea of dialogue and the name of love, only to qualify ironically both of these staple models of interpretation, Ricoeur does more than produce an awful silence, or even a sly smile. What he is doing in this passage, and what he has done in all his works since *Fallible Man* (1960), is to remind us of the figure of Eros in Plato's *Symposium* and to suggest that perhaps it is the most fitting representation for that genius of creation which is involved in all interpretation. Ricoeur's hermeneutic phenomenology does recognize the dimension of self-interest in interpretation. But such a recognition causes him neither to revel in the possibilities for interpretive abuse, nor to banish the imaginative interpreter from his republic. What he has done is to attempt to project with an ever increasing power of discrimination "a hermeneutic style" capable of doing justice to the demands of the text and the desires of the hermeneut.[13]

In "Fatherhood: From Phantasm to Symbol," Ricoeur has developed the implications of his hermeneutic phenomenology in the most useful way—so far—for the literary critic. In this essay, Ricoeur examines three models of authority suggested by the idea of fatherhood: the Freudian model of neurotic phantasm ("Big Daddy"), the Hegelian model of legal institution (the "Penates"), and the Christian model of self-sacrificing partner, who on the basis of a free election of friendship, allows himself to be named in a Covenant relationship by the creative word of his self-designating Son ("The Form of a Servant"). Ricoeur suggests that the shift from the Old to the New Testament can best be seen as the transformation of the Freudian phantasm of the murdered and mortifying father, via the dialectic of figures instituted by the Covenant relationship ("King," "Saviour," "Jealous Lover"), into the rich paradoxes of the symbol of the Father in the Christian experience. As Ricoeur wryly puts it, "a father who is a spouse is no longer a progenitor (begetter), nor is he any more an enemy to his sons: love, solicitude, and pity carry him beyond domination and severity."[14]

The point to be taken from Ricoeur, then, is that one need not see the intertextual dimension of literary works, which Bloom,

Eliot, and Derrida all recognize, precisely in any of their terms. The relationship between Joyce's *Ulysses* and Homer's *Odyssey* need not be seen simply as the creative equivalent of either the Oedipal conflict, or the bildungsroman of the Western Spirit as it winds its way down a dead-end street, or the solitary game of charades that since time immemorial language plays with itself. Ricoeur suggests that linguistic symbols, precisely because they are overdetermined and irrational, make repeatedly necessary the work of interpretation, a work that includes both a constructive and a deconstructive phase. In such work the individual ego of the interpreter is transformed by the structures of the text being read, transformed—if only for a climactic moment—into a self like that suggested by the figure of a god who would die so that all of us might live in the imaginative light cast by his exemplary love: "Soon the whole earth will dance and sing."[15]

If Bloom's notion of interpretation strongly reminds one of Freud's tragic family romance, and Eliot's position sounds remarkably like a literary version of Hegel's idea of dialectical development, then I suggest that Pater's "imaginary portraits" bear some resemblance to Ricoeur's understanding of the Christian model of authority. An investigation of such possible affinities between Ricoeur's hermeneutic phenomenology and Pater's many fragments of a great romance may also prove exemplary, if only, finally, in a negative way.

The Aesthetic Ideal

Conceive the possibility of such a man: of middle-class, Broad Church origins, his father a Victorian surgeon, his mother a Victorian wife, Walter Pater is orphaned by the time he reaches the age of reason and then is raised by aunts in an old country estate, about which he is left to wander in pursuit of objects for his dreams. Pater is a shy, sensitive child, fastidious, obsessively formal, a lover of ritual, a natural aristocrat in an age of all-too-common minds, hypersensitive to criticism, as well as to the shifting colors and forms of objects, and often sickened by the spectacle of suffering even in dumb animals. This child is, indeed, father to the man. Is it any wonder, then, that in the age of " the relative spirit," he would invent for his culture and ours the classic expression of the aesthetic ideal, a style of life in which one seeks perfection in being rather than in doing. Perfection in being requires becoming, via the impassioned contemplation of beauty in all its forms, the most refined and exquisite receptacle of the accumulated imaginative capital of the world; the economy of means and ends, means that must be seen as ends, informs Pater's ideal of creative energy. Every Beatrice calls forth her Dante, and every Dante must become in turn another Beatrice, when the sensuous mind, liberated in its impotent solitude, attempts to feed itself, before the assembled excellence of past ages, upon the seductive images of its own sublime vacancy.

The questions which I would put to Pater are these: what exactly is the aesthetic ideal, how is it meant to work, and why did it emerge when it did in late Victorian culture? In trying to get Pater to answer these questions, I hope to suggest an answer to the question with which I began: why is Pater reappearing now as a figure of significance in literary history?

According to Pater's earliest essays, "Diaphanëite" (1864), "Coleridge" (1866), "Wincklemann" (1867), and "Aesthetic Poetry" (1868),[16] the aesthetic ideal would seem to be a self-conscious quest for that symbolic vision of absolute beauty in which the innocent joy of childhood and the unhappy experience of maturity are reconciled in the idea of the wise creator who can give, on the model of sacred history, whether Greek or Christian, a transcendent imaginative significance to life. In pursuit of this impossible vision, one must be willing to see others as Goethe saw Wincklemann and Pater sees Flaubert: as martyrs to the aesthetic view of life. One must learn to delight in their courting of disaster if one is going to see them in the spirit of art, that is, as transformed into symbols of that perfection which only exists for a climactic moment in the highest examples of Greek tragedy—a perfection of personal style in which one recognizes a sense of freedom amidst the intolerable play of fateful circumstance.

What else are we to make of figures who are able, in Yeats' phrase, to "come/ Proud, open-eyed and laughing to the tomb?"

> In those romances of Goethe and Victor Hugo, in some excellent work done *after* them, this entanglement, this network of law becomes the tragic situation, in which certain groups of noble men and women work out for themselves a supreme Denoument. Who, if he saw through all, would fret against the chain of circumstance which endows one at the end with those great experiences?[17]

This is what it means "to burn always with that hard, gemlike flame," to be always at that "focal point" where the tragic dividing of forces is taking place. Much as Plato does in his *Dialogues,* one must sublimate the death of a man into the symbol of an idea, thereby translating oneself in the process into the genius of interpretation, the daemon Eros.

Not only must the quester after the aesthetic ideal see others as living metaphors and mythical symbols, then, but he must himself become more and more impersonal, universal, archetypal, until he can play Apollo to their Dionysus:

> The artist and he who has treated life in the spirit of art desire only to be shown to the world as he really is; as he comes nearer and nearer to perfection, the veil of outer life not simply expressive of the inward becomes thinner and thinner. . . . Such a character is like a relic from the classical age, laid open by accident to our alien modern atmosphere. It has something of the clear ring, the eternal outline of the antique.[18]

Ideally, of course, one would be the dramatist of one's own tragedy, an Oedipus and Sophocles both, a hollow Laocoön, which, when opened reveals the shining image of a god.

Thus the aesthetic ideal, as Pater sees it, requires the cultivation of an ironic detachment, a studied indifference, to the direct phases of life. This ironic pose is best shown in Pater's contention that one must view all phases of Western culture, Classic, Medieval, and Modern as necessary to the progressive development of the human spirit. But unlike Hegle, from whom he takes his Romantic view of history, Pater celebrates a type of personality rather than a form of metaphysical speculation. For Pater it is Goethe, as portrayed by his works, who best embodies the aesthetic ideal since only Goethe, of all moderns, creates himself out of himself by struggling concretely with each of the great forms of human genius in turn, until the secret of each form's strength is won and the discovery of his own strength is thereby insured, and he leaves each inherited form of genius "fall back," like an exhausted lover, "into its place in the supreme artistic view of life." It is to this strange romance of interpretation and "self-culture" that Pater summons us.

The best example of Pater's interpretive method is the study of Leonardo da Vinci from *The Renaissance* (1873).[19] At an early point in the essay, while trying to define the formula for expressing Leonardo's particular power as an artist over our minds, Pater recalls from Vasari's original study that Leonardo early on and throughout his career was fascinated by "the image of smiling women and the motion of great waters." This fascination wholly informs Pater's formula for Leonardo's genius: the shifting interplay between the desire for beauty and the scientific curiosity for knowledge. What is important about this discovery is not the originality of the thought but the resonant force of the expression:

> And in such studies or art and nature some interfusion of the extremes of beauty and terror shaped itself, as an image that might be seen and touched, in the mind of this gracious youth, so fixed that for the rest of his life it never left him.[20]

This image, of course, will return fully developed in "The presence that rose thus so strangely beside the waters," Pater's most famous purple passage on *La Giaconda*.

What Pater has done in this study is to make a continuous drama of self-discovery out of the various elements of Leonardo's life. First, he creates an antithetical structure for that life which shows Leonardo torn between the desire of the aesthete and the curiosity of the scientist. Then he imposes this structure on every facet of the life, in order to make it yield the original sources of its unfolding, the secret of its power. Finally, Pater re-creates those origins in the image of his own aesthetic ideal, wresting from Leonardo in the form of this prototype of the Mona Lisa as he will revise it in his own unique manner, a sign of his own imaginative strength. But this is not all of what Pater does in this passage. For, as the whole tenor and style of it suggests, there is another figure that Pater has peering through the diaphanous lineaments of that image of terrible beauty, a figure whose language has influenced Pater's own formulation of Leonardo's genius.

> Fair seed-time had my soul, and I grew up
> Fostered alike by beauty and by fear:
> Much favoured in my birthplace, and no less
> In that beloved Vale to which ere long
> We were transplanted—there were we let loose
> For sports of wider range . . . .
> Dust as we are, the immortal spirit grows
> Like harmony in music; there is a dark
> Inscrutable workmanship that reconciles
> Discordant elements, makes them cling together
> In one society. How strange that all
> The terrors, pains, and early miseries,
> Regrets, vexations, lassitudes interfused
> Within my mind, should e'er have borne a part,
> And that a needful part, in making up
> The calm existence that is mine when I
> Am worthy of myself! Praise to the end!
> Thanks to the means which Nature deigned to employ;
> Whether her fearless visitings, or those
> That came with soft alarm, like hurtless light
> Opening the peaceful clouds; or she may use
> Severer interventions, ministry
> More palpable, as best might suit her aid.[21]

What are we to make of this rather clear affinity between Pater's interpretation of Leonardo and Wordsworth's self-interpretations? One thing that we can observe is that there is an extraordinarily great amount of condensation and refinement in Pater's passage, as if his prose were becoming like the aesthetic poetry he praises so highly: "Like some strange second flowering after date, it renews on a more delicate type the poetry of a past age, . . . as from a lower to a higher degree of passion."[22] Imag-

ination expresses itself in Pater as an urge to an intensified re-
arrangement and revision of past works of literature, almost as if
Pater were giving expression to the dreams of a scholar. Should
we say, as Harold Bloom most likely would, that in this passage
on Leonardo's youth we have another example of the anxiety of
influence at work? Pater, in order to overcome the influence of
Wordsworth, transforms him, via Shelley's convenient fictionalization of the Medusa of the Uffizi,[23] into the muse that inspires
Pater's own genius, so that he might give birth to his own imaginative father and thereby to the essential features of his poetic or
creative self. Or should we say, as Eliot might have if his own
anxieties had permitted him to confront the presence of Wordsworth in Pater, that it is the peculiar collocation of literary styles
inherited from the past which gets in the way of Pater's seeing the
object under discussion "as in itself it really is"? Pater is, according to such a possible account, neither fish nor fowl, neither
critic nor poet, but just an annoying amphibian.

What the hermeneutic phenomenology of Paul Ricoeur suggests about such an interpretive dilemma is that both views of
interpretation depend upon a faulty notion of the text and its
relationship to history. As Ricoeur puts it, "interpretation is the
process by which disclosure of new modes of being—of new
forms of life—gives to the subject a new capacity for knowing
himself. The reader is rather enlarged in his capacity for self-
projection by receiving a new mode of being from the text itself."[24] In the "fusion of horizons" which results in any act of
interpretation, despite the reciprocal blindnesses of both Eliot
and Bloom, the interpreter is dispossessed of the narcissistic desires for grandeur and so appropriates a new power of imaginative
sympathy capable of demystifying the loftiest sublimation.
Wordsworth may have become Pater's muse, but first he had to
become the young Leonardo. Similarly, Pater may have become
Oscar Wilde's muse as he chants the famous passage on the *Mona
Lisa* before the imperturbable smiling portrait on the Louvre
wall,[25] but what could be a finer testament of the power of what
of what Pater calls "imaginative loves"?[26] There is a dialectic of

idealization and deconstruction at the heart of the interpretive process and where one leaves off and the other begins, or who is being victimized by whom, are perhaps, in the final analysis, moot questions.

But the question concerning the nature of the world projected by Pater's text is provocative. For it is the particular structures of history, the social discourses of a culture at a particular time, which inspire the creation of textual ideals. What were those structures like in Pater's time which allowed him to project and promote the aesthetic ideal? What was the nature of the discourse, the institutional alignment of interests and forces at work then to make Pater and his ideal seem necessary? As Ricoeur does with Freud, one must excavate the site of texts that exist, as it were, alongside Pater's own, not just those that stand in a line some place before or immediately after him.[27]

By far the most illuminating text of this sort is John Henry Newman's *The Development of Christian Doctrine* (1845). For in its opening sections Newman describes how an idea develops, taking possession of men and revising their aims and values, until it has mastered a space of intellectual and actual territory in the history of a people:

> This process is called the development of an idea, being the germination, growth, and perfection of some living, that is, influential truth, or apparent truth, in the minds of men during a sufficient period. And it has this necessary characteristic—that, since its province is the busy scene of human life, it cannot develop at all, except either by destroying, or modifying and incorporating with itself, existing modes of thinking and acting. Its development then is not like a mathematical theorem worked out on paper, in which each successive advance is a pure evolution from a foregoing, but it is carried on through individuals and bodies of men; it employs their minds as instruments, and depends upon them while it uses them. And so as regards their existing opinions, principles, measures, and institutions, it develops in establishing relations between them and itself, in giving them a meaning, in creating what may be called a jurisdiction over them, in throwing off from itself what is heterogeneous in them. It grows when it incorporates; and its purity consists, not in isolation, but in its continuity and sovereignty. This it is which imparts to the history both of states and of religions

its especially turbulent or polemical character. Such is the explana-
tion of the wranglings whether of Schools or of Parliaments. It is the
warfare of ideas, striving for the mastery, each of them enterprising,
engrossing, imperious, more or less incompatible with the rest, and
rallying followers or rousing foes according as it acts upon the faith,
the prejudice or the interests of individuals.[28]

In this extraordinary passage analyzing the place of the
"warfare of ideas" in the politics of cultural institutions, Newman seems to recall Hegel even as he clearly anticipates Darwin
or Foucault. Ultimately, of course, Newman wants to argue that
belief in the traditional doctrines of Christianity can be given the
validity of a social custom, a cultural idea, since they do possess
in England particularly a "natural" history of the kind referred to
in the above passage. But what I find fascinating about Newman's insight is that one can use it to describe, by way of analogy,
the progress of what Pater terms the aesthetic ideal as he defines,
refines upon, and traces its imaginative development in the culture from its origins with the Greeks, through its sacrificial death
in the medieval period, to its glorious return in the Renaissance,
like "buried fire" breaking out from under the glaciers of a
frozen world—only to need yet another resurrection, after the
debacle of the French Revolution and all that followed it, in
Pater's own time.

In his "imaginary portraits" Pater is attempting, in his own
sublte ironical way, to become the midwife of an idea whose time
has come round once again. Pater sees his time as mean and
vulgar, too engrossed in material pursuits to take the Romantics
and the Victorian prophets seriously, a time in which both the
commercial interests and the fledgling socialists and trade union-
ists are all dizzy with jingoism and smugly satisfied with their
power to compromise their principles in the interest of utility.
Yet in this millieu Pater conceives of the emergence of "the relative spirit," with its emphasis upon the scientific analysis of
"types of life evanescing into each other by inexpressible refinements of change," as an opportunity for the reassertion of the
aesthetic ideal as he sees it:

But the child of whom I am writing did not hate the fog because of
the crimson lights which fell from it sometimes upon the chimneys,

and the whites which gleamed through its openings, on summer mornings, on turret or pavement. . . . And thinking of the very poor, it was not the things which most men care most for that he yearned to give them; but fairer roses, perhaps, and power to taste quite as they will, at their ease and not task-burned, a certain desirable, clear light in the new morning, through which sometimes he had noticed them, quite unconscious of it, on their way to their early toil. . . . Angels might be met by the way, under Engish Elm or birchtree.[29]

Pater's purely aesthetic version of Carlyle's metaphysical idea of "natural supernaturalism," with its emphasis upon the sensuous forms of objects, is a secular vision of the world, the latest revision of the religious tradition, that is made to stand as the final, necessary embodiment of the essence of Western culture. It is this aesthetic justification of modern existence that one must preserve and defend, it is this that one must sacrifice oneself for.

For Pater, the aesthetic critic must become the interpreter of the Greek ideal for the modern world, being careful to impress the vision of classical taste on the latest generation of readers and to uncover for all to see the way in which the tragic vision of the Greeks has taken possession of the Western mind:

> The supreme artistic products of succeeding generations form a series of elevated points, taking each from each the reflexion of a strange light, the source of which is not in the atmosphere around and above them, but in a stage of society remote from ours. The standard of taste, then, was fixed in Greece, at a definite historical period. A tradition for all succeeding generations, it originates in a spontaneous growth of the influences of the Greek Society. what were the conditions under which this ideal, this standard of artisitic orthodoxy was generated? How was Greece enabled to force its thought upon Europe? In Greek tragedy . . . man finds himself face to face with rival claims. It shows how such a conflict may be treated with serenity, how the evolution of it may be a spectacle of the dignity, not of the impotence of the human spirit . . . capable of thus bringing joy out of matter in itself full of discouragements. . . . It is the highest expression of the indifference which lies beyond all that is relative or partial. Thus what modern art has to do in the service of culture is to rearrange the details of modern life, so to reflect it, that it may satisfy the spirit. And what does satisfy the spirit in the face of modern life? The sense of freedom.[30]

What Pater is arguing for here is the use of the historical imagination in the interest of recovering for the modern world an aesthetic version of an absolute, an imaginative vision of an ideal way of living and interpreting one's life.

Faced with the conflicting claims of science and religion, of the "relative spirit" and Christian forms of belief, one can gain "a sense of freedom" by following the model of the Greeks and turning such conflict into sublime tragedy. But, of course, this "sense of freedom" that results from the self-consciously ironic interpretation of existence is a privilege of the ideal spectator of world history who, trained by his studies, can "discriminate every moment some passionate attitude in those about us, and in the brilliancy of their gifts some tragic dividing of forces on their ways." Like Hegel in his *History of Philosophy* when he views the death of Socrates as a tragic necessity in the development of the Absolute Spirit, Pater would have us become that which we behold here: the solitary indifferent seer of all those " 'images. . . of man suffering amid awful forms and powers' " that the history of the human spirit so luxuriously affords.[31]

The Idea of the Creator

"It is the image of what the history it symbolizes has more and more become for the world, paler and paler as it recedes into the distance." With these words dismissing Christianity, Pater concludes his discussion of Leonardo da Vinci's *Last Supper.* In this discussion Pater sums up all the qualities of his idea of the creator. Ironically enough, given Pater's proclivity for the Greeks, it is the "figure . . . the faintest, most spectral of all," which consummates the design of the painting of Christ:

> On the damp wall of the refectory, oozing with mineral salts, Leonardo painted the *Last Supper.* A hundred anecdotes were told about it, his retouchings and delays. They show him refusing to work except at the moment of invention, scornful of whoever thought art was a work of mere industry and rule, often coming the whole length of Milan to give a single touch. He painted it, not in fresco, where all must be *impromptu,* but in oils, the new method which he had been one of the first to welcome, because it allowed so many after-thoughts, so refined a working out of perfection. It turned out that on a plastered wall no process could have been less

durable. . . . It was another effort to lift a given subject out of the iron age of its conventional associations. . . . We recognize one of those symbolical inventions in which the ostensible subject is used not as matter for definite pictorial realisation, but as the starting point of a train of sentiment, as subtle and vague as a piece of music.[32]

Pater weaves all the characteristic traces of the creator around this suggestive symbol of the incarnated god: the imposition of great formal beauty upon a perpetually deteriorating world; the mysterious influence of the creator's work over the minds of men, so strong that it actually creates history; the scrupulously self-conscious attending upon the event of inspiration; the insatiable pursuit of formal experimentation; the tragic fate of the work itself; and, most importantly of all, the well-orchestrated system of symbolism, at the center of which, most transparent of transparent shadows, appears that ghostly figure suggestive of the Creator behind the creation himself—a Christ made in the image of the first English critic to write an appreciation of Dionysus.

Like David Strauss' study of the development of the figure of Christ in the New Testament, Pater in his "imaginary portraits," his testament of aestheticism, traces the history of his idea of the creator, its origins, development, death, and rebirth. Rather than making Pater's task virtually impossible, then, the "relative spirit" of the higher biblical criticism actually provides inspiration for Pater's work: "Criticism came with its appeal from mystical unrealities to originals, and restored no life-like reality but these transparent shadows [Christ and his apostles] which have not flesh and bones,"—but which are therefore all the more useful in filling the space of sunlight on the wall with the outlines of Pater's own highest desire: "The angel may still be seen in Florence. . . . It is a face of doubtful sex, set in the shadow of its own hair, the cheek-line in high light against it, with something voluptuous and full in the eyelids and the lips."[33] Just as he believes (in *Plato and Platonism*) that the ardent study of natural history will make it possible for the faithful student to see "legible on the surface of a shell" the whole history of its evolution and so will perfect rather than deaden his appreciation of the curious fusion of beauty and truth that the spectacle of life presents to the discriminating eye, so Pater finds in the results of the higher criticism of art and of the Bible a model for his own interpretations of the idea of the creator in cultural history.

Pater thus makes a virtue of necessity by inventing the modern form of romance, the spiritual form of fiction in which the life of the central figure—whatever his ostensible lineaments and origins—exists solely as the vehicle for the expression of the author's own desires for symbolic immortality, for the perfection of style, in the Greek manner: "Fresh, unperplexed, it is the image of a man as he springs first from the sleep of nature, his white light taking no odour from any one-sided experience. He is characterless, so far as character involves subjection to the accidental influences of life. . . . This colourless, unclassified purity of life, with its blending and interpenetration of intellectual, spiritual, and physical elements, still folded together, pregnant with the possibilities of a whole world closed within it, is the highest expression of the indifference which lies behind all that is relative or partial."[34] As in Derrida's understanding of metaphor, the Dionysian creation must die in some sense if the Apollonian idea is to live. In order to embody this idea of the creator in his texts, Pater must become both father and mother, husband and wife to himself. "No mind can engender until it is divided in two," as Yeats puts it. But the goal of self-division is, in Steven's phrase, "to evolve a man," a master of historical repetition who is not the Nietzschean "exceptional monster," but the crystalline "central man": "A touch of the poet, that Bloom has. Yes," as Joyce puts it. It seems that Ricoeur's continuous insistence upon the figure of Eros as the sign under which the interpreter must operate finds support in Pater's adaptation of Goethe's romance of interpretation, a late Victorian revision of the Romantic tradition that has been definitive for modernism as well.[35]

In fact, Pater's *Studies in the History of the Renaissance* (1873) represents the first stage in the re-creation of his vision of the creative personality for the modern world. The first four studies—"Two Early French Stories," "Pico della Mirandola,"

"Sandro Botticelli," and "Luca della Robbia,"—define, respectively, the Paterian formula of sweetness and strength which characterizes the aesthetic ideal of the Renaissance; the dialectical method of interpretation for realizing this formula concretely in each of the studies; the symbolic type of highly suggestive beauty associated with the aesthetic view; and the imaginative goal of perfect self-expression for which the aesthetic man strives. The next four studies—"The Poetry of Michelangelo," "Leonardo da Vinci," "The School of Giorgione," "Joachim du Bellay"—trace the progress of this aesthetic ideal in the modern world, demonstrating the shifting balance of "sweetness and strength," creative style and power, operative throughout the course of its development, until its virtual disappearance, amidst the mandarin refinements of early eighteenth-century France.

In this way Pater justifies his contention that in Winckelmann one can see the essence of the aesthetic idea, the Greek love of form in all its manifestations, translated back into the world, with all its original force and beauty still intact, for the nourishment of the modern creator par excellence, Goethe. Pater thereby places himself at the climax of his historical study, in a position analogous to Winckelmann. "That marriage of Faust and Helena, of which the art of the nineteenth century is the child," is made possible by the vision of Hellenic art that Winckelmann left to Goethe: "Goethe, then in all the pregnancy of his wonderful youth, still unruffled by the press and storm of earlier manhood, was awaiting Winckelmann with a curiosity of the worthiest kind." Both in this study and in the preface and conclusion to *The Renaissance*, Pater is shown to be, like Winckelmann, an embodiment of the modern critical mind full of longing for a creative renaissance: "Can we bring down that ideal of the Greeks into the gaudy, perplexed light of modern life?"[36]

I suppose the example that best sums up Pater's vision of the modern psyche, which so desperately needs to see the rebirth of the idea of the creator, is his famous purple passage on the *Mona Lisa*:

The presence that thus rose so strangely beside the waters, is expressive of what in the ways of a thousand years men had come to desire. Here is the head upon which all "the ends of the world are come," and the eyelids are a little weary. It is a beauty wrought out from within upon the flesh, the deposit, little cell by cell, of the strange thoughts and fantastic reveries and exquisite passions. Set it for a moment beside one of those white Greek goddesses or beautiful women of antiquity, and how would they be troubled by this beauty, into which the soul with all its maladies has passed! All the thoughts and experience of the world have etched and moulded there, in that which they have power to refine and make expressive the outward form, the animalism of Greece, the lust of Rome, the reverie of the middle age with its spiritual ambition and imaginative loves, the return of the Pagan world, the sins of the Borgias. She is older than the rocks among which she sits; like the vampire, she had been dead many times, and learned the secrets of the grave; and had been a diver in deep seas, and keeps their fallen day about her; and trafficked for strange webs with Eastern merchants: and, as Leda, was the mother of Helen of Troy, and, as Saint Anne, the mother of Mary; and all this has been to her but as the sound of lyres and flutes, and lives only in the delicacy with which it has moulded the changing lineaments, and tinged the eyelids and the hands. The fancy of a perpetual life, sweeping together ten thousand experiences, is an old one; and modern thought has conceived the idea of humanity as wrought upon by, and summing up in itself, all modes of thought and life. Certainly Lady Lisa might stand as the embodiment of the old fancy, the symbol of the modern idea.[37]

In this passage Pater invents the symbol of the modern psyche, presenting it as an Anima Mundi in possession of a particular culture at a particular time. It presides over a cultural world hopelessly divided between a religious and a scientific view of life and painfully self-conscious of the refinements of its alienation. Most significantly, this terrible smiling beauty stands for a kind of mind which feels itself to be the climactic development in the evolution of world history. It is a mind ironically suspended in the interstices of such a monumental text and fatally in love with a vision in which for a privileged, epiphanic moment all its memories might come together in a system of symbolic correspondence. This system would contain all the traces inscribed in such a mind by history, at the center of which appears the master-trace of its own weary self-image. In this passage, Pater discloses the ironic muse of modern literature, the femme fatale who is "the image of the god within," of the dying god within: the creator's purely academic mask. "He is so possessed by his genius that he passes unmoved through the most tragic events, overwhelming his country and friends, like one who comes across them by chance on some secret errand."[38] Behind every successful modern creator, Pater would seem to say, stands such a symbolic self-portrait as that represented in *La Gioconda,* a mind's self-portrait, a mind that lives all the past in an "eternal" revisionary present and has perhaps written off the future.

In *The Renaissance* Pater uses the elements of the scholarly study of the period and its most representative figures to shape a highly self-referential text whose aim is the narration of Pater's own myth of self-development. By wooing from each figure in these "imaginary portraits" the secret of his imaginative power, Pater is able to articulate the various influences at work upon the modern critical intelligence. In this way Pater can rearrange the museum world of his time according to his desire to make possible the reemergence of that "impossible possible philosopher's man," the creative individual who will owe allegiance to neither side in the many conflicts of the day, whether it be that of religion and science or culture and anarchy, but who therefore will be able to hover ironically above the "play of circumstance" in the webs of his own devising. In fact, the reason that Pater gives for selecting the Renaissance as his ideal period is precisely its freedom from the kind of controversy, extant in the modern world ever since the French Revolution, which appears to be naked will to power in the service of an ideology that has no place for what Yeats, following Pater, calls "unity of being":

> But in the *House Beautiful* the saints too have their place; and the student of the Renaissance has this advantage over the students of the emancipation of the human mind . . . in the French Revolution, that in tracing the footsteps of humanity to higher levels, he is not beset at every turn by the inflexibilities and antagonisms of some well-recognized controversy, with rigidly defined opposites, exhausting the intelligence and limiting one's sympathies. . . . Here there are no fixed parties, no exclusions: all breathes of that unity of culture in which "whatsoever things are comely" are reconciled, for the elevation and adorning of our spirits.[39]

For Pater, the critic reads cultural history and analyzes the most representative forms of its expression solely for the inspiration they afford to the solitary individual in his pursuit of contemplative perfection. "The *Interpreter* of the *House Beautiful,* the true aesthetic critic, uses these divisions [of history] only so far as they enable him to enter into the peculiarities of the objects with which he has to do." Thus the critical interpreter of the wonders of the Western world might become like "the painter of the *Last Supper* who lives, "with his kindred," in a "land where controversy has no breathing-place." But, of course, such a land has more in common with the unclassifiable splendor and sublimity of the pyramids, than with any land of the living. Only the great dead can "refuse to be classified" by the myriad interests of the day which called their creativity into action. Or those among the living who seem already dead, so willing, as Pater presents his Leonardo as being, to sink into the arms of the secular power and give full rein to his anxious desire to satisfy "the last curiosity" by desperately trying to fathom the fatal allure of the perfect self-knowledge that comes only in death.[40]

The pattern that emerges from the study of Pater's first major work in the genre of "imaginary portraits" is deceptively simple—with that kind of simplicity often found in myth, and found particularly evident in Pater's favorite myth, that recorded in the "golden book" of Apuleius, the myth of Eros and Psyche.[41] Believing himself to be "the composite result" of all the previous ages, a passive latecomer, and to live in a time in which all the traditional structures of Western culture are being dissolved in the acid bath of historical criticism, the study of influences, Pater becomes what he beholds when he reads himself into da Vinci's *Mona Lisa.* Pater becomes a resident of the House Beautiful, where the mental furniture, while lovely and precious, stifles the creative impulse, smothering it as its first breath is taken, with the crystalline refinements of the world historical spectacle, the damp haze of disorderly reveries and resentful nightmares; but then in the midst of tragic crisis, the idea of the creator announces itself to Pater like the movement of the autumnal breeze over the waters, takes possession of the darkened mind and penetrates into its most secret recesses. Together, the ideal beauty of the critic and the powerful love of the creator produce the pleasure of the text. And this romance of interpretation repeats itself with every act of writing, as if Pater in his "imaginary portraits of past genius" were fusing the Keats of the "Ode to Psyche" with the Goethe of *Dichtung und Wahrheit*.

For Pater, then, the critical interpreter, when confronted by the inherited culture, the amassed imaginative capital of the ages, suffers a painful self-division, a psychic wounding. How can he ever hope to compete with such Fathers? The interpreter thus becomes a belated man, even an ironical academic. But at the same time, if he perseveres in his work of interpretation, he can seduce the genii of his Fathers from their secret hiding places, as it were, by disclosing how every strong Father was once a weak son and that a weak son may just become a strong Father, if he allows the structures of the text—in Ricoeur's phrase—"to give a self to the ego" as part of the disciplining of the imagination.[42] Then, perhaps, the Fathers will in return be seen as a possible spouse, a composite muse to his own genius, that "image of the god within." Only by first submitting to the forms of textual beauty that veil such knowledge can one learn of the shaping spirit that informs their every lineament.

Pater's *Marius the Epicurean* (1884) is his most systematic fictional development of this pattern of self-interpretation. I cannot hope to do justice to its allusive intricacies. What I would like to do, however, after briefly outlining its structure and commenting on its central vision, is to focus on a single passage in which Pater attempts to justify his hero's acceptance of the institutions of his time, expressed by Wallace Stevens as "things as they are,/ Only changed upon the blue guitar." My intention is to show how Pater's kind of romance leads inevitably to a surrendering of the very imaginative power for which he searched so long and hard.

Marius the Epicurean is the result of seven years of painstaking labor. Pater intends it, as we know from the note which he attaches to the conclusion of *The Renaissance* in 1888, to be the justification of the aesthetic view of life, of the Greek ideal of sensuous form and spiritual power, put forward in that work originally published in 1873. Attempting to resolve the conflict between Christian and Classical worlds, Pater places his skeptical young man, Marius, in second-century Italy during the peace of the Antonine emperors, the great imperial students of the Stoic philosophy. This is a time when, to Pater's eyes at least, the early Church and the late Pagan mysteries agree on one thing, that the appeal of religion must be through the forms of worship, the rituals of divine service. But before Marius is allowed to make this discovery, Pater moves his central figure, like a silhouette in a fire-lit cave, past a shadowy background of shifting cultural forms and beliefs: the Patriarchial religion of Numa, the literary Euphuism of Apuleius, and the Stoicism of Cornelius Fronto, the great Sophist to the emperor, Marcus Aurelius.

In each instance, Pater embodies the formula that best expresses the particular virtue of a worldview in one of Marius' friends or relations: Marius' dead father, his friend Flavian, and his employer Aurelius himself. He also presents the way of life represented by each view by means of an appropriate muse-figure: Marius' devoted widow-mother, Apuleius' irrepressibly inquisitive Psyche, and the Emperor's cynical, beautifully evil Faustina. After working through these worldviews, a process marked both by the death of a major representative of each view and an exhaustive essay on the topic by Pater (as in Hegel, one hardly knows which is more tragic) Marius confronts in the refined and chaste joy of Cornelius, a young Roman officer who seems to prefigure medieval chivalry, the secret equation of Christian love. Similarly, when Marius meets the widowed Cecilia holding her child in her arms during the celebration of a mass in the catacombs—a Christmas service commemorating the birth of Christ into an essentially dead world—he sees the archetype of Madonna and Child that is about to take possession of the human spirit. Pater, however, does not have his hero come full circle completely and suffer a new birth by converting to Christianity. Instead, he has him engage in an endless self-debate, a case of infinite suspense and voluptuous hesitancy, until circumstances force the moment to a crisis.

One day, after an earthquake, the persecution of Christians is resumed as a form of propitiation to the apparently jealous Pagan deities. Marius and Cornelius are both captured, and Marius, presuming that Cornelius is to become the husband of Cecilia, substitutes himself for his friend and dies from fever on his way to being executed among a group of simple believers. In this ironic way, Pater grants Marius the form of a martyr's death, even as he withholds judgment on its ultimate significance:

> In moments of his extreme helplessness their mystic bread had been placed, had descended like a snow-flake from the sky, between his lips. Gentle fingers had applied to hands and feet, to all those old passageways of the senses, through which the world had come and gone from his, now so dim and obstructed, a medicinable oil. It was the same people, who in the gray, austere evening of the day took up his remains, and buried them secretly with their accustomed prayers; but with joy also, holding his death according to their generous view of this matter, to have been of the nature of a martyrdom, and martyrdom, as the church had always said, a kind of sacrament with plenary grace.[43]

With the finesse of the most accomplished virtuoso or brilliant devil's advocate, Pater plays his solemn music of dispersal.

The main focus of the book, of course, is chapter 19, "The Will As Vision," in which Pater tries to justify belief in some kind of divinity, some form of personal immortality, some sense of freedom, however general, vague, and improbable, on the basis of the will-to-believe in such things throughout history: "Might the will itself be an organ of knowledge, of vision?" But the supreme fiction of Marius' will-to-believe is his famous vision amid the Alban hills of "an unfailing companion," an Eros-figure, a mind like his own behind the mechanical show of things, some infinitely gentle, infinitely suffering Creator, who would take possession of the swept and garnished sanctuary of the soul, and lift the habitual burden of sadness from one's being:

> Might not this entire material world, the very scene around him, the immemorial rocks, the firm marble, the olive-gardens, the falling

water, be themselves but reflections in, or a creation of, that one indefectible mind, wherein he too became conscious, for an hour, a day, for so many years?

Pater makes it clear that Marius' experience of "a sense sublime of something far more deeply interfused" owes as much to the will-to-believe in such a possibility as to any other factor. Moreover, "the divine companion," that exalted, invisible double, is Marius' own best self—that self which he discovers when he identifies with what Coleridge calls the Imagination, Blake calls the Human Form Divine, or Yeats suggests is the Daemon:

> That divine companion figures no longer as but an occasional way-farer beside him, but rather as the unfailing "assistant," without whose inspiration and concurrence he could not breathe or see, instrumenting his bodily senses, rounding, supporting his imperfect thoughts.

Finally, it becomes obvious that the idea of the creator which Pater puts into Marius' mind formulates almost too perfectly the intention informing Pater's text with regard to satisfying his own chronic longings:

> How had he longed, sometimes, that there were indeed one to whose boundless power of memory he could commit his own most fortunate moments, his admiration, his love, Ay! the very sorrows of which he could not bear quite to lose the sense:—one strong to retain them even though he forgot, in whose vigorous consciousness they might subsist for ever, beyond that mere quickening of capacity which was all that remained of them in himself: "Oh! that they might live before Thee." Today at least, in the peculiar clearness of one privileged hour, he seemed to have apprehended that in which the experiences he valued most might find, one by one, an abiding place.

What we have in this last self-referential passage is Pater's ideal image for the coercive play, the dialectical spiral of textual creation: "instrumenting his bodily senses, rounding, supporting his imperfect thoughts." As Paul Valéry notes in his "Introduction to the Method of Leonardo da Vinci" (1894), the human mind, when confronted by the many, diverse influences of the past upon the present, naturally wishes "to place a being in our likeness at the heart of the system [of history] we impose upon our-

selves."[44] What I would say, using Valéry's notion as a helpful
analogy,[45] is that here in *Marius* Pater is giving a local habitation
and a name to the system of essay, myth, history, and romance
that *is* his text, in a Romantic, Wordsworthian vision of the Creative Logos as the ultimate monumental presence. Furthermore,
Pater is having Marius express the wish for that creator-figure
into which Pater would wish to be transformed with regard to his
own fictional character. And finally, sensing the unlikelihood of
that far-off divine event, Pater himself, like Emerson in his essay
"The Poet," articulates his yearning to give birth, in turn, to
some future text which would have at its center a figure made in
his own best image: "The artist, like the God of the creation. . . ." Such are the curious ways in which literary history
gets produced.

So, if Pater can be said to have invented the modern psyche in
The Renaissance, then in *Marius,* if one is allowed a further hyperbole, he has revised the "ideal of the Creator" as he calls it,
found in Greek philosophy and Christian scripture, by making
him the genius of loving creation, the Imagination as seen after
Coleridge, by one of the "last romantics." "Do they never come
down again from the heights, to help those whom they left here
below?—And we too desire, not a fair one, but the fairest of all.
Unless we find him, we shall think we have failed."[46]

Despite all of Pater's careful, well-modulated qualifications
(for example, his use, in the final pages of the book, of a conversation between the ironic Roman writer Lucian and a young
enthusiast of Stoicism, to balance his enticing vision of the creator with an acute awareness of his failure to resolve the conflict
between morality and art) Pater in the end falls prey to his own
beautiful idealizations, becomes victimized by his impossible
dreams, and so appears as the perfect object of attack, awash in
the sea of his own fantastic impotence. For when one asks what
idea of society and of the individual's relation to society does this
vision of the creator reinforce, one finds that the answer involves
a rationalization, exquisitely phrased, of the need to capitulate to
the structures of power at work in the world whatever the historical epoch. And the rationale? Such structures help to promote,

despite their unjust foundations, good taste and the expansion of imaginative sympathy:

> A wonderful order, actually in possession of human life!—grown inextricably through and through it; penetrating into its laws, its very language, its mere habits of decorum, in a thousand half-conscious ways; yet felt to be, in part, an unfulfilled ideal, and, as such, awakening hope, and an aim, identical with the one only consistent aspiration of mankind! In the apprehension of that, just then, Marius seemed to have joined company once more with his own old self; to have overtaken on the road the pilgrim who had come to Rome, with absolute sincerity, on the search for perfection. It defined not so much a change of practice, as of sympathy—a new departure, an expansion, of sympathy. It involved, certainly, some curtailment of his liberty, in concession to the actual manner, the distinctions, the enactments of that great crowd of admirable spirits, who have elected so, and not otherwise, in their conduct of life, and are not here to give one, so to term it, an "indulgence." But then, under the supposition of their disapproval, no roses would ever seem worth plucking again.

When one stops to consider that Pater is here talking about the Roman bureaucracy and its "rhetoric of life" by which the empire imposes its laws and its rituals, some of them quite nasty, upon millions of people, then the argument for accepting things as they are—whether in Rome or in Victorian London—because such acceptance will educate one's taste and sympathy, begins to appear specious. Is it an expansion of sympathy to open oneself to the pieties of empire, the rites of imperialism? Must one compromise one's principles because they do not square with those in authority? Pater would seem to think so, for he goes on to justify Marius' acceptance on the basis that such acceptance is after all in harmony with the aesthetic view of life, since one must appreciate beauty in all its forms, even that of empire, "that wonderful order, actually in possession of human life!"

> The authority they [Roman bureaucrats] exercised was like that of classic taste—an influence so subtle, yet so real, as defining the loyalty of the scholar; or of some beautiful and venerable ritual, in which every observance is become spontaneous and almost mechanical, yet is found, the more carefully one considers it, to have a reasonable significance and a natural history.[47]

Even if one argues that Pater sees in such organizations as the Roman bureaucracy and its avatar, the English academy, the prefigurement of the religious ideal of the community of saints, of the Church in heaven, still one must admit that Pater has succumbed to one of the most familiar of scholarly temptations. Given the scholar's training to see in events the inexorable logic of necessity working itself out in the spectacle of history, one could justify any established order at any time on the basis of the beauty of the spectacle, the perfection of the interpolated logic, however tragic the consequences in terms of actual lives lost or ruined. To put it another, perhaps less tendentious way, if one must always taste and see before one can begin to judge, one may end up drugged or poisoned by the vision partaken of. The vision of power presented by this essentially Arnoldian idea of the State is the case in point. For the latter can even begin to resemble a dramatic text, perhaps performed by indifferent actors at best, but competently orchestrated at least by an invisible hierarchy of self-hypnotists.

Suspended Judgment: The Pater Problem Again

During the year 1889 Pater published six of the seven chapters that make up *Gaston de Latour: An Unfinished Romance*.[48] Pater conceives of the work as a companion piece to *Marius,* only this time dealing with the developmental crises of a sceptical young man from a century closer to Pater's own: sixteenth-century France. Gaston feels caught between the innocent beatitudes of his childhood religion and the sensuous allure of the Renaissance critical spirit. Gaston's quest is to find the human embodiment of the kind of ideal creative mind, the unfailing Logos, the idea organizing one's sensations, that Marius perceives behind the shifting veil of things:

> Was there perhaps somewhere, in some penetrative mind in this age of novelties, some scheme of truth, some science about men and things, which might harmonise for him his earlier and later prefer-

ence, "the sacred and the profane loves," or, failing that, establish, to his pacification, the exclusive supremacy of the latter? (p. 41)

As in Marius, Pater sends his protagonist on a voyage of discovery, in search of some ideal model of selfhood, a search which has him drift past a variety of intellectual backgrounds and social milieus, even meeting along the way Montaigne and becoming an enthusiastic reader of Giordano Bruno. Traditional belief, radical scepticism, Renaissance Neoplatonism and pantheism: these are some of the cultural forms with which Gaston's mind conjures itself into being.

At one point early in the work, Pater describes the sense of loving stillness and perfect peace that descends over Gaston as he climbs the tower stairs in "Our Lady's Church," the Cathedral of Chartres:

> At such times of crisis, to recall the winged visitant, gentle, yet withal sensitive to offense, which had settled on his youth with so deep a sense of assurance, he would climb the tower of Jean de Beauce, then fresh in all its array of airy staircase and pierced traceries, and great uncovered timbers, like some gigantic birdnest amid the stones, whence the large, quiet, country spaces became his own again, and the curious eye, at least, went home. He has become well aware of the power of those familiar influences in restoring equanimity, as he might have used a medicine or a wine. At each ascending storey, as the flight of the birds, the scent of the fields, swept past him, till he stood at last amid the unimpeded light and air of the watch-chamber above the great bells, some coil of perplexity, of unassimiliable thought or fact, fell away from him. He saw the distant paths, and seemed to hear the breeze piping suddenly upon them under the cloudless sky, on its unseen, capricious way through those vast reaches of atmosphere. At this height, the low ring of blue hills was visible, with suggestions of that south-west country of peach-blossoms and wine which had sometimes decoyed his thoughts towards the sea, and beyond it to "that new world of the Indies," which was held to explain a certain softness in the air from that quarter, even in the most vehement weather. (pp. 42–43)

Here is the justification of the aesthetic ideal, at least as far as Pater is concerned. Beginning in a sudden return to familiar influences, the vision moves up and out to encompass the possibility of the sublime, and in the process—as each resonant figure appears and takes its place in Pater's sinuous prose—another Romantic ghost, another coil of perplexity, drops off and is laid to rest. The echoes of Shelley, Coleridge, and Keats are so abundant, and yet Pater manages to weave his own music out of their different songs, that one almost believes in the composition of peace orchestrated here. The solemnly ecstatic movement out of oneself to hover freely above the coils of experience as one's imagination first recognizes itself in remembered places and then expands to the absolute limits of known horizons—this moment of vision, intimate self-possession, and mental simplicity—a dream of innocence recaptured from childhood and reenacted in the present: this is the end of impassioned contemplation for which Pater strives. It is this aesthetic ideal which the idea of the creator allows Pater to arrange.

So it causes some real surprise that the vision goes on to include the awareness of other kinds of experience not usually intimately associated with such privileged moments.[49] It is as if the moment were condensing into itself, by means of Pater's ironic narrative structure, the extremes of innocence and experience:

> Amid those vagrant shadows and shafts of light must be Deux-manoirs, the deserted rooms, the gardens, the graves. In mid-distance, even then a funeral procession was on its way humbly to one of the village churchyards. He seemed almost to hear the words across the stillness. They identified themselves, as with his own earliest prepossessions, so also with what was apt to present itself as being the common human prepossession—a certain finally authoritative common sense upon the quiet experience of things—the oldest, the most authentic, of all voices, audible always, if one stepped aside for a moment and got one's ears into what might after all be their normal condition. It might be heard, it would seem, in proportions as men were in touch with the Earth itself, in country life, in manual work upon it, above all by the open grave, as if, reminiscent of some older, deeper, more permanent ground of fact, it whispered then oracularly a certain secret to those who came into such contact with it. Persistent after-thought! Would it always survive, amid the indifference of others, amid a thousand doubts?
> (p. 43)

It seems that Pater in the above passage begins to approach Wordsworth's vision of "the still sad music of humanity," as Nature's check upon his visionary hubris, a power to chasten and subdue imagined flights of the would-be phoenix. For Pater takes a strange delight in the signs of human limitation and mortality, our attachment to the earth in a literal sense, and is actually worried that mankind, amidst the intricate refinements of intellectual speculation, might forget the vacant ground that underlies all. Only by persistently remembering the fact of human existence can one remain in touch with the common wisdom of the people and so with the earth itself. After ascending the tower of vision, then, to escape the torturous network of cultural influences that intimate life's self-divisions and insignificance, and gazing out upon an opening expanse that stretches even farther in the mind's eye, Gaston is called back down to earth to recognize the paradoxical echo of his vision in the oracular voice that chants the lesson of the grave.

What follows now, however, comes as an even greater surprise. For Pater has Gaston focus and embody his vision of renewed innocence and perennial wisdom in the figure of a little child who first had led him here and would soon lead him back. Pater sees the child as possessed by the voice of vision:

> It seemed to have found, and filled to overflowing, the soul of one amiable little child who had a kind of genius for tranquility, and on his first coming hither had led Gaston to what he held to be the choicest, pleasant places, as being impregnable by noise. In his small stock of knowledge, he knew, like all around him, that he was going to die, and took kindly to the thought of a small grave in the little green close, as to a natural sleeping-place, in which he would be at hand before-hand. Descending from the tower, Gaston knew he should find the child seated alone, enjoying the perfect quiet of the warm afternoon, for all the world was absent—gone forth to receive or gaze at a company of distinguished pilgrims. (pp. 44–45)

In this last passage the interfusion of perspectives, that of Gaston, child, and narrator, in behalf of a beautiful morbidity, is uncannily reminiscent. Pater's being "half in love with easeful Death" summons the distant music of Joyce's "The Dead."

What is happening throughout this entire section from *Gaston de Latour*? Why is it typical of Pater's "imaginary portraits"? And how does it bear upon the relationship between the essentially conservative spirit of the aesthetic view of life and the recent resurgence of interest in Pater?

Pater begins with Gaston in a state of crisis, a chronic sense of incapacity. Gaston is simply unable to negotiate between the shifting world views and models of behavior, the cultural codes and styles that confront him in his time—at least as Pater makes that time resemble his own. Pater then has Gaston seek temporary refuge from that world by winding his way to the top of a tower, at each turn of whose stairs another perplexity, like another piece of snake skin, drops off. By alienating himself from his culture and its history, by holding it ironically at a distance, Gaston is able momentarily to regain his self-possession while gazing at a familiar domesticated scene that yet reflects back at him the sense of sublime immensity still possible as an ideal representation of the invisible world of his dreamy imagination. Then Gaston is called back to the earth, the simple natural world of human work and mortality, that aboriginal ground of fact underlying and so often obscured by the mandarin spinnings of solitary thinkers. The agent of such sobering recollection is the voice of the grave. The latter is part of the final turn of irony, this time directed at his own presumptive flight as well as at the airy nothings from which he would so anxiously flee. Yet quite clearly Pater approves of both the ascent of desire and the descent of love, this ironic dialectic of Eros, which describes not only the axis of human experience but also the act of interpretation, the critical performance, that hollows out conventional figures only to create in them even more refined images of the unfillable void, the insatiable abyss of representation.

Then, in the figure of the little child, Gaston, and Pater, through him, appear to recover what seems to be the original source, the imaginative father to all that the man has become and, becoming, sees: "the necessary angel of earth" who brings "relationship and love" even where none, seemingly, can exist. The child and the interpretation put upon him suggest the paradigmatic impression of Wordsworth's poetry from "We Are Seven" of *Lyrical Ballads* (1798) to the "Boy of Winander" set

piece as placed finally in *The Prelude* (1850). Such an intense
suggestion highlights a further irony, viz., that the figure of past
origin which he discovers in the present scene, that little child
who would lead him, is not simple but is hauntingly composite,
like the "twin-born" duality of "thought and word" in "the perfect style" of Flaubert or Plato. The features of both parents,
Wordsworth and Pater, are still plainly visible in the face of the
child that Gaston, and we, contemplate. And yet in so identifying
with the figure that we hear Pater's sympathy break through
Gaston's impersonal inflections, we begin to feel stirring the father's love for his child. In this paradoxical, perhaps perverse
way, Wordsworth, Pater's imaginative father, becomes, so very
tentatively, like a little child again, so that he once more might
lead the aging man to a vision of the creator that would suffice.

This section from *Gaston de Latour* is a more concentrated
instance of the kind of irony generally at work, over larger portions of narrative, in Pater's "imaginary portraits." Eliot's Arnoldian judgment that Pater cannot see the object "as in itself it
really is," is not demonstrated since the object clearly is not the
action of people in society nor the forms of nature so much as it is
the mind that delights in brooding over the texts of others in
which, "like the monkish scribe," it sets in the margins of such
discourse emblematic figures of its own, filling the blank spaces
of perfected illusion with so much "truth of the earth." Nor does
this section support Harold Bloom's pessimistic vision of the
influence of the past upon the present, his belief that such influence becomes more and more burdensome and productive of an
almost unbearable anxiety until each new effort at original imaginative creation can be at best only a Pyrrhic victory, a case of
diminishing returns in the downward spiral of growing solipsism
and alienation. The purpose of Pater's writing, in which he gives
into the temptations of the scholar just enough but not too much,
is to make possible the renewal of the literary tradition. By incor-
porating the languages of art criticism, the higher criticism of the
Bible, science, and German metaphysics—and by using such a
renovation in style to show our imaginative fathers becoming like

little children again—Pater is establishing the foundation for a generation of creators who will see themselves becoming fathers in their turn. And Pater's role? Perhaps to be seen as one of the ever-weaving "Mothers."

> "There, skated my son, like an arrow among the groups. Away he went over the ice like a son of the gods. Anything so beautiful is not to be seen now. I clapped my hands for joy. Never shall I forget him as he darted out from one arch of the bridge, and in again under the other, the wind carrying the train of my fur coat behind him as he flew."

That is Goethe's mother. All of Pater's *Imaginary Portraits* (1887) lead up to this scene of apotheosis of innocence, as described by her words. Pater's wish, in his romance of interpretation, is that he might see the birth of the creator in his own time, a "resurgam" of the imaginative on the model of the "aufklärung," the enlightenment in Germany: "In that amiable figure of the young Goethe I seem to see the fulfillment of the Resurgam on Duke Carl's empty coffin—the aspiring soul of Carl himself, in freedom and effective, at last."[50] And, no doubt, Pater's fulfillment as well.

All of Walter Pater's work may be said to aspire to the condition of creation. His blending of "art and literary criticism, belles lettres, classical scholarship, the *journal intime,* and the philosophical novel"[51] has one aim: "that . . . form . . . should penetrate every part of the matter" until, as in a piece of excellent music, the content becomes one with the form. That is, the content becomes so much a pure trace of the way something is being imagined, so open to interpretation from different perspectives, that, like a dish of peaches seen by Cézanne, it appears as "a space of fallen light" upon the walls of the ideal spectator's mind, illuminating as it fades the virtually empty traces of signification previously decorating the imagined original tabula rasa. Like the borrowed figures from classical mythology made to suggest Christ on the catacomb walls in *Marius,* such etching and interleaving of figures should produce in that spectator's mind, by juxtaposition and repetition, an intimation of the image of the hidden god, the underlying form of "reasonable music," of the creative Logos, that permeates the production of the text.

Pater hopes to educate a public by such suggestive symbolic means, educate them to the appreciation of the idea of the creator so that they might also become creators themselves in their own right. The aid of such education is to get them to see like the poet sees, an aim still very much at the center of the interpretive act as defined by Paul Ricoeur:

> Would not the poet be the one who perceives power as act and act as power? He who sees as whole and complete what is sketchy and in process, who perceives . . . things as not prevented from becoming, seeing them as blossoming forth . . . every form attained as a promise of newness: In short, he who reaches "this source of the movement of natural objects, being present in them somehow, either potentially or in complete reality" (Metaphysics Δ, 1015 a 18–19), which the Greeks called *phusis*.[52]

Or in Pater's own words, "to watch," with full appreciation, "for its dramatic interest, the spectacle of a powerful, of a sovereign intellect, translating itself, amid a complex group of conditions which can never in the nature of things occur again, at once pliant and resistant to them, into a great literary monument.[53] But at what cost such vision, one still is tempted to ask.

The initial price of Pater's vision can be seen in a passage from *Plato and Platonism* (1893) in which he effectively reduces all the great oppositions that inform and illuminate knowledge, morality, and culture purely to a question of style, with the duty of the artist of one's own life simply being to impose the perfection of ideal form upon the chaos of experience:

> Only, remember always in reading Plato—Plato, as a sincere learner in the school of Pythagoras—that the essence, the active principles of the Pythagorean doctrine, resides, not as with the ancient Eleatics, nor as with our modern selves too often, in the "infinite," those eternities, infinitudes, abysses, Carlyle invokes for us so often—in no cultus of the infinite (Tò ἀπειρον) but in the finite (Tò πέρασ). It is so indeed, with that exception of the Parmendean sect, through all Greek philosophy, congruously with the proper vocation of the people of art, of art as being itself the finite, ever controlling the infinite, the formless. Those famous ουστοιχίαι Tων εαντιων,

or parallel columns of contraries: the One and the Many: Odd and Even, and the like: Good and Evil: are indeed all reducible ultimately to terms of *art*, as the *expressive* and the *inexpressive*. Now observe that Plato's "theory of ideas" is but an effort to enforce Pythagorean πέρασ, with all the unity-in-variety of concerted music,—eternal definition of the finite, upon Tò απειρον the infinite, the indefinite, formless, brute matter of our experience of the world. (pp. 59–60)

The aesthetic view of life comes down to this: a far from blessed rage to order, a question of style, the terrible beauty of art, like Pater's *Mona Lisa*, absorbing and reformulating all the cultural forms of the past within the once radiant circle of the work of art, for the expression of a vacant smile, a splendid torpor, prevading one's own separate world.

A further expense is incurred if one, in emulating the master, desires to become, again like Plato, the focal point where the energies of the past ignite into a white radiance that will open up and people the undiscovered kingdoms of the future with crystalline self-reflections:

> Now it is straight from Plato's lips, as if in natural conversation, that with itself, in that inward dialogue which is the "active principle" of the dialectic method as an instrument for the attainment of truth. For, the essential, or dynamic, dialogue, is ever that dialogue of the mind with itself, which any converse with Socrates or Plato does not promote. The very words of Plato, then, challenge us straightaway to larger and finer apprehension of the processes of our own minds; are themselves a discovery in the sphere of mind. It was he made us freemen of those solitary places, so trying yet so attractive: so remote and high, they seem yet are naturally so close to us: he peopled them with intelligible forms. Nay more! By his peculiar gift of verbal articulation he divined the here hollow spaces which a knowledge, then merely potential, and an experience still to come, would one day occupy. And so, whose who cannot admit his actual speculative results, precisely *his* report on the invisible theoretic world, have been to the point sometimes, in their objection, that by sheer effectiveness of abstract language, he gave an illusive air of reality or substance to the mere nonentities of metaphysic hypothesis—of a mind trying to feed itself on its own emptiness.[54]

In the above passage, as in that more famous one on the *Mona Lisa*, Pater's mask slips and reveals his highest desire: to be a determining influence on succeeding generations by virtue of his power to revise the past and to imagine the myriad alternatives of any possible future according to the suggestive symbolic and ironically self-referential designs of his accomplished prose. Pater wants to create the critical language in which men will speak for a thousand years, to leave to us, as Wallace Stevens puts it concerning his poetic desire, "the look of things," what he felt at what he saw in the way of its being said. But as the final image in the passage suggests, such imperious delusions and (self-) deceptiveness must reflect back on one's own growing imaginative poverty, a reflection Pater is acutely sensitive to. Overcoming the past and divining the future in a way Pater claims Plato has done condemns one to the vicious circle of self-interpretation, that endless dialogue of the mind with itself, than which, in most cases, no conversation could be less imaginative.

If, however, one survives the first temptation to transform the stones of life into stylish croissants and even manages to outgrow the second temptation to possess, in potentiality, all the kingdoms of the intellectual world, then one must face and resist the final and greatest temptation, that which exacts the highest interest. Like Oscar Wilde, for example, you can become so beguiled or exhausted by your own genius for irony that you will cast yourself down from the top of any convenient temple of art to see, if indeed as has been prophesied, some ministering angel has been put in charge of your life, lest you dash your foot against a stone. Or, to use Pater's formula for such willed disasters:

> Everyone knows the legend of Abelard, . . . how as Abelard and Heloise sat together at home there, to refine a little further on the nature of abstract ideas, "Love made himself one of the party with them." You conceive the temptations of the scholar, who in such dreamy tranquility, amid the bright and busy spectacle of the "Island," lived in a world of something like shadows; and that for thought, those restraints which lie on the consciences of other men had been relaxed.[55]

In living out the script of an imagined tragedy one perhaps will feel purely and simply again—at least for a moment as the tightrope begins to sway. If, as nothing else, a *cri du coeur* is seen as a nice change of pace.

Perhaps this is why Pater has suffered a renaissance in our time: he discloses, in the words of Heidegger, that "the essence of mortals calls upon them to heed a call which beckons toward death," dying as he did, like Plato, pen virtually in hand. What other figure of the modern mind could call forth such authentic fellow feeling from the latest products of our "refined and comely decadence"?[56]

CHAPTER THREE
THE GENIUS OF IRONY: NIETZSCHE IN BLOOM

Nietzsche until he went mad, did not confuse
himself with his own Zarathustra.
Bloom, Poetry and Repression

A poet writes always of his personal life, in his finest work out
of its tragedy, whatever it be, remorse, lost love, or mere loneli-
ness; he never speaks directly as to someone . . . there is always
a phantasmagoria. . . . He is never the bundle of accident and
incoherence that sits down to breakfast; he has been reborn as
an idea, something intended, complete.
Yeats, "A General Introduction For My Work"

HAROLD BLOOM has been a controversial figure in Ameri-can critical circles ever since the publication in 1959 of his
first book, *Shelley's Mythmaking*. It set itself squarely against the
ruling critical orthodoxies of the time (New Criticism and Aristo-
telian neo-humanism) by challenging the common view, derived
from Arnold, that Shelley was "an ineffectual angel" beating
golden wings vainly in a void of idealistic abstraction. Bloom
argued that Shelley was instead more of a self-conscious visionary craftsman in the manner of Northrop Frye's Blake. No matter what the dominant opinion has been, one can count on Bloom
to oppose it. Consider the first and still most original of his
theoretical utterances, *The Anxiety of Influence* (1973). Just when
his Yale colleagues (de Man, Hartman, and Miller) were adapting
Derridean deconstruction and Lacanian psychoanalysis to the
interpretation of literary texts within an American context; and
his former mentors (M. H. Abrams and Walter Jackson Bate)
were defending the conventional methods and values of literary

history against the neophyte American deconstructors by refining well-established views of the Romantic tradition's Christian
and humanistic origins; Bloom returned to Nietzsche, Emerson,
Freud, and occult or once heretical forms of speculation (Kabbalah and Gnosticism) to propound a radically subversive position on why and how poetry gets written and literary traditions,
especially that of Romantic visionary poetry, impress themselves
so effectively on our minds. In essence, then, in *The Anxiety of
Influence* Bloom redefined the contexts of the various critical debates and developments in his own influentially eccentric fashion.

For Bloom, the poet in the line of vision (or the poet of the
sublime) must wrestle with all the specters of his elected and
partially repressed precursors, in order to win the right to his
own distinctive imaginative identity. Bloom in his practical criticism repeatedly traces the manner in which the will to revision
appears in the major texts of our modern literary culture. He is
fascinated by the many different ways an author, as Wordsworth
found when crossing the Alps (see *The Prelude*, VI), is brought to
the brink of "blank disertion," unable to counter with his own
original image the sudden memory of a precursor's long-re-
pressed words, and yet can finally rise to the occasion and seize
the opportunity such a radically disjunctive moment makes in a
text. Into this semantic gulf, the strong creator projects a sublime
representation of himself as an inspiring heroic master of influence, a new image of the prophetic voice to be reckoned with.
This sublime self-image is, of course, necessarily the result of
the belated poet's unconscious measurings of the difference between himself and all those distorted or "misread" recollections
of literary ancestors that constitute the modern mind's round
of touchstones. This process of measurement, repression, and
compensation, appearing in a poem as certain distinctive rhetorical, psychological, and imagistic effects, comprises Bloom's no-
torious ratios of revisionary defense: *clinamen, tessera, kenosis,
daemonization, askesis,* and *apophrades*.[1]

Consequently, every significant poem is, for Bloom, another
strategic move in the great wrestling match with the mighty

dead, an achieved anxiety concerning the difference in priority and spiritual authority between the latecomer poet and precursor, a defensive invention of the former's necessary stance in relation to the latter's reimagined sublimity. That is, Bloom's theory is a kind of literary judo intended to turn the formidable strength of one giant of the imagination after another to one's advantage. In addition, I think it is fair to say that Bloom's theory is not only a hyperbolic generalization of his own readings of the Romantics and their modern heirs, but is also a speculative allegory of his relationship to, and readings of, his critical and scholarly rivals. Theory, in short, exemplifies itself as method, and vice versa, thereby creating for Bloom his own separate world.

In this opening section I will briefly discuss the contributions two of Bloom's latest volumes, *Agon* and *The Breaking of the Vessels*, make to his theory. Then, I will take a detour into Joyce, Nietzsche, Shelley, and Longinus to discuss how the sublime manifests itself as a certain kind of destructive influence, revisionary irony. With this meaning of irony defined and illustrated, I will then return to Bloom to analyze how his theoretical practice manages to handle, almost successfully, one of his major critical precursors, Nietzsche.

Agon and its companion volume *The Breaking of the Vessels* complete Harold Bloom's more than decade-long brooding on the sorrows of revisionism that began with *Yeats* (1970) and *The Anxiety of Influence* (1973), reached a peak of theoretical elaboration with *A Map of Misreading* (1975), *Kabbalah and Criticism* (1975) and *Poetry and Repression* (1976), and bore practical interpretive fruit in his massive study of Wallace Stevens, *The Poems of Our Climate* (1977). But these new volumes are more than just refinements of the "system," for they are also acts of self-revision that look forward to what promises to be a definitive literary analysis of Freud, *Transference and Authority*. In this respect, *Agon* is of particular interest, as two of its longer and better chapters treat the work of this master in self-revision. And even though nearly every chapter here has appeared previously since 1977 as a separate essay, *Agon* nonetheless makes a unified impression, one not solely dependent on the obtrusive strength of the critic's personality.

For Bloom, a Jewish devotee of the Gnostic Alien God, that primal forefather who is also an all-devouring abyss (or foremother), the revisionary moment is a repetition of the original creation-fall that plunged the Gnostic pneuma or divine spark into the prison of time, historical cycles, and the decaying human body. Yet this repetition, as an inventive lie against its own belated status, also defines the aim of the writer's quest for sublimity, which is to identify oneself with and then to transfer authority to oneself from all those fabulous images of his precursors—from Yeats and Blake, say, back to Jehovah and the Demiurge—with which the would-be creator has lovingly terrorized himself. The critic's task, therefore, is to ask over and over again what Bloom wickedly terms "the triple question: more? less? equal?" That is, the critic must interrogate and measure the competing sublimities of precursor and ephebe, in an attempt to settle the issue of who really deserves canonical status among the other grand cultural monuments. Given such a prodigiously tendentious vision and such a delightfully malicious (if reductive) critical approach, it is no wonder that *Agon,* for all its apparent heterogenity, produces a singular effect in the reader's mind: that of a holograph of Bloom's critical heterocosm.

The essays in *Agon* range from a theoretical discussion of how one makes oneself an influence ("Agon: Revisionism and Critical Personality") and a close reading of an ancient Gnostic text ("Lying Against Time: Gnosis, Poetry, Criticism") to energetic encounters with Freud ("Freud and the Sublime" and "Freud's Concepts of Defense and the Poetic Will") and a series of essays on nineteenth-and twentieth-century American literary figures, the most important of which are the discussions of Emerson ("Emerson: The American Religion") and of Whitman ("Whitman's Image of Voice: To the Tally of My Soul"). These fifteen essays, considered in groups of five, illustrate the three antithetical models of poetic invention, the three models for world-making, which Bloom now proposes. He analogizes poetic invention with a catastrophe theory of creation derived from Gnosticism, with a psychoanalytic perspective on the family romance, and with a rhetorical, transumptive procedure of reversing images of earliness and belatedness found in critical and poetic texts alike. In addition, *Agon* stands as a marker of what Bloom calls "the American difference," a difference that evades by its willful extravagance both traditional, Arnoldian forms of humanism and all recent deconstructive forms of antihumanism imported from the Continent. Bloom concludes that only a truly strong, totally antithetical stance can serve the American critic as he faces an American canon of great writers in this time of America's obvious decline.

The most significant feature of these essays is their revision of Bloom's dialectic of revisionism first formulated in *A Map of Misreading* and most fully worked out in *Poetry and Repression*. In these works, Bloom argues that the pattern of revisionary interpretation discernible in all post-enlightenment texts worth the effort of reading could be reduced to an endlessly recurring cycle of three phases or acts: an initial moment of *limitation* or ironic self-reduction; a second moment of *substitution* in which the writer develops his sense of identity by reinventing the beloved masks of his precursors; and a final moment in which the writer produces a sublime *representation* of himself as the only begetter of his fathers and so of himself and his textual world as well. (The ultimate source of this pattern, as Bloom contends in *Kabbalah and Criticism,* is Isaac Luria's revision of the *Kabbalah*.) In *Agon* this dialectic of limitation, substitution, and representation (or restitution) becomes the antithetical triad of negation (or cancellation), evasion (or self-preservation), and extravagance (or exaltation).[2]

The significance of this self-revision is really twofold; the triad of negation, evasion, and extravagance is more in line with Bloom's three models of poetic invention discussed previously, and, as now formulated, his revisionary triad would seemingly be harder to assimilate to more conventional notions of the dialectic as drawn from Hegel or Marx. Bloom thus gives more coherence to his baroque theoretical meditations and defends them against possible critiques from deconstructive sources. For deconstructors delight in nothing more than exploding the progress of the dialectic wherever it is operative by exposing its specious logic and its unexamined metaphorical basis.

Thus, since the discordant notes of *The Anxiety of Influence* Bloom has added to, revised, refined, elaborated, and relentlessly applied his theory in a series of volumes that have made him the first literary critic in the American tradition—I associate Frye with more broadly British and European strains—to rival the greatest of the nineteenth-century masters of English prose, such as Carlyle, Ruskin, Emerson, and Pater—truly cultural presences, each of whom also created their own heterocosms. The irony of Bloom's achievement, for all its curiously representative status is, however, that, given the highly compartmentalized disciplines in the humanities, Bloom can never exercise the kind of influence in our time that these earlier figures once could and did. But, as I shall explain, this irony is, perhaps, really a fortunate one after all.

For Harold Bloom's latest volume, *The Breaking of the Vessels*, represents as *Agon* does his drive for originality in its decline. The book strikes a series of antithetical poses both more extreme than struck in the past and more predictable given the general outlines of his theoretical project as found in *The Anxiety of Influence* and the speculative books that followed it in the mid-seventies. It is as if the perennial "bad boy" of American literary criticism has suddenly become old overnight, moving from precocious and prolific youth to decadent and despairing ancientness without ever attaining critical maturity along the way. Bloom's concern in *Vessels* is, as usual, "neither self nor language but the utterance, within a tradition of uttering, of the image or lie of voice, where 'voice' is neither self nor language, but rather spark or pneuma, as opposed to self."

Consequently, for this self-confessed Jewish Gnostic, a poem can only be "spark and act" and criticism must ape its subject or "else we need not read it at all." Bloom's concern, that is, is all for image: "How can one measure the disruptions of a tradition as they occur within an individual poem? . . . What was the poet attempting to do for himself by writing this particular poem?" One can measure those disruptions with Bloom's six-fold revisionary ratios (clinamen, tessera, kenosis, daemonization, askesis, apophrades), his strange amalgam of traditional rhetorical figures of speech and Freudian mechanisms of defense, which *A Map of Misreading* most successfully articulates. And one can discover what the poet was trying to do for himself if one remembers that "the figure that a poet makes, not so much in or by his poem but as his poem relates to other poems," is the figure one must seek "to isolate, define, and describe by adequate graduations."[3] This spectral figure, part poet's phantasmagoria, part reader's projected phantasm, haunts those interstices in a text, those spots of rhetorical disjunction and semantic indeterminacy, which have always been and always will be Bloom's critical focal point, since his exclusive wish is to learn how to become as if ex nihilo an influence himself, and so achieve the status of symbolic immortality as a cultural monument. Thus, Bloom would become, if only he could through his theoretical exertions, one of those spectral figures he conjures up in his antithetical readings of canonical texts.

If this makes Bloom sound like the critical descendant of Yeats with all his occult aesthetic speculations or of Pater in "The Will as Vision" section of *Marius,* this is as it should be. Bloom openly confesses that his critical project is "an aestheticism," one that endorses "the language of Gnosis" and private visions over the language of reason and social effectiveness. But it is a curious aestheticism to which he confesses, because unlike Yeats and the other aesthetes such as Pater, Oscar Wilde, or Lionel Johnson, Bloom, like Frye, does not care overly much about the particulars of style and poetic form. For example, Bloom quotes Emerson from "The Oversoul" with obvious enthusiasm: "The soul is superior to its knowledge, wiser than any of its works. The great poet makes us feel our own wealth, and then we think less of his compositions." In other words, Bloom's critical vision must be considered a belated form of Romantic irony, that self-conscious post-enlightenment form of the sublime, in which the literary work exists almost solely for the opportunity it gives its author to imagine himself superior to the various conflicts he has drama-tized, parodied, and so apparently overcome in his text. The most famous modern instance of such a vision of Romantic irony is, ironically enough, put in the mouth of a failed poet. In chap-ter 5 of Joyce's *A Portrait of the Artist as a Young Man*, Stephen Dedalus waxes visionary and compares the artist to "the god of creation" indifferently paring his fingernails; he evokes a vision of the Demiurge enshrined by the very New Critics who hated Shelley for being pinnacled in the intense inane. Although Bloom still wars with the New Critics he also continues to echo them when he argues repeatedly in *Vessels* and in *Agon* that the strong poet necessarily becomes the latest version of the Demi-urge who first produced the creation-fall in the Gnostic cosmol-ogy.

The most significant new wrinkle that *The Breaking of the Vessels* puts into Bloom's theory emerges, as in *Agon*, from his discussion of the three paradigms of poetic invention that he proposes the critic should use to measure the effectiveness of the poem he is reading. These paradigms are (a) a catastophe theory of imaginative creation drawn from Gnostic speculation concern-ing the origins of the cosmos; (b) Freud's understanding of the workings of what he termed "the family romance"; and (c) Bloom's own rhetorical transcription of Freud's notion of the transference. In brief, Bloom believes that each strong or truly successful poem must be seen on the model of the original crea-tion-fall proposed by the Gnostics; sparks of the unknown Alien God fell and were ensnared in the forms of this world when the anxiety-ridden and envious Demiurge made the cosmos to con-tain his fear of the primal abyss. Similarly, each strong poem, Bloom contends, must be seen as another reinvention of the liter-ary father the poet would like to revise and appear imaginatively greater than, as if the later poet were, somehow, the earlier poet's spiritual progenitor and the precursor's "corpus" could become material for the ephebe's textual construction. Bloom also argues that each strong poem enacts a transference of power from earlier to later poet, primarily by means of a "transumptive" interplay of images of earliness and belatedness, in which the later poet introjects the former quality and projects the latter fate back on his poetic father: "When a strong poet revises a precursor, he reenacts a scene that is at once a catastrophe, a romance, and a transference. . . . The catastrophe is also a creation; the romance is incestuous; the transference violates taboo and its ambivalences."[4]

In this fashion, Bloom again revises himself and his own earlier understanding of the dialectic of revisionary interpretation found in *A Map of Misreading* and *Poetry and Repression*. Bloom's earlier theory was that the belated poet ironically limits himself, in order to substitute his own image of the precursor for the established one, an act of interpretive sleight of hand which actually results in the precursor's imaginative diminishment even as it beefs up the later poet's own self-representation. This revisionary dialectic of limitation, substitution, and representation has become in *Vessels* as in *Agon* the three full-scale paradigms of poetic originality—catastrophe creation, family romance, and transference—just discussed. The consequence of such self-revision is that Bloom's dialectic of revisionism appears now to be less indebted to contemporary continental versions of the Hegelian dialectic. In fact, as conceived here, Bloom's dialectic is less of a reductive system of interpretation and more of an imaginative revisionary paradox. One surmises that all this coincides with Bloom's intentions in *The Breaking of the Vessels*, a volume ultimately about the critical cost of such self-revision.

This last notion—the cost of self-revision—really stands at the heart of any evaluation of Bloom's work. For the cost seems to involve the necessity of ruthless self-parody, a baleful prospect that Bloom repeatedly invokes in *Vessels*. The reason that Bloom's kind of criticism must end in a demonic celebration of self-parody, of radical and interminable self-revision, lies in his operating assumption that poetry speaks the language of the will, and that the will is an apocalyptic antithetical force at odds with all that is not its anti-natural self—even with its own earlier representations—since this antithetical will desires the impossible: above all else to be itself alone, the great original to top all great originals, like that Alien God the Gnostics relentlessly attempted to envision as joyfully lost in the beauty and power of the pleroma. "By uttering truths of desire within traditions of uttering, the poetic will also gives itself a series of overdetermined names." Such a vision of the motive for metaphor overlooks entirely the interpersonal and social functions of poetry, pinnacling the world-be visionary critic not so much in the intense inane as on the barren heights of his own guilty if still idealized solitude, a self-tormenting creature who is unable to tell his desire from his despair:

> Any mode of criticism, be it domestic or imported, that would defraud us of this true contect [of suffering] must at last be dismissed with a kind of genial contempt. Perhaps there are texts without authors, articulated by blanks upon blanks, but [the strong poet] has the radical originality that restores our perspective to the agnostic image of the human which suffers, the human which thinks, the human which writes, the human which means, albeit all too humanly, in that agon the strong poet must wage, against otherness, against the self, against the presentness of the present, against anteriority, in some sense against the future.[5]

Bloom's point is really a quite chilling one for contemporary criticism. It suggests that the critic, like the image of Kafka's Father in "The Judgment," must project for his heir the ultimate fate of endless self-revision, self-destruction. With this in mind, I shall present a digression on modern irony, the sublime, and Joyce, in order to suggest, why Bloom's revisionary project is representative in its failure to subsume and assimilate what the figure of Nietzsche here stands for: that revisionary madness which, like Shelley's Alastor, haunts all those antithetical questers after their own fires who spurn Nature's common sun.

Parables of the Demon: Understanding Irony

Twin epiphanies conclude Joyce's story "Eveline." The initial epiphany concerns her mother's fate and Eveline's possible future:

> As she mused the pitiful vision of her mother's life laid its spell on the very quick of her being—that life of commonplace sacrifices closing in final craziness. She trembled as she heard again her mother's voice saying constantly with foolish insistence:
> —Derevaun Seraun! Derevaun Seraun!
> She stood up in a sudden impulse of terror. Escape! She must escape! Frank would save her. He would give her life, perhaps love, too. But she wanted to live. Why should she be unhappy? She had a right to happiness. Frank would take her in his arms, fold her in his arms. He would save her.[6]

Eveline senses in her mother's last craziness an intimation of the life to come for her if she remains in Ireland as housekeeper to her irresponsible and vindictive father and as surrogate mother to the younger children of her family. Her mother's tortured Gaelic refrain, though semantically unintelligible to Eveline, is clear enough emotionally. In Ireland "the end of pleasure" is "pain."[7] So Eveline, quite naturally, yearns in desperation for the opportunity to realize her dream of escape, and she sees in Frank, her romantically envisioned sailor-boy, the lineaments of the saviour who would rescue her from "paralysis."

The second epiphany, more familiar perhaps, shows Eveline clutching the iron bars of the dock gate, refusing to answer the entreaties of her lover to join him on the ship that will take them away from the repressions of Irish culture to a new life in Buenos Aires. In this posture of the terror-stricken animal that prefers the security of the cage to the unknown, Eveline becomes the perfect emblem of the "paralysis" that is Joyce's theme in *Dubliners*. Apparently fear of her own sexuality and guilt over leaving her family in the lurch prevent her at last from even acknowledging her lover's frantic injunctions:

> No! No! No! It was impossible. Her hands clutched the iron in frenzy. Amid the seas she sent a cry of anguish.
> —Eveline! Evvy!
> He rushed beyond the barrier and called to her to follow. He was shouted at to go on but he still called to her. She set her white face to him, passive, like a helpless animal. Her eyes gave him no sign of love or farewell or recognition.[7]

A powerful "nausea" has her in its grip. It is a dread of the unknown so strong that it is as if "all the seas of the world" menace her. Frank, she now feels, "would drown her." So, like an Eve who would remain in a familiar Eden, no matter how hellish it is now, rather than risk starting a new life, Eveline refuses her saviour's hand. Apparently, her saviour would plunge her beneath, rather than lift her above, the murderously innocent waves.[9]

I begin this section with the conclusion to a story by Joyce not out of perversity, but because it is a powerful modern example of the genius of irony at work. No matter how many times and how closely one reads the story one cannot help but feel that the lucid formulation of her mother's fate must compel Eveline to leave Ireland at all costs. Yet Eveline does not leave. She cannot leave. Fear of the overwhelming unknown and guilt at breaking the promise she made to her now dead mother, to keep the family together whatever the price, seize her just as she would be drawn by her girlish love for a carefree sailor out of her "hard life."

What finally keeps her in Ireland, however, is not simply fear and guilt in any ordinary sense. Rather, it is primarily the inexorable attraction of that image of her own potential fate—"that life of commonplace sacrifices closing in final craziness." Sublime pathos captures and imprisons her Romantic imagination. Eveline, for a moment, sees into the life of her mother as her creator and the reader see into her life. Joyce even allows Eveline to think to herself this magic formula for what, if she stays at home, must become her mode of paralysis. Such insight and articulation would seem to be beyond the capacity of a nineteen-year-old Irish girl in turn-of-the-century Dublin who can still think of her lover's face as being one "of bronze" and can still speak of her father's occasional patronizing gestures of tenderness and concern as signs of his being "very nice."[10] Yet in saying this I don't mean to imply that Joyce is simply violating the realistic conventions of his story. Rather, I suggest that he has Eveline think the story's marvelously apt motto or "touchstone"—"that life of commonplace sacrifices closing in final craziness"—because he wants the reader to understand how the memorable forms of language can taken on, even for such a one as Eveline, a self-induced hypnotic power which, ironically enough, the meanings of those forms are often meant to dispel.

The irony of the conclusion to this story, then, resides not only in the disjunction between reader expectation and final catastrophe. It resides primarily in this insight into the subtly paradoxical operations of guilt on the imagination. For it is her promise to her pathetic old mother that grants a safely familiar local habitation and a name to her anxieties: her father's house, her future of commonplace sacrifices. In our culture one is schooled in such demonic images as the one Eveline conjures up as she recalls her mother's dismal end. We are taught, as Yeats claims, to love the forms of our "self-victimage." Self-sacrifice is noble, and tragic, even as we are also reminded that it is so terribly wasteful. As Joyce puts it in the mind of the boy-narrator of "The Sisters," the first, programmatic story in *Dubliners*, the "paralysis" that devastates lives and empowers memory and desire with the most awesome of phantasms, is like "the name of some maleficent and sinful being." This "paralysis" is the demon or "genius" of irony. It is as if the sharp differences between rhetorical figures and between these figures as literary and ideological codes are staged by the text as traces of a repeatedly grimacing mental smile. This is why one longs so strangely to be near the "deadly work" of "paralysis," even as one fears the fatal contamination: What Joyce has written in *Dubliners* are parables of the demon, ironic exorcisms of his own possession by the "genius" of irony. For Joyce, irony, paralysis, characterizes the particular form of Irish life he experienced as it has been shaped by the uncannily destructive influences of family, church, and nation on the imagination, and replicated in turn by the various discourses of his time: religious, political, literary. This irony is as much Harold Bloom's theme as it is Joyce's. And the great original on this topic, for Bloom at least, is Nietzsche. For Bloom argues that a "philosophy of composition" is necessarily a "genealogy of the imagination" and thus "a study of the only guilt that matters to a poet, the guilt of indebtedness." For Bloom, "Nietzsche is the true psychologist of this guilt."[11] And such guilt inspires all forms of revisionary madness that would substitute a self-destructive Romantic alienation for the reality and risks of human passions.

The genealogy of irony's destructive influence is, of course, Nietzsche's major topic, especially in his splendid polemic, *On the Genealogy of Morals.* The vision of cultural formation and cultural history offered there is anything but comforting. For Nietzsche, "the entire history of a 'thing'" whether an object of knowledge or art, a custom or an institution, or even a bodily organ, is nothing but "a continuous sign-chain of ever new interpretations whose causes do not even have to be related to one another but, on the contrary, in some cases succeed and alternate with one another in a purely chance fashion." A will to power repeatedly rises up and imposes ever new characteristics on "a thing, a custom, an organ," making each object of this will over into yet another serviceable type or antitype in the ruling interpretation of a culture.

> The "evolution" of a thing, a custom, an organ is thus by no means its *progressus* toward a goal, even less a logical *progressus* by the shortest route and with the smallest expenditure of force—but a succession of more or less profound, more or less mutually independent processes of subduing, plus the resistances they encounter, the attempts at transformation for the purpose of defense and reaction, and the results of successful counteractions. The form is fluid, but the "meaning" is even more so.[12]

Whether the ruling interpretation or ideology is the creation of aristocrats or plebians, the strong or the weak, conservatives or radicals, an Eveline or a Bloom, does not, in the final analysis, really matter. The hermeneutical practice of the will to power of a self-selecting group—whether of critics or spiritual "paralytics"—functions, according to Nietzsche, to establish both its "hegemony," to use the current formulation for mastery, and, of course, the servitude of other groups.

But what is particularly apropos in Nietzsche's analysis is his subsequent description of the typical form in which the will to power manifests itself in Western culture. Thanks to the centuries-long hegemony of the priestly class and its ascetic ideal over the natural aristocrats and their noble values, the morality of self-sacrifice rules. I quote now the relevant passages in full from the *Genealogy of Morals,* passages which Bloom in *The Anxiety of Influence* and elsewhere makes much of.[13]

> The conviction reigns that it is only through the sacrifices and accomplishments of the ancestors that the tribe *exists*—and that one has to *pay them back* with sacrifices and accomplishments: one thus recognizes a *debt* that constantly grows greater, since these forebears never cease, in their continual existence as powerful spirits, to accord the tribe new advantages and new strength. In vain, perhaps? But there is no "in vain" for these rude and "poor-souled" ages. What can one give them in return? Sacrifices (initially as food in the coarsest sense), feasts, music, honors; above all, obedience—for all customs, as works of the ancestors, are also their statutes and commands: can one ever give them enough? The suspicion remains and increases; from time to time it leads to a wholesale sacrifice, something tremendous in the way of repayment to the "creditor" (the notorious sacrifice of the first-born, for examples; in any case blood, human blood). The *fear* of the ancestor and his power, the consciousness of indebtedness to him, increases, according to this kind of logic, in exactly the same measure as the power of the tribe itself increases, as the tribe itself grows ever more victorious, independent, honored, and feared. By no means the other way around! Every step toward decline of a tribe, every misfortune, every sign of degeneration, of coming disintegration always *diminished* fear of the spirit of its founder and produces a meaner impression of his cunning, foresight, and present power. If one imagines this rude kind of logic carried to its end, then the ancestors of the *most powerful* tribes are bound eventually to grow to monstrous dimensions through the imagination of growing fear and to recede into the darkness of the divinely uncanny and unimaginable: in the end the ancestor must necessarily be transfigured into a *god*.[14]

Self-sacrifice is thus the devotion of oneself to the work of paying back to the ancestors the debt one owes them for existence itself. This primitive guilt and fear, Nietzsche contends, continues to haunt the religious, moral, scientific, and even aesthetic values of modern culture. For Nietzsche, this ascetic ideal is not weakening because Christianity is dying. It has only become associated more intimately with science and art.

What the meaning of this ascetic ideal is could not be clearer. It means that one would rather have the void of self-destruction for an ultimate purpose, through the mad devotion to one form of cultural work or other, than to be void of all useful purpose, and so be compelled to invent one's own life-affirming purpose for oneself and to persuade others of its revisionary power for life. Nihilism is only the growing communal recognition of the suicidal essence of the ascetic ideal, which, so far, has been the only (ironic) meaning that man has given to existence. "We can no longer conceal from ourselves *what* is expressed by all that willing which has taken its direction from the ascetic ideal: this hatred of the human, and even more of the animal, and more still of the material, this horror of the senses, of reason itself, this fear of happiness and beauty, this longing to get away from all appearance, change, becoming, death, wishing, from longing itself—all this means—let us dare to grasp it—*a will to nothingness*, an aversion to life, a rebellion against the most fundamental presuppositions of life; but it is and remains a *will*! . . . And, to repeat in conclusion what I said at the beginning: man would rather will *nothingness* than *not* will."[15]

To summarize: one could say that the gist of Nietzsche's critique of values in most of his writings from 1882 to 1888 is that, despite the many different attempts at revising the ideals of Western culture, the will to power over the past in setting up new ideals to propitiate the increasing demands of the ancestors inevitably takes the form of self-sacrifice, even if the meanings of each new set of ideals do in fact shift, and seem to represent a liberation from guilt or fear. Like a script composed by an unknown ironic author, the tragedy of Western culture claims Nietzsche himself, of course, when, in the end, he knowingly and with demonic laughter, embraces in *The Antichrist* and *Ecce Homo*, the vision of a new aristocracy of warrior-philosophers who would put down decadence by elevating the noble values Nietzsche celebrates: "Have I been understood?—*Dionysus versus the Crucified!*"[16] Thus Nietzsche becomes a prime example of his own theory of revisionism. To revise the past in the assumed interests of the present on the basis of a demonic or utopian vision of the future inevitably results in one becoming the latest Sancho Panza who would also see, out of a desperately guilty emulation, the sublime windmills of some deluded master's tragic romance. All the parables of the demon, irony, then, appear necessarily to be variations on this Quixote Syndrome.[17] Harold Bloom, like Nietzsche before him, will both critique and fall victim to the demonic form of revisionism.

Before turning to Nietzsche's current influence on postmodern critics, and particularly on Harold Bloom, I shall digress briefly on this notion of "parables of the demon." Shelley in his *Defense of Poetry* most succinctly expresses what I intend by the term. Commenting on the power of poetry to "enlarge the circumference of the imagination," Shelley remarks that the thoughts provoked by the poetic phantasmagoria are those "which have the power of attracting and assimilating to their own nature all other thoughts, and which form new intervals and interstices" in the grand cyclic poem to which all writers are contributing. These "new intervals and interstices" form a "void" that "forever craves fresh food." Commenting a few pages earlier on what Nietzsche will call "the gay science" of the Provençal troubadours, Shelley gives an even clearer statement of his idea: "It is impossible to feel" the spell of their verses "without becoming a portion of that beauty which we contemplate."[18]

What Shelley is saying is that the new poem disrupts the configuration of texts in the tradition as it overturns, so as to revise, the habitual patterns of thinking—those personal "touchstones" of perfection we all carry around with us in our heads. Yet this process is not simply a joy, as Shelley's own poem, *Alastor*, can attest. For the new configuration that results from revisionism is a realignment of "intervals and interstices whose void *forever craves fresh food*," or new revisions—an image of the abysmal "god" of poetic creation that does suggest the more unspeakable rites of sacrifice. In any event, this "void" is given a local habitation and a name by each writer. Each writer's "feary father"—or "mother"—that "familiar compound ghost," whether Rousseau/ Nietzsche, Yeats/Stevens, Hardy/Heidegger, or Wordsworth/Pater, comes to stand for that insatiable void of the revisionary impulse—the will to power. And those portions of a writer's texts

that, whether openly or not, attempt to revise the void by installing there one's favorite demon by displacing from its center the
favorite demon of another writer, such writings are "allegories of
reading," as Paul de Man would say, that tell the story of irony.
This is in part what I mean by "parables of the demon."

But I also mean something much more, and a passage from
Longinus on the Sublime can help to illustrate what I am after. In
chapter 9, section 13 of "On the Sublime," Longinus tries to
explain his sense of *The Odyssey* as a work of less magnitude than
The Iliad. Unable to do anything more than repeat his assertion
of the difference, Longinus must resort to figures of his own
invention intended to persuade the reader of Homer's failing in
The Odyssey. As he attempts to represent, by staging, his understanding of the defect or privation that haunts Homer's later
epic—that unfortunate rhetorical disjunction between heroic and
fabulously comic figures and scenes—Longinus begins to use
language that is an instance of the apocalyptic discourse he has
claimed is one of the hallmarks of the grand style as it appears in
Homer's *Iliad* or Plato's *Republic:*

> Accordingly, in *The Odyssey* Homer may be likened to a sinking
> sun, whose grandeur remains without its intensity. You seem to see
> henceforth the ebb and flow of greatness, and a fancy roving in the
> fabulous and incredible, as though the ocean were withdrawing into
> itself and were being laid bare within its own confines.[19]

As the writer looks into the web of the tradition, the figures of
speech that he would use to cut out his own space and to reshape
the web invariably catch him up in the web, so that he produces
texts that show him becoming in turn a tragic demon to the next
generation of readers. This happens because his texts, too, contain voluptuous "intervals and interstices" that seduce one into
attempting to replenish the beauty of the void by renewing one of
the archetypes of the literary universe, which necessarily means
that one must sacrifice one's imaginative integrity to this project,
in order to assume representative or "typical" status.

In reading texts and revising the tradition according to one's own designs, then, one is always in danger of becoming what one beholds: the brilliant creator of one's own shiny prison, whose writings are "parables"—"superhuman mirror-resembling dreams"—that recount what has become since Shelley's time the demonic nightmare of revisionism—or what Nietzsche might characterize as the guilty hermeneutics of power. By a logic as apparently inescapable as it is certainly perverse, a writer who would reinterpret the past in terms of the needs of the present, seem inevitably to become a self-caricature, the comedian of his own ideal, the monstrous puppet of his own creation: a divine void. Such seem to be the contours of the romance of interpretation. For who else can Longinus be ironically referring to in the above passage but himself wearing the sublime mask of his failing Homer?

Returning to the story "Eveline," we can see how this process of self-victimization works out. The image of her mother "saying constantly with foolish insistence" "Derevaun Seraun! Derevaun Seraun!" ("the end of pleasure is pain! the end of pleasure is pain!"), operates like a curse on Eveline's life. This image installs itself, as it were, at the center of the disjunction between her fear of repeating her mother's fate—"the pitiful vision of her mother's life laid its spell on the very quick of her being"—and her desire for "Escape! She must escape!" The result is that she remains in Ireland held captive by a mediating phantasmagoria of her own fitful production: "that life of commonplace sacrifices closing in final craziness." (With this formulation Eveline "authors," as it were, her one and only "epitaphic" text.) So, too Joyce seems to be saying, the writer who would break out of the tradition by reformulating the sacred hollows of his literary idols, must end up repeating the void of that tradition in its most regressive forms by his installing there images of his own private hell, that "agenbit of inwit," that broken tooth of conscience, or Harold Bloom's "sufferings of history," which under the guise of the loftiest and most impersonal of rhetorics, sweetens time with self-destructive, Nietzschean revenge.

The Master of Creative Parody: Approaching Bloom

The irony of revisionism, then, is my theme. But let me illustrate how this irony works more particularly with an example from Nietzsche:

> *Epicurus,*—Yes, I am proud of the fact that I experience the character of Epicurus quite differently from perhaps everybody else. Whatever I hear or read of him, I enjoy the happiness of the afternoon of antiquity. I see his eyes gaze upon a wide, white sea, across rocks at the shore that are bathed in sunlight, while large and small animals are playing in this light, as secure and calm as the light and his eyes. Such happiness could be invented only by a man who was suffering continually. It is the happiness of eyes that have seen the sea of existence become calm, and now they can never weary of the surface and of the many hues of this tender, shuddering skin of the sea. Never before has voluptuousness been so modest.[20]

Nietzsche reads into the figure of Epicurus a disjunction between the tragic need that inspires the hedonic philosophy and the serene and happy vision recommended and produced by it. A potentially paralyzing insight into the continuity of suffering creates an unwearyingly happy regard for the shuddering skin of the sea of existence. Pain has become pleasure; Dionysus has invented Apollo out of the void of pure need to transfigure existence.

What Nietzsche has done is to project this disjunction between need and vision onto Epicurus in the form of an ironic antithesis, a Dionysian commentary, arising out of Nietzsche's own need, on the Apollonian process of transfiguration. Nietzsche has recreated the void out of which Epicurus as a figure projected by his own philosophy has emerged, and so Nietzsche has completed Epicurus by remaking him in his own image of the suffering philosopher who would transfigure need into vision by means of his "gay science." Thus, in revising the past, one becomes *like* the figure one would understand as one revises that figure. Like a passive-aggressive magic mirror, the irony of revisionism reconstructs and projects the very things it says it would represent and reflect, or renew and supplement.

But, clearly, the materials for my interpretation of the irony of revisionism are self-consciously planted in Nietzsche's own text. The framing statements from the above passage tell the tale of how we are to understand Nietzsche's studious wink: "Yes, I am proud of the fact that I experience the character of Epicurus quite differently from perhaps everybody else" and "Never before has voluptuousness been so modest." What could be more voluptuously modest than Nietzsche's singular pride here?

By such ironic remarks Nietzsche breaks the illusion of serious critical representation, and nods in our direction to indicate that, of course, he knows that what he is saying of Epicurus is also being enacted by the imitative form of his text as a kind of creative parody of himself. This parody is a reflexive shadow of the need out of which he has created this bright vision of a kindred spirit so like Pater's "Divine Companion" in *Marius*—a need that is, perhaps, his and his alone. As Nietzsche puts it in a later aphorism from *The Gay Science:* out of the deceptive chaos of space, "I want to create a sun of my own."[21] But first one has to create the chaos.

In the process of such self-creation, however, the irony of revisionism subverts the project from within. One is defined by that which one would revise. Nietzsche's Epicurus is defined by the tradition Nietzsche would reverse. Similarly, Nietzsche's vision is defined by his need, and so, his art of transfiguration is defined by the vision of guilt and nihilism found in the *Genealogy of Morals.* To put it in even more graphic terms: Eveline's dream of escape, though hopelessly banal and virtually unselfconscious, in being defined by the paralysis she senses, is essentially no different from Nietzsche's powerfully sophisticated vision. The only difference, as his ironic revision of the following Zarathustra passage suggests, is that Nietzsche knows the shape of his determination and would joyfully affirm it:

> "I walk among men as among the fragments of the future—that future which I envisage. And this is all my creating and striving, that I create and carry together into One what is fragment and riddle and dreadful accident. And how could I bear to be a man if

man were not also a creator and guesser of riddles and redeemer of accidents. *To redeem those who lived in the past* and to turn every it was into a thus I willed it—*that alone should I call redemption.*"[22]

So, one could say, Nietzsche would transfigure every Eveline into the Joyce of her own situation, and every Epicurus would become another mask of the tragic god who laughs at himself and all existence as he is being torn to pieces once again. One must become the artist of one's own fate, the stylist of one's own demise—or at least one must create the fictions that enable one to claim such status. The aim is to become the tragic master of creative parody, even as one knows that the origin of that aim is the irony of revisionism, which consists of the knowledge that one knows such mastery must become one's greatest creation.

I think that it is due to Nietzsche's exemplary irony, his playing Joyce to his own Eveline, as it were, knowing all the while that both master and slave are captives of a fate they cannot escape—I think it is this "tragic knowledge" which has made Nietzsche an influence on American criticism again.

In fact, Nietzsche's influence on American literary criticism has never been greater than it is now, not even in the heyday of James G. Huneker and his *Overtones*.[23] The chief conduit for this influence is undoubtedly Jacques Derrida. Bloom, de Man, Hartman, and Miller, among the Yale critics, have particularly attempted to assimilate and to turn to their own purposes the inspired Nietzschean clowning of the frivolous trace.[24] For Derrida and through him, for the Yale group of critics generally, Nietzsche has become the genius of irony, the self-canceling simulacrum of an authority figure (a trace) that occupies even as it discloses the places in their texts where rhetorical discontinuities and conceptual aporias threaten to explode these texts from within, shattering them into fragments as openly meaningless as "I have forgotten my umbrella." The work of revision is thus undermined as it gets underway. The tower of vision is deliberately built on sand, out of sand, at high tide.

Like Joyce in "Eveline" or Nietzsche himself in the passage on Epicurus, the deconstructive writer would turn the irony of revisionism back on itself. By staging parodies of his own parables of the demon even as he writes them, such a critic would subvert all movements to posit a single, final value, ideal, or style in place of the predicament of "paralysis" or "need" or "textual" implication in the web of tradition. Like Joyce and Nietzsche, this deconstructive critic refuses to identify with the simulacrums of his own tracing. He thereby refuses to become simply an unwitting character in his own play. Or at least that is the announced strategy or style so far: "if there is going to be style, there can only be more than one."[25]

To summarize my position here: there are places in a text of rhetorical disjunction, conceptual contradiction, and ideological conjuncture, such places of ironic representation as "the tender, shuddering skin of the sea" from Nietzsche's revision of the figure of Epicurus cited earlier. That passage is an ironic representation because it echoes, thematically and formally, the very idea of "continual suffering" it is meant to repress and transfigure. I say "formally," and mean by the term "structurally." The metaphor, "the tender, shuddering skin of the sea" revises the words "a man who was suffering continually," which, for Nietzsche, is itself a metaphor that appears to be purely literal, a "dead" metaphor which we have forgotten. The result of the resurrection of this metaphor as metaphor, and its continued life in the living tomb of "the tender, shuddering skin of the sea," is not a dialectical sublation of antitheses, but an emerging blankness, a spectral smile haunting the most serious work of transfiguration. Such spots of apparent and momentary indeterminacy, such "intervals and interstices" whose "void forever craves fresh food," draw out a writer's revisionary tendencies and define the scope and the master-figures of the interpretation he would impose upon that void. This is why Derrida, like Nietzsche and Joyce, attempts to disrupt this process repeatedly, to keep it going, to keep flushing out the hollows of the text with figures of his own that parody the revisionary impulse in the act as it were. If the irony of revisionism can be compared (as Harold Bloom has compared it) to Milton's Satan copulating with his own offspring, Sin, to produce the horrible giant, Death, then Derrida's Nietzschean or Joycean deconstructive project—the irony of irony as it were—can be likened to a simulated coitus interruptus, after repeated artificial stimulation of an eccentric kind.[26]

The Vision of the Riddle: Nietzsche in (to) Bloom?

At last we approach Harold Bloom, who, as it turns out, has been in our midst from the outset. For Bloom, unlike Derrida or *his* Nietzsche, believes that the writer, if he is to become creative, and a source of influence for later generations, must periodically repress his self-consciousness and identify with the redemptive imagination of a precursor, if only so he can ransack the tomb and gnaw on the bones of the dead. Bloom's project is to murder and (re-)create:

> Uncovering the Cherub, as Yeats momentarily sees, can be accomplished by the act of becoming one with the redemptive imagination of the precursor. . . . (Thus) the imaginative gift comes necessarily from the perversity of the spirit, and so the living labyrinth of literature is built upon the ruin of every impulse most generous in us. So apparently it must be.[27]

For Bloom, the irony of revisionism appears as the anxiety of influence rather than as "allegories of reading" or as the play of "différance." The ephebe, to become strong, must repress his knowledge of indebtedness for a moment and assume the stature of his poetic father by revising his images, defenses, and rhetorical patterns in ways that make the belated poet the ancestor god, and the precursor the heir apparent burdened by the overwhelming riches of the new fictional ancestor: "Every forgotten precursor becomes a giant of the imagination."[28] That is, every would-be Aeneas has heavier and many more fathers than he can possibly bear to admit. Or imagine Eveline with Joyce as her father.

Bloom's topic, then, is the sublime and how one would compose a counter-sublime to best the precursor at his own game, in the endless agon of poetic history that no one can ever win, a contest in which the later poets are like the guilt-ridden descendants in Nietzsche's portrait of cultural history from the *Genealogy of Morals* or are like the failing genius of Longinus in his revision of Homer. One can only learn how to lose with a greater degree of nobility or honesty; and, in the end, intentional self-caricature, the fictions of the self that result from the feeling for the lost sublime, can be the only result:

> There are no longer any archetypes to displace: we have been ejected from the imperial palace whence we came. . . . For us, creative emulation of literary tradition leads to images of inversion, incest, sado-masochistic parody, of which the great, gloriously self-defeating master is Pynchon.[29]

Like a band of little Satans each of us would mate with our own Romance-daughters, and so mock our loves by the production of our own deaths. Pynchon's only rival, in such a romance, besides Bloom himself perhaps, is Nietzsche.

Surveying the ways in which Bloom has revised and plotted the figure of Nietzsche for his own purposes over the course of his career tells us a great deal about Bloom and the irony of revisionism. In the essay on Walter Pater's career collected now in *Figures of Capable Imagination* but written and revised in the early 1970s, we see enshrined Bloom's very early swerve away from Nietzsche's influence. At this stage in his career Bloom essentially sees Nietzsche as an aesthetic critic of our culture who, like Pater and Emerson, longed for a creative renaissance that never quite came, a Scholar-Gipsy of philosophy whose spark from heaven came in the parodic form of the "mocking laughter of Zarathustra," which smacks too much of *hysterica passio:* "The aesthetic man, surrounded by the decaying absolutes inherited from [the tradition], accepts the truths of solipsism and isolation, of mortality and the flux of sensations, and glories in the singularity of his own peculiar kind of contemplative temperament."[30]

But in the production of the tetrology, Bloom's view of Nietzsche begins to shift radically and repeatedly. In *The Anxiety of Influence* (1973) Bloom sees Nietzsche as a genealogist of the imagination and a critical historian of the anxiety of influence:

> Nietzsche and Freud are, so far as I can tell, the prime influences upon the theory of influence presented in this book. Nietzsche is the prophet of the antithetical, and his *Genealogy of Morals* is the profoundest study available to me of the revisionary and ascetic strains in the aesthetic temperament. . . . Both Nietzsche and Freud underestimated poets and poetry, yet each yielded more power to phantasmagoria than it truly possesses. . . . Nietzsche was a master psychologist in seeing that poets are far more intense in their Dionysian self-deceptions than in their share of our common Promethean guilt.[31]

Then in *A Map of Misreading* (1975) Bloom declares that Nietzsche is the prophet of deconstruction and the prototype of Paul de Man's "Überleser" (over-reader). That is, Nietzsche now is no longer the flawed but great ancestor; he is now in part a comrade in arms, in part an Esau whose legacy one can usurp for one's own purposes if one is resourceful and deceptive enough:

> This fictive reader simultaneously somehow negatively fulfills and yet exuberantly transcends self, much as Zarathustra so contradictorily performed. Such a reader, at once blind and transparent with light, self-deconstructed yet fully knowing the pain of his separation both from text and from nature, doubtless will be more than equal to the revisionary labors of contradiction and destruction, but hardly to the antithetical restoration that increasingly becomes part of the burden and function of whatever valid poetry we have left or may yet receive.[32]

Not unsurprisingly, *Kabbalah and Criticism* (1975) discovers Bloom reading Nietzsche as the secret heir of Kabbalah and Gnosis, as Bloom himself now revises them:

> For Nietzsche, every trope is a change in perspective, in which outside become inside. . . . [In this light] poetic language makes of the strong reader what it will, and it chooses to make him into a liar [against time and its "it was."][33]

Finally, in *Poetry and Repression* (1976), Nietzsche has become for Bloom a master of "creative parody" that is, a master of the unwittingly self-caricaturing effects of poetic language, who, unlike Emerson and Stevens but like Blake and Yeats, never *fully* identifies himself with his own creations—never does so, that is, until he goes mad:

> I myself, perhaps wrongly, tend to read *Zarathustra* as a highly deliberate Nietzschean parody of the prospective stance that frequently distinguishes the High Romantic poet. . . . Like Emerson and Whitman before him, Stevens persuades himself by his own rhetoric that momentarily, in his poem, his ontological self and his empirical self have come together. Nietzsche, until he went mad, did not confuse himself with his own Zarathustra. . . . Yeats, like Nietzsche, implicitly decided that he too would rather have the void as purpose than be void of purpose.[34]

Bloom's point is simply this: Nietzsche, rather like Yeats and Blake, and unlike Emerson, Whitman, and Stevens, refuses to identify himself completely with the phantasm of the precursor's imagination as revised and projected by his own defensive rhetoric. Consequently, Nietzsche becomes a master of creative parody, but cannot become, in Bloom's scheme of things, a sublime creator in the grand style of Milton or Whitman who identify totally with God and Emerson, respectively.

I have rapidly sketched the descent of the Nietzschean demon in Bloom's writings with the intent of suggesting that Bloom's six-fold pattern of revisionism is in full operation. Early in his career, Bloom swerved from Nietzsche's influence by seeing him as a version of Pater and Emerson as seen through the eyes of an antithetical Arnold figure. Nietzsche was an aesthetic critic in need of the redeeming poet who is yet to come. Then, rapidly in the tetrology, Nietzsche is, first, a precursor whose insights into critical history Bloom would complete by his own antithetical theory of influence. But then Nietzsche becomes a brother who one claims is greater than one in certain ways, only so such self-humbling may win one the fruits of the other's labors. Next, Nietzsche's sublime intuitions concerning the will to power as "the necessity of misreading" are put into their proper light by Bloom's own hyperbolic counter-sublime of Kabbalah and Gnosis. Finally, however, Bloom sees Nietzsche as the master of creative parody, the giant of irony who dwarfs de Man and Derrida and whom Bloom knows best. This Nietzsche can hollow out

any pose, dart to any new perspective, in an endless round of
ironic self-cancellings of the ruling metaphors of the Western
tradition of philosophical discourse. Nietzsche thereby becomes
as formidable and as graspable as the smile of the Cheshire cat.

Thus, Bloom's revisionary ratios (clinamen, tessera, kenosis,
daemonization, and askesis) do in this way truly describe the
irony of revisionism as it works itself out in Bloom with regard to
Nietzsche's influence. Bloom has, therefore, striven mightily,
with this one figure at least, to exorcise the demon by creating a
multitextual heterocosm to contain him and to reflect back at the
critic his own heroic image. This version of Satan—this correction of error—must have a Hell of his own, and Bloom has assumed the role of the divine architect who, ironically enough,
would build for him over the void of critical substitutions that
stretches between ironic reductionism and mythic representation
Nietzsche's own Pandemonium. Given this demon, Bloom is of
God's and the Covering Cherub's party, and knows it full well.
For Bloom, every would-be strong writer identifies with the
Gnostic Alien God, only to end up wrongly transformed by his
misreading of tradition into the latest version of the demented
Demiurge of the Gnostics.[35]

But, naturally, the question arises: what about the final turn of
the revisionary screw? Where is the apophrades? Or has Bloom,
like Ashbery in relation to Stevens, only managed to become yet
another instance of some giant shadow's last embellishment?

Nietzsche does make one last major appearance in Bloom's
writings. In *The Flight to Lucifer: A Gnostic Fantasy* (1979),
Nietzsche shows up momentarily under the guise of Valentinus,
who, having forgotten his original need and his intended vision,
seeks advice on the matters of origins and aims from Olam, the
Gnostic Aeon, whose wisdom echoes Nietzsche's in *Zarathustra,* but does so in the prophetic tones of Bloom's own most
recent esoteric rumblings:

> The vision faded away again. Valentinus looked hard at Olam, who
> was impatient to depart. "Aeon, if error and the failure belong to
> the truth itself, then what is divine is degraded. How will going

back to the origin restore me, or even you?" Olam would not answer. Valentinus went on, but speaking now more to himself. "Or, is this the measure of our strength? That we admit to ourselves, and without perishing, that the world of original being has ceased to be true?" Olam, provoked to a reply, seized a stone and threw it, underhand but with amazing force, far into the sky. It did not descend. He grinned cheerfully and spoke with assurance: "You are a stone of wisdom, and I sling them. We are both star-destroyers! You threw yourself so high, when first you found me! But every thrown stone—must fall! The aim is not to return to the Pleroma at it was, at the origin! For that All was less than All, that Fullness proved only an emptiness. The aim must be to gain a past from which we might spring, rather than that from which we seemed to derive."[36]

As we shall see in some detail, the above scene derives from Nietzsche's chapter, "Of the Vision and the Riddle," in part 3 of *Thus Spoke Zarathustra*. Ironically enough, the mocking reductive discourse of the Spirit of Gravity, Zarathustra's enemy, is staged in Bloom's text as the wisdom of Olam. Bloom has striven to become one of his own critical fathers here by staging a scene of instruction for Nietzsche, a scene that would instruct Nietzsche in the wisdom he has repressed and that Bloom has single-handedly resurrected. In the passage from *The Flight to Lucifer* Bloom aims to give birth to himself as an authentically creative writer by representing Nietzsche as a worn-out master of creative-parody who needs the Gnostic wisdom, that spark from heaven, which only Bloom can provide. But in the process Bloom recreates himself as another, later version of the Spirit of Gravity, Nietzsche's figure for what Bloom himself earlier derided as the Covering Cherub. Such is the revisionary comedy of errors as staged in Bloom.

We have all seen this irony of revisionism before in Bloom, in connection with Yeats. Bloom argued in his book on *Yeats* (1970) that the Irish poet had sought to correct the vision of his imaginative fathers, Blake and Shelley, by supplementing their "naive" prophetic humanism with his own more "mature" tragic vision of the irremedial evil of human existence. But, Bloom argues, in the process of working out this vision of evil, Yeats ironically becomes the antithetical fulfillment of that humanism through his embrace of a Gnostic Sophia—in Celtic garb—thirsty for the blood of Jerusalem and Asia.

But, as we now see, Bloom has become a living example of his theory of the anxiety of influence. In the name of the aesthetic humanism of Blake and Shelley, the supposed naturalistic "morality" of Stevens and Freud, and the mystical existentialism of Martin Buber, Bloom criticized severely Yeats' supernatural hijinks in *A Vision* and in the great poetry written in its baleful light as "the worship of the composite-god of historical process."[37] Yet by decade's end Bloom himself became an academic revision of what he had beheld in Yeats: a "professor" of humane letters espousing what according to Bloom in *Yeats* is the modern form of Gnosticism: historical determinism. For Bloom's theory calls for the growing solipsism of the poet and so, in the final analysis, for the "death" of poetry in the "birth" of "poetic" criticism. It seems that, as Oscar Wilde might say and the work of Cervantes and Flaubert or Joyce might demonstrate, life does truly imitate art far more than art imitates life, and in more complex and paradoxical ways than any writer can begin to imagine. For the final danger of the irony of revisionism is, of course, that one will become the antithetical image of all that one originally held dear.

This question of the irony of revisionism haunts Nietzsche's *Zarathustra,* and particularly its centerpiece, "Of the Vision and the Riddle." Not the least of the difficulties of this chapter is the impossibility of deciding wherein lies the vision, wherein the riddle.

There are two clearly defined parts to this chapter. Both are sections of Zarathustra's address to the sailors on board the ship that is taking him from the Blissful Isles to his lost companions on the mainland. The first half of his address recollects his bitter vision of the Spirit of Gravity, Zarathustra's devilish nemesis, who appears to him as a demon, part dwarf, part mole, that perches on his shoulder. From that position the Spirit of Gravity mocks Zarathustra's every effort to affirm life, especially his heroic posture that would seem to exclaim homerically, "'Was that life? Well then! Once more!'"[38] One cannot very easily dance up to the sublime heights from which even tragedy appears comic, when the Spirit of Gravity hangs on one's shoulder and pours into one's ear the mocking remark: "'You stone of wisdom! You have thrown yourself high, but every stone that is thrown must—fall'" (p. 179). (I would recall to you the passage from Bloom's *Flight to Lucifer* cited previously, and as well the central image of the goal of Nietzsche's revisionary project, viz., that of becoming like a new star in the cultural firmament: "'You must be full of chaos to give birth to a dancing star!'" [p. 44]). Thus the Spirit of Gravity mocks Zarathustra's every effort to become himself, to transfigure himself into a living touchstone, a living philosopher's stone of creative health.

The second part of this chapter concerns Zarathustra's hypothesis of the "Eternal Recurrence" and its riddling illustration. At the gateway of the "Moment" an eternity rolls out behind and an eternity rolls on ahead—a notion that "The Spirit of Gravity immediately parodies with his sing-song vision: 'Everything straight lies,' mimics the dwarf-mole-demon disdainfully, 'All truth is crooked, time itself is a circle'" (p. 178). But their spat is interrupted by a dog howling nearby which recalls a time from Zarathustra's past, from his childhood in fact, when he heard a similar howling and he was moved to pity for a dog so fearful of the ghostly moon. But when Zarathustra looks up now from his reverie, the dwarf and the gateway of the Moment—all the former visionary and mock-visionary scenes are gone, vanished enigmatically. He tells the sailors that it was as if he had been dreaming and had then awakened, or perhaps it was just the opposite? For all at once, Zarathustra reports, he was standing between wild cliffs, alone, desolate in a most desolate moonlight.

What follows is the riddling allegorical vision of the most solitary man, the ironic illustration of the visionary hypothesis of the Eternal Recurrence that has just been articulated and mocked

earlier in the chapter. I quote this ironic allegory at length because paraphrase cannot convey its terrible dramatic effectiveness:

> *But there a man was lying!* And there! The dog, leaping, bristling,
> whining; then it saw me coming—then it howled again, then it *cried
> out*—had I ever heard a dog cry so for help?
>
> And truly, I had never seen the like of what I then saw. I saw a
> young shepherd writhing, choking, convulsed, his face distorted;
> and a heavy, black snake was hanging out of his mouth.
>
> Had I ever seen so much disgust and pallid horror on a face? Had
> he, perhaps, been asleep? Then the snake had crawled into his
> throat—and there it had bitten itself fast.
>
> My hands tugged and tugged at the snake—in vain! they could
> not tug the snake out of the shepherd's throat. Then a voice cried
> from me: 'Bite! Bite! Its head off! Bite!'—thus a voice cried from
> me, my horror, my hate, my disgust, my pity, all my good and evil
> cried out of me with a single cry. (pp. 179–180)

What are we to make of this vision, so riddling, so clear? That's
what Zarathustra now asks the sailors as he concludes his account.

> You bold men around me! You venturers, adventurers, and those of
> you who have embarked with cunning sails upon undiscovered seas!
> You who take pleasure in riddles! Solve for me the riddle that I saw,
> interpret to me the vision of the most solitary man! For it was a
> vision and a premonition! What did I see in allegory? And *who* is it
> that must come one day? *Who* is the shepherd into whose mouth the
> snake thus crawled? *Who* is the man into whose throat all that is
> heaviest, blackest will thus crawl? The shepherd, however, bit as
> my cry had advised him; he bit with a good bite! He spat far away
> the snake's head—and sprang up.
>
> No longer a shepherd, no longer a man—a transformed being,
> surrounded with light, *laughing!* Never yet on earth had any man
> laughed as he laughed!
>
> O my brothers, I heard a laughter that was no human laughter—
> and now a thirst consumes me, a longing that is never stilled. My
> longing for this laughter consumes me; oh how do I endure still to
> live! And how could I endure to die now!
>
> Thus spoke Zarathustra. (p. 180)

Thus, also, spoke the vision and the riddle. But what does it still
say to us?

Well, Nietzsche's translator, R. J. Hollingdale in this case, in a footnote to this section informs the reader that this scene incorporates some of Nietzsche's own personal memories of and fantasies concerning the time his father was found lying unconscious on the ground after a fall from a horse, a fall which turned out to be the occasion of Pastor Nietzsche's death. In addition, the conjunction of imagery here can suggest the retelling of several myths: that of Christ's death and resurrection, that of Ulysses' return to Ithaca, that of Hamlet's speculation on the poisoning of his father by Claudius. And more contexts could be adduced, but to what end?

Such contexts cannot, I think, account for the powerful, unceasing reverberations of this passage. How are we to interpret this desire on Zarathustra's part of such demonic laughter? What weight are we to give to his questions which besiege the sailors to solve, if they can, this riddle for him? Why is the act of biting off the snake's head so decisive? And so easily accomplished? Does it suggest that the ideas of the eternal recurrence, whose traditional symbol is the uroborus, the will to power over the past, time and its "it was", and the übermensch, do not cancel each other out, leaving one with the sense that time is only the medium for the repeated disclosures of human impotence? How does this unnatural act relate to Nietzsche's assertion that man has unwittingly killed God and so made possible a Dionysian appreciation of the innocence of becoming? In short, can the critic really make a significant difference, for himself, for his discipline, for his culture, by means of his provocative, riddling questions and allegorical visions, that are truly open-ended and not merely rhetorical, that are like Nietzsche's riddling vision here, and unlike Bloom's self-indulgent revision of Nietzsche? Can the critic's self-conscious reflections of his unknown fate actually educate others? Can the fictions of the critic, like those of the poet, make a difference by humanely reshaping the very being of others?

As we have seen, of all the Yale critics only Bloom in chapter 39 of *The Flight to Lucifer* has confronted this central scene of instruction from Nietzsche's *Zarathustra*. But his confrontation is in the form of a reductive, antithetical condensation and gnomic abstract formulation of Nietzsche's riddling vision as if produced by a demonic version of Pater's aesthetic critic. Bloom would simply incorporate Nietzsche into his own critical romance, but he does so in a way that explodes Bloom's inadequate world of revisionary discourse and shows Nietzsche *in full bloom:* "The aim must be to gain a past from which we might spring, rather than that from which we seemed to derive." Bloom's invented past, his adopted Gnostic heritage, dissolves here to reveal Olam as a belated revision, not of Zarathustra or of Nietzsche but of the Spirit of Gravity. Bloom's revisionism invariably appears as the antithetical reduction and inversion of the vision of his fathers, a process that judges Bloom even as he would judge others. Bloom becomes what he beholds—not Blake's Los, but his Spectre, not the Real Man the Imagination, but the Covering Cherub:

> Literary tradition . . . is now valuable precisely because it partly blocks, because it stifles the weak, because it represses even the strong. To study literary tradition today is to achieve a dangerous but enabling act of the mind that works against all ease in fresh "creation." Kierkegaard could afford to believe that he became great in proportion to striven-with greatness, but we come later. Nietzsche insisted that nothing was more pernicious than the sense of being a latecomer, but I want to insist upon the contrary: nothing is now more salutary than such a sense. Without it, we cannot distinguish between the energy of humanistic performance and merely organic energy, which never alas needs to be saved from itself.[39]

What might Nietzsche's rejoinder be to this anti-natural, paralyzing gloom? "Bite! Bite!," I think.

I will not attempt to answer here the questions raised by Nietzsche or dodged by Bloom. I want to propose a certain perspective to adopt for discussing how at the moment when he appears to have most successfully internalized and reversed Nietzsche by having him in *The Flight to Lucifer* return as a spokesman for his own antithetical wisdom, Bloom has in fact been reduced by the influx of Nietzschean vision that makes Bloom's text just another riddling commentary on a problem given classic formulation by Nietzsche. To answer the question why it is that Bloom cannot successfully negotiate the turn of apophrades, or the return of the dead in our own colors, when this passage announcing the eternal recurrence is involved, requires that we see clearly what the romance of interpretation and the irony of revisionism necessarily entail.

Northrop Frye characterizes "romance" as a narrative genre in which an idealized hero, associated analogically with a Messiah figure, engages in a quest for redemption from the sterility that is afflicting him and the land of his adopted people. This quest involves a ritualized contest with all the enemies of fresh creativity, a confrontation with death, and the virtual apotheosis of the hero. Frye goes on to note that romance thus idealizes the rites of initiation of a ruling class group, presenting in the best possible light all those conventions and disciplines that determine the ideological justification for why some are assimilated into and many others are excluded from the "best" society. Only those, whatever their origins, who buy the favored story of the ruling group, who are willing to invest belief in a heroic dream known to be only a dream, will be admitted into the ranks of the group:

> The romance is nearest of all literary forms to the wish-fulfillment dream, and for that reason it has socially a curiously paradoxical role. In every age the ruling social or intellectual class tends to project its ideals in some form of romance, where the virtuous heroes and beautiful heroines represent the ideals and the villians the threats to their ascendency.[40]

In short, like Eveline, we work at learning our roles in such a self-victimizing text. For this formulation of romance holds true, I believe, even for our modern culture of suspicious unbelief and the facile fictionalization of reality, since that culture promotes the ironic and parodic reenactment of all past mythic forms as the primary means for maintaining at least the perverted semblance of intellectual order and social cohesion. The result is rather naturally bizarre, a comic spectacle to end all comic spectacles, as if a host of Touchstones who would each be Tiresias turn out to be all playing, badly, the role of Oedipus all over again, in a production staged for our amusement by the various disciplines, discourses, and medias of our culture.

Both Nietzsche and Bloom, throughout their writings but particularly in *Zarathustra* and the tetrology of theoretical works and *The Flight to Lucifer,* are engaging, one knowingly and satirically, the other reductively through his absurdist parody of Nietzsche, in the ironic repetition of the central plot of the romance of interpretation for the critic of our culture. This plot is the one that tells the story of how modern individuals would save the appearances of the religious representation of reality by transferring its prestigious aura to secular texts. In this fashion, the critic replaces the priest as mediator of a (now) humanistic vision portraying man as in the process of a becoming god through the power of his imaginative productions. Such a plot goes back to the Enlightenment, and can even be found in the apparently most sensible and rational of philosophers in the aesthetic tradition:

> Humanity (as an ideal), in its complete perfection, implies not only all essential qualities belonging to human nature, which constitute our concept of it, enlarged to a degree of complete agreement with the highest aims that would represent our idea of perfect humanity, but everything also which, beside this concept, is required for the complete determination of the idea. For of all contradictory predicates one only can agree with the idea of the most perfect man. What to us is an ideal, was in Plato's language an *Idea of a divine mind*, an individual object present to its pure intuition, the most perfect of every possible beings, and the archetype of all phenomenal copies.[41]

What Kant is arguing for here is the revision of the Platonic idea of the divine mind as the measure, the origin, and the end of all phenomenal reality. This revision, in accord with Kant's critical project, must represent the Platonic idea as a regulative ideal or fiction: Shelley's "void that forever craves fresh food." The goal of the critical quest is to approximate in one's life of writing the ideal of this divine mind. Textual production creates what Wallace Stevens calls the image of "the impossible possible philosophers' man," "the man of glass" Descartes originally used in his *Meditations* to figure madness.

Nietzsche and Bloom, in their own critical projects, wrestle with this Kantian dragon. Nietzsche attempts to use it by creatively revising it and by substituting for it the idea of the transfiguration of the human species according to his vision of the übermensch, a transfiguration which would make us all capable of the demonic laughter he envisions. Bloom, in his turn, would parody and reductively invert Nietzsche's own revision: "Nietzsche, until he went mad, did not confuse himself with his own Zarathustra."[42] But the irony of revisionism which stems from Kant and his critical and aesthetic projects, is an irony that cannot be avoided no matter how self-conscious the critic of Kant or how intentionally repressive and sublime the would-be critic of such critics. The oppositional critics of our culture would critique the last vestiges of the ascetic ideal—as it makes its appearance both in the work of art of our culture and in the latest models of revisionary interpretation—by ironically mating or identifying with their own self-created phantasmagoria "found" in the "voids" of past texts. The aim is to reproduce themselves as the divine children of yet another potentially liberating vision that deserves, ultimately, to be parodied, too. The ultimate word on this irony of revisionism which plagues the critic's romance of interpretation is, perhaps, not Nietzsche's or Bloom's, or Kant's, but Joyce's from the Ithaca chapter of *Ulysses*.

As Leopold Bloom settles into bed, he examines the reasons why apparently he no longer can feel anger at his wife's repeated infidelities, but instead only feels a superior kind of amusement:

> If he had smiled why would he have smiled? To reflect that each one who enters [the bed] imagines himself to be the first to enter whereas he is always the last term of a preceding series even if the first term of a succeeding one, each imagining himself to be first, last, only and alone, whereas he is neither first nor last, nor only or alone in a series originating in and repeated to infinity.[43]

Could it be that that bed is the text, and Molly, the unfaithful wife, is the void that forever craves fresh food, and her lovers are the line of oppositional critics that stems from Kant? And that Bloom, Leopold Bloom that is, is? And Joyce is? Perhaps my title can suggest answers to these questions?

In summary, then, one could say that the irony of revisionism inevitably entails a guilty rebellion against the present decadence (however defined), in the name of a more creative future which is fearfully envisioned according to the most archaic of phantasms from the past. But for Nietzsche and Joyce, unlike for Bloom (Harold Bloom that is), one can master this irony of revisionism by masterfully parodying it—by sublimely representing it as the eternal recurrence of the perverse romance of interpretation of the would-be uroboric critic of modern culture. But can one imagine it really: the eternal moment of paralysis that so afflicts those who would act must be repeatedly bitten off with a bloody smile? Could any of our theoretical Evelines ever really revise their fathers in this fashion?

CHAPTER FOUR
AFTERWORDS:
GEOFFREY HARTMAN ON THE
CRITIC'S DESIRE
FOR REPRESENTATION

The past cries to be recognized and the present to be transformed.
Hartman, *Criticism in the Wilderness*

Critique du Mal

Reality explained.
It was the last nostalgia: that he
Should understand.

Esthétique du Mal

AT ONE POINT near the end of the first edition of *The Gay Science* (1882), Friedrich Nietzsche confesses openly that in a time when the god of metaphysics and morality has been murdered by the will to truth fostered by the faith in this god, existence can be justified—to use the formula from *The Birth of Tragedy* (1872)—"only as an aesthetic phenomenon." In such an ironic world only an open-eyed will to illusion that calls for the perfection of one's own individual "style" can redeem an otherwise ugly and brutish life: "To 'give style' to one's character—a great and rare art! It is practiced by those who survey all the strengths and weaknesses of their nature and then fit them into an artistic plan until every one of them appears as art and reason and even weaknesses delight the eye."[1] If the individual is going to withstand the pressures of an indifferent world, he must produce the *appearance* of a unifying taste. This appearance or illu-

sion of style becomes for Nietzsche, in this period of his
thinking, the "one thing needful."[2] The isolated critic of an increasingly "nihilistic" culture must become, in Nietzsche's view,
the quester after a perfection of style that would pervade both life
and work with the representation of a sublime unity of personal
taste.

By 1887, however, Nietzsche is singing a different tune. In the
third essay of the *Genealogy of Morals*, "What is the Meaning of
the Ascetic Ideal?", he traces with a terrifyingly consistent logic,
the various transformations of "the ascetic ideal," which, in the
name of philosophical, religious, ethical, humanistic, scientific,
and aesthetic *values* has pitted man against nature, on an impossible quest to know and master reality, however conceived. Despite the persistent changes, this antithetical drive informing the
ascetic ideal means one thing—"nihilism," a will, for lack of any
other goal, to nothingness: "That, the ascetic ideal has meant so
many things to man, however, is an expression of the basic fact of
the human will, its *horror vacui: it needs a goal*—and it will rather
will *nothingness* than *not* will."[3] The ironic contradiction implicit
in his earlier valorization of style now becomes clear, and
Nietzsche explodes his aesthetic justification of existence by
pointing out how it is just another example of the ascetic ideal—
the drive to sacrifice all, even oneself, to the antithetical work of
human culture. But, of course, in demonstrating how "discipline
of style" (based primarily on Goethe's example) is also an instance of the ascetic ideal, Nietzsche perfects an individual unity
of style and vision so powerful as to be unforgetable.

Now, as Stanley Corngold has brilliantly demonstrated, one of
the most attractive of Nietzsche's features is the way he always
provides readers with ample opportunities for discovering in him
"unceasingly . . . a rhetoric for restating attractively" one's own
position for or against this or that, in a manner that makes
Nietzsche into clairvoyant precursor, unwitting fool, or sadly
mad victim of his own ironic genius, all, naturally, according to
the exigencies of the reader's current situation.[4] Nietzsche's
ceaseless experiments with perspective, his repeated trying out

of the logic of one cluster of metaphors after another, produces texts in which one can find just about what one likes, even a baleful developmental pattern of increasing insight into what can be called, after the example of Nietzsche's own practice cited above, the irony of revisionism.

In my own defense, however, I must say that I offer the characterization of one aspect of Nietzsche's writing during the final period of his creative life with none of the usual motives in mind. Rather, I find Nietzsche's self-revision, whether one thinks of it as separated by the space of years or by the space of an ellipsis, conveniently clarifying. It throws a certain distinctive light on one feature of modern cultural life, *viz.*, the ironic position of the critic of our culture, his will to truth or un-truth as the case may be, his romance-like quest for symbolic immortality via the perfection of style. The oppositional critic, whether "aesthetic," "modern," or "postmodern," whether literary, philosophical, or political, aims to expose the illusions of the present in the name of a future transformation, which yet would redeem the hard-won achievements of the (carefully selected) past—such a critic necessarily condemns himself, as Nietzsche knew, to repeating, at best perhaps in a finer tone, the Romantic pattern of idealization and disillusionment, the dialectic of (self-) interpretation, that he intends to bring to a halt or to explode.

But all this exists on the level of theoretical argument. What does it mean in practice, for the literary artist and his critic? For the beginnings of an answer to that question, let us once again turn to Joyce.

Early in Joyce's "Araby," the narrator formulates his first experience of "love" in terms of an internalized romance that he cannot help, no matter how comically incongruous the circumstances, but act out:

> Her image accompanied me even in places the most hostile to romance. On Saturday evenings when my aunt went marketing I had to go to carry some of the parcels. We walked through the flaring streets, jostled by drunken men and bargaining women, amid the curses of labourers, the shrill litanies of shop-boys who stood on guard by the barrels of pigs' cheeks, the nasal chanting of street-

singers, who sang a *come-all you* about O'Donovan Rossa, or a
ballad about the troubles in our native land. These noises converged
in a single sensation of life for me: I imagined that I bore my chalice
safely through a throng of foes. Her name sprang to my lips at
moments in strange prayers and praises which I myself did not
understand. My eyes were often full of tears (I could not tell why)
and at times a flood from my heart seemed to pour itself out into my
bosom. I thought little of the future. I did not know whether I
would ever speak to her or not or, if I spoke to her, how I could tell
her of my confused adoration. Buy my body was like a harp and her
words and gestures were like fingers running upon the wires.[5]

This romantic image of a girl known only as Mangan's sister
proves so attractive for boy and narrator because she has remained a suggestively open figure (at once Virgin and Temptress)
that focuses the boy's otherwise chaotic energies and shapes his
story, along the lines of what is for the narrator an impossibly
silly quest to appear different. When the boy finally gets to the
bazaar, he recognizes the repetition, within the banal roman-
ticized context, of the very reality he would prove himself
"above." The boy's desire for a present to give Mangan's sister as
a token of his love represents his (and the narrator's continuing)
desire for a bizarre self-representation:

> Gazing up into the darkness I saw myself as a creature driven and
> derided by vanity; and my eyes burned with anguish and anger.[6]

As Nietzsche recognized, the motive for metaphor is the desire to
be elsewhere, which means to appear to oneself, at least, as someone else. And it is comforting, after all, isn't it, to be able to
intimate, via studied allusions to the Romantic Agony, that one
has been as big a fool as Satan?

My point is this: the Romantic internalization of the quest-
pattern has been ironically exposed by and used to produce many
now "classic" modern texts, whether of literary or philosophical
origins. (Oscar Wilde, unfortunately, anticipated this ironic
modern development in both his life and his art.) Thanks to
Northrop Frye and Harold Bloom (and ultimately, I suppose, to
Eliot's notes to *The Waste Land*), the romance of interpretation
has been carried into literary criticism, not only as a theme to be

discovered (or exposed) in poetic texts, but also as a principle of construction animating critical texts and entire careers. Although the picture has been made more complicated by the introduction of structuralist and now post-structuralist tints, which give to the critic's face the appearance of a self-conscious suspicion of all inherited patterns and values, it still can be said that "postmodern" literary criticism in America, especially if one thinks of the Yale School and its recent graduates as representative, repeats the modern (and previously Romantic) round of idealization and disillusionment, the dialectic of paralysis and escape, dramatized so powerfully, for example, in Pater, Nietzsche or in Joyce.

Quite clearly, this is a question of the application and exhaustion of a cultural code or paradigm, an ideology of romance, that promises to grant the individual (philosopher, poet, critic, etc.) the possibility of symbolic immortality among the giants of the cultural past, the other great heroes, as it were. The writer, for instance, need only operate as if the fiction were necessary (even if not true), and he becomes thereby the redemptive knight, the muse becomes his lady fair, the course of his career becomes his perilous journey, writer's block becomes his favorite repressive dragon, and the textualization of his (already encoded) psyche becomes his (and his community's) ultimate salvation. I have put this point reductively to underline the silliness of this nonetheless compellingly simple narrative, which does permit work to get done. As Nietzsche discovered, the absurdity of a phenomenon does not prohibit its popular effectiveness, nor does it hold out the prospect that it may yield to analysis, no matter what perspective one adopts. In this context, one could say, without exaggeration, that "deconstructive" criticism, American style, constitutes the last gasp of modernism, and so, perhaps, the final revision of Romanticism.

A brief digression is in order here. The way the internalized quest works in criticism nowadays, on the level of practice, goes something like this. (First, recall the last stanza of Yeats' "Lapis Lazuli.") Just as Yeats, in a fit of playful hysteria, reads into

"Every discoloration of the stone,/ Every accidental crack or dent," some aspect of his personalized poetic romance, his "phantasmagoria," so, too, the critic pinpoints those places in a literary text where, due to the action of time or the imperfection of the artist's craft—or to its very perfection—a space of semantic indeterminacy can be produced. A context (literary, philosophical, psychoanalytic, etc.) can now be (re-)constructed, which permits the critic to fill in the gap. Here the critic can stage the "critical" sublime, by conjuring up some antithetical speculations of his own, which have been drawn reflexively from his current reserve of defensive "fictions," as Wallace Stevens would say. These "fictions" are clearly recognized as such, in a playful "crisis" atmosphere, and their ironies can never be resolved except formally within the open-ended dialectical vision produced by the critic's text, into which the connoisseur of contemporary criticism compulsively peers.[7] Hence the current praise of "différence," "free-play," "indeterminacy," and "irony," in the most advanced circles, which sounds like a reprise of the New Critical virtues of "tension," "ambiguity," "paradox," and, of course, "irony." But, naturally, there is a critical difference. The former terms compose a rhetoric of (generally) anti-humanistic subversion, while the latter terms compose a rhetoric of (generally) humanistic and religious reaction.[8] But more of this difference later. Let me, finally, turn to Geoffrey Hartman.

He must be doing something right. After all, critics on the "right" (who are for humanism) and critics on the "left" (who are against humanism) have, for remarkably similar reasons, simultaneously appreciated and attacked his recent work, especially *Criticism in the Wilderness: The Study of Literature Today.* Denis Donoghue, in his Sunday *New York Times Book Review* article, praises Hartman's brilliant mind, broad range of literary and philosophical reference, and often engaging style, but must nonetheless wonder aloud what kind of influence the book will have on its intended audience (it is dedicated to Hartman's students). Revising his favorite passages from Pope and Swift on the ridiculous fate of lesser talents, Donoghue summons up the prospect of hordes of graduate students with monstrous reams of unpublishable poetry snatched from their desks to be shredded, as they now rush into interpretation, vainly attempting to emulate Hartman's occasional self-consciously "literary" effects, his witty, recondite, playful, inspired, hermeneutic hijinks. In this ("realistic"?) manner—Oh, for a single horde of graduate students!—Donoghue isolates what he feels is the matter with the book. It is Hartman's announcement, in a time void of literary masters of the stature of Yeats or Joyce, of the critic's intention to occupy that void. Donoghue thinks Hartman is wrong to suggest in this age of mass-culture that contemporary criticism, continental style, is successfully "crossing the line" and becoming a new form of literature (with, of course, nineteenth-century precedents), that is, becoming "philosophical" (as opposed to remaining "practical") criticism:

> To a well-defined problem it [*Criticism in the Wilderness*] suggests a bizarre solution. The problem is what good is literary criticism in a time of mass education? . . . Mr. Hartman's answer seems desperate to me . . . I find it alarming that the only thing Mr. Hartman can recommend, in such a case, is that critics should leap into poesy. . . . My own view is that, short of inheriting a fortune, teaching is the best way of making a living, and the conditions we find in university classrooms are pretty tolerable, as conditions go.[9]

Unlike Hartman, apparently, Donoghue embraces the status quo with a clear conscience. For him, criticism, like remedial comp., is one of the venerable service functions of the profession, and it should demonstrate, as well as preach, "the decency of communication."[10] (Which means that Hartman should write so that Donoghue's students can understand him?) In short, Donoghue, the Henry James Professor of Letters at New York University, recognizes Hartman's own remarkable achievement over the course of a brilliant career, but must find fault with him for failing to relate his most recent criticism meaningfully to the needs of his time.

Michael Sprinker makes essentially the same type of criticism of Hartman, but from a position far different than Donoghue's. But first of all the requisite praise of Hartman's insights and style. Sprinker finds, quite rightly, that of all Hartman's works, *Criticism in the Wilderness*, "observes so judiciously the demand for plainness, lucidity, and purity," found in the Arnoldean wing of the profession. (Donoghue would cringe at such a position.) In addition, Sprinker argues that, of the Yale group, Hartman is clearly the most sensible, witty, enjoyable, and original writer. Yet Sprinker, too, finds a flaw in this potential idol. Feigning an extreme astonishment, Sprinker cannot accept Hartman's claim, at the conclusion of the book, that, for humanistic poet and critic alike, aesthetic contemplation, taking time over art, constitutes a valuable, perhaps, the most valuable form of "materializing activity" in our culture, an authentically human "mode of praxis."[11] Sprinker, like Donoghue in his way, cannot abide such a radical claim for art that would demand from the critic a response in kind:

> Whatever else humanism may do, it scarcely materializes culture. . . . Surely the problem facing contemporary criticism is not to preserve art from devastations by politics, but rather to create a politics of art that serves human and democratic rather than mechanical and totalitarian ends.[12]

One begins to doubt the efficacy of that "surely."

For are Sprinker's reasons for criticizing Hartman's position essentially different from Donoghue's? After such praise of Hartman's "purity" of style, can a call from Sprinker for a kind of "decency" be far behind? Admittedly, Sprinker's critique does come from a less enfranchised, "left" point of view, and it does sound more informed about the actual conditions of life in university classrooms, but is his "how can criticism take itself so seriously that it aspires to the condition of praxis" attitude substantially distinguished from Donoghue's "how can criticism take itself so seriously that it aspires to the condition of art" attitude? Are not these attitudes of Donoghue and Sprinker just different deployments, apparently antithetical, of the same ironic devaluation of interpretive activity, which includes the interpretive activity of poetry as well as criticism?

If I am correct in my suspicions here, what is the significance of this solidarity of opinion within the critical establishment, whether "right" or "left," against interpretation? Could it be the anti-intellectual strain of American culture at work again? Or is it more likely to be, given especially Donoghue's Irish origins and Sprinker's critical sophistication, the romance of interpretation jousting against interpretation itself? For in order to put an end to the dialectical spiral of interpretation, one position must be privileged, if only temporarily, and the other positions, consequently, must be proportionally devalued. The shape of the interpretive outcome is thus fairly well fixed, or predetermined in advanced, as it were, even as the particular content of the interpretation, in the service of which the text is brought to an end, may change repeatedly.

That is why Donoghue and Sprinker sound so much alike, despite the surface differences. To put an end to their own interpretations, they both have chosen to rely on one strand in the discourse of modern criticism, the one that from Arnold to the present, privileges "reality" or "praxis" as the final arbitrator of the pretentions of art or culture, even if that "reality" is envisioned along less rather than more barbaric and undemocratic lines. That Donoghue's "decency of communication" and Sprinker's "politics of art" together disclose the fundamental similarity in form, strategy, and attitude that still exists within the Anglo-American tradition of literary criticism justifies my contention that in his recent work Geoffrey Hartman must be doing something right. He has touched a nerve. Why this should be so, specifically in Hartman's recent work, requires an understanding of his career within the discipline of criticism, a career in which Hartman has attempted to avoid blind idealization and cynical disillusionment, the Quixote-like romance of interpretation and the Panzaic irony of revisionism, two sides of the same hermeneutic coin.

The Purification of Romance

> But who is that on the other side of you?
> Eliot, *The Waste Land*

Geoffrey Hartman's recognition of the tremendous power over us of the figures of romance occurs in its pure form in his very first book, *The Unmediated Vision* (1954). At the conclusion of his chapter on Valéry, Hartman discusses how Valéry's critics, especially with regard to "Le Cimetiere Marin," attempt to reduce the poet's metaphors to simple allegorical counters, and so, instead of clarifying Valéry's actual achievement, betray their own limitations. For example, one critic claims that the "doves" of "Le Cimetiere Marin" definitely refer to the sails of the fishermen of Sète. But then, he revises himself and claims that these "doves" must be metaphors for the Holy Ghost. This revision occurs not according to the dictates of the poem, but according to the needs of the critic's developing argument. Hartman's response to this ironic situation is revealing and prophetic of much that is to come in his work and in contemporary criticism generally:

> The critic is not absolutely wrong, but he has not understood that the concept of dove is in Valéry subordinate to a visual idea which never submits to complete conceptualization or, conversely, to an idea that desires but never attains visibility. This fact forces the poet to a continual change of metaphor. The sails are now doves and now sails, now perhaps the saucers of sunlight on the palpitating sea, now the whiteness of marble trembling in the shaded graveyard, now mysteriously sheep, vain thoughts, inquisitive angels. It is the play that matters, *"le jeu supreme"* of a mind haunted by an inexhaustible visual desire.[13]

So before Derrida's "différance" or "free-play," before de Man's "rhetoric of temporality" or "irony," before Bloom's revisionary "ratios," Hartman's inexhaustible desire for visual representation was. One could say that Hartman's own shifting positions, his pointed, parabolic, pensée-like style, his range of interpretation (from Christopher Smart and Goethe to Raymond Chandler and Derrida), and his recent diverse and playful theoretical formulations ("beyond formalism," "the fate of reading," "the scene of nomination," "a hermeneutics of indeterminacy," etc.) are examples of Hartman's self-conscious recognitions of this critical desire for representation. These formulations are his own constantly changing, self-revising conceptual metaphors for that inexhaustible visual desire that haunts his texts, which may be in his case the sublime idea of such an impossible "unmediated vision" itself. For such an "unmediated vision" is the goal, whether espoused or parodied, of any romance, from *Beowulf* to *The Moving Target*, from *Oedipus Rex* to *The Anxiety of Influence* —for it is, of course, an "unmediated vision" of oneself as supremely different.

Paradoxical as it may at first sound, I think it is fair to say that Hartman believes that the desire for representation fuels both mimetic and anti-mimetic aesthetics (or "psychoesthetics," as he likes to term the subject). As Hartman put it in his preface to a recent collection he edited, *Psychoanalysis and the Question of the Text* (1978):

> The question that moves to the center [in recent criticism] is that of the character of the written character: its ambiguous origin and uncertain effect, its metaphorical energy however restrained or purified, its residual bodily or hieroglyphic aspect, its irreducible "soundance" (Joyce).[14]

Hartman continues in this line of thinking, expanding on what he means by "the character of the written character," in his own contribution to the collection, "Psychoanalysis: The French Connection." In this essay Hartman posits at the origin of the desire for representation "a scene of nomination," in which the writer "first" fantasizes "a specular image" of his identity, an idealized mirror-image, at odds radically with his "proper" name as exemplified in his signature:

> Like a child who will not believe his parents are his real parents but engages imaginatively in a "family romance" [inventing the loins from which he would like to have sprung] so the proper name or signature [in every act of writing] is always being "torn up" in favor of a specular name, whether or not it can be found [i.e., definitively represented].[15]

Whether the writer in question is Arnold Bennett or Virginia Woolf, John Gardner or Gabriel Márquez, Matthew Arnold or Jacques Derrida—or Geoffrey Hartman—this desire for sublime representation, for repeating in a perfected form the original phantasm of the scene of nomination—one's fantasized "election" to the vocation of writing—deforms one's every word, as any conception of an impossible quest must. That is, this desire for representation makes necessary the repeated attempts at changing perspectives and creating (or revivifying) metaphors, at producing new texts, in a vain attempt to fulfill by exhausting this desire. Or at least so Hartman has consistently maintained, despite all of his own dartings and shiftings, over the course of his career.

If we grant the figurative power of romance-structures over our minds and actions along these lines, the issue raised by Hartman's own practice, as well as by his theories, is this: what role does our knowledge of such power play in our lives? Do we embrace our revisions of the ruling figures of romance by making everything over into grist for our visionary mills? Or do we suffer our Romantic (self-) interpretations to be exposed, at least indirectly, by our critical meditations on the texts which we read and in which they are so differently dramatized? In short, do we play the part of character or author, Madame Bovary or Flaubert? And even given such self-conscious knowledge, do we really have a choice anyway? Does it finally make a difference, after all, one distinctive enough to tell from our own despair at the comical spectacle, within and without the profession, of life repeatedly imitating art?

Hartman, like Wordsworth in his Preface to the *Lyrical Ballads,* does think that knowledge can make a difference. As you recall, Wordsworth thinks that a natural hierarchy of minds can be composed from observing the kinds of response people make to the kinds of stimuli presented to them:

> For the human mind is capable of being excited without the application of gross and violent stimulants; and he must have a very faint perception of its beauty and dignity who does not know this, and who does not further know, that one being is elevated above another, in proportion as he possesses this capability.[16]

Wordsworth goes on to say that the task of the writer in a time of urbanization and industrialization, when people are condemned to spiritual torpor by the routine of their labor and so crave gross and violent stimulants, especially that of newspapers and gothic romances—his task is to educate public taste by purifying the language of men, by selecting judiciously from it the truly imaginative common features.

Hartman makes Wordsworth's project his own in the preface to his 1970 collection *Beyond Formalism*, by acknowledging the dominating presence of romance-structures within the culture at large and specifically within criticism. Hartman calls for the critics to emulate the Romantic poets who sought to purify these structures of their magical power over the imagination:

> If we denominate as Romance the field of all strong illusions—of all myths that have claimed, for good or bad, the mind of man—then art cultivates that field, bringing forth food out of the eater and sweetness out of the strong. With the Romantic poets the purification of Romance moves into the center of the literary enterprise.[17]

Hartman's point is not that such an effort never existed before the Romantics—one need only think of Ariosto or Cervantes. It is, rather, that with the Romantics the complex question of the purification of romance, how *this* quest can purify, or be purified, and so become a new project of romance itself—it is this complex question that "moves into the center of the literary enterprise" and has remained there since the Romantic poets.

Of course, no one individual can purge entirely from the language the mythic, archaic and religious structures of romance. Even if one person would attempt to do so, such a project would be inadvisable. It would be like trying to speak while swallowing one's tongue. Yet without a critical effort at purification of some kind, the consequences can become as disastrous and self-parodic as those that dog the footsteps of every Quixotic figure: "Born into Romance, we replace one illusion with another, until the pain of being is the pain of imagination."[18] Like Kierkegaard's demonic seducer in volume 1 of *Either/Or*, the writer is periodically tempted to seduce his readers into a similar paralyzing impasse, to hand it down to them, by offering interpretations and recounting stories that his readers can never really be sure are not specifically directed at them. And so such readers are forever condemned to play Eve to the writer's Satan, Mortimer to his Oswald.

Let me be clear about this entire situation, even at the risk of redundancy. Despite the Faustian risk of such a belief, Hartman essentially shares the Renaissance and Romantic humanist faith in the redemptive or liberating power that knowledge of the conditioning structures of our culture grants to individuals. One can be made "free" by such "humane" enlightenment and so, perhaps, wiser in action as well, whether that action takes the form of writing or revolution. For his generation of critics, this means that knowing about the formative activity of romance-structures in the critic's own discourse is better than repressing the very possibility of coming upon such knowledge in the name of some neoclassical principle of decorum. Knowing, for example, that when in *Plato and Platonism* Walter Pater insists that the naturalist's lore concerning shells, their perfect types and imperfect instances, grants the naturalist the possibility of a pleasure in contemplating any single specimen far more intense and complex and so greater than the delight of a "curious schoolboy" playing hookey—knowing that Pater's own vision here has been ironically conditioned by the perfect type of the opposing literary view, should enable the critic to avoid blindly repeating the pattern of Pater's response:

> I have seen
> A curious child, who dwelt upon a tract
> Of inland ground, applying to his ear
> The convolutions of a smooth-lipped shell;
> To which, in silence hushed, his very soul
> Listened intensely; and his countenance soon
> Brightened with joy; for from within were heard
> Murmurrings, whereby the monitor expressed
> Mysterious union with its native sea.
> Even such a shell the universe itself
> Is to the ear of Faith; and there are times,
> I doubt not, when to you it doth impart
> Authentic tidings of invisible things;
> Of ebb and flow, and ever-during power;
> And central peace, subsisting at the heart
> Of endless agitation.[19]

But, on second thought, endorsing the idea that knowledge possesses the power to liberate one would mean, in this instance, recognizing what Pater himself apparently did not know—or at least has not represented—even as he endorsed the very same idea we would espouse. Pater's ideal of knowledge is, therefore, founded on a defensive ignorance. Consequently, we *would* be repeating Pater's pattern, after all, in our own self-conscious quests to improve, via knowledge, our capacities for aesthetic delight, delight best exemplified in such a different vision as Wordsworth's.

But, I think, this is precisely Hartman's ironic point. Staying with such paradoxes of interpretation, refusing to subsume one term, either knowledge or power, for example, to the other, refines the critic's interpretive drive and permits him to resist any easy solutions, such as courting the abyss or mounting the barricades. As Hartman himself notes with approval when quoting Valéry on this point, the patient intellectual intentionally hesitates between extremes and so does indeed mark (also in the sense of measure) time by producing in his writing the kind of "durée" or internal time-sense less and less available to modern man since the beginnings of the industrial era. For purposes of clarification, I quote Valéry:

> As for the most central of our senses, our inner sense of the interval between desire and possession, which is no other than the sense of duration, that feeling of time which was formerly satisfied by the speed of horses, now finds that the fastest trains are too slow; and we fret with impatience between telegrams. We crave events themselves like food that can never be highly seasoned enough. If every morning there is no great disaster in the world we feel a certain emptiness: "There is nothing in the papers today," we say. We are caught red-handed. We are all poisoned. So I have grounds for saying that there is such a thing as our being intoxicated by energy, just as we are intoxicated by haste, or by size. . . . We are losing that essential peace in the depths of our being, that priceless absence in which the most delicate elements of life are refreshed and comforted, while the inner creature is in some way cleansed of past and future, of present awareness, of obligations pending and expectations lying in wait.[20]

Valéry's rhetoric of intoxication and rapture, like Nietzsche's Dionysian insights, betrays how the whole of modern life is pervaded by a desire for sublime representation, a desire so powerful and chronic that if it is not fulfilled, we feel empty. We no longer can recall what contemplation, especially aesthetic contemplation (as opposed to enthusiasm of one kind or another) once meant. Hartman's comment on this passage and on Valéry's poem "L'Abeille" suggests that the value of Valéry's achievement in poetry and prose resides in its "prolonged hesitation" which makes time for consideration possible and so tries to mediate some of the more monstrous effects of a sensationalistic culture.

In Northrop Frye, Hartman sees both promise and danger— the promise of increased knowledge (his "sweet science" to echo Hartman's application of Blake's trope to Frye) and the danger of paralysis and repetition such knowledge also permits:

> [Frye's] great achievement is the recovery of the demon or the intrinsic role of romance in the human imagination. His importance to literary history proper is as a topographer of the romance imagination in its direct and displaced forms. . . . His idea of displacement [of mythic forms into increasingly realistic mediums or contexts] reveals the permanence of romance. One can no more remove the romantic element from art than natural instincts from man.[21]

Thus Hartman essentially accepts Frye's "Copernican revolution" in American literary studies, as well as his great "system" with its seasonal rhythms and lineal descent of an original mythic vision which has passed through romance, high-mimetic, low-mimetic, realistic, and ironic incarnations in the course of literary history.[22]

Yet while Hartman can accept and admire Frye, he, like Pater, resists in his own work the temptation to succumb (as Frye and Bloom have not) to the charms of romance by forming, on the model of Blake or Yeats, a textual heterocosm of one's own, a sublime critical identity as "system" that necessarily precludes discovery in favor of self-confirmation ("That, too, I must have known"). The more systematic the critic the more likely he is to condemn himself to an endless replication of his vision throughout the field in trial after sublime trial of his will to master text after precursor text by a self-justifying series of coercive interpretations:

> I do not lay claim, however, to a special theory of consciousness: of how one achieves that degree of self-awareness firm enough to be called an identity or authentic enough to be honored as destiny. Perhaps the very ideas of identity, destiny, etc. are among the beliefs a mature mind renounces.[23]

Hartman's irony in this passage is so muted as to be in danger of being missed. What seems to be a confession of lack, even of an impoverishing need, is actually testimony to the possibility of his greater maturity, a possibility that is represented in the text here as perhaps just dawning on our critic.

Like Keats, Hartman proposes to remain as long as possible in a state of "negative capability," since authentic creativity is only a reality for a writer who, Shakespeare-like, possesses no hard and fixed identity. This desire for mobility of self-representation, Hartman realizes, *is* a desire, one that requires, even as it enacts, the self-conscious modification of the critic's desire for sublime representation. Yet, on the other hand, one cannot simply will oneself into a posture of radical openness without appearing comically pathetic. In fact, Hartman quotes Yeats, of all poets, on the difficulty of so purifying romance that one could stand free of the husk of meanings inherited from the personal and cultural pasts: "Yeats comments on the difficulty of such a step: having demythologized ourselves, 'the last kiss is given to the void.'"[24]

The obvious question that arises now is how does Hartman propose that the writer, whether poet or critic, both expose and use the structures of romance embedded in his language or discourse without becoming either so contaminated by what he would employ and purify that he would end up entangled in the coils of his own artifice; or so suspicious of himself that he could not act at all. How to avoid both blind (or obsessive-compulsive) repetition and self-conscious paralysis (to the point of bad parody)—that is, as Nietzsche and Joyce knew, the question. Like

Pater's, Hartman's answer, or provisional solution, involves a corollary question of critical strategy.

The Subject of Style

> The artist discriminates, that is, between one kind of inde-
> finability and another, and poetry is a very complex art.
>   Pound, *I Gather the Limbs of Osiris*

At the end of his brilliant essay on I. A. Richards in *The Fate of Reading* (1975), Geoffrey Hartman enacts a strategic answer to the question of avoiding the twin dangers of the interpreter, anxious self-effacement and cynical self-assertion. After examining Richards' "ideal" of "perfect reciprocity" between text and interpretation, stimulus and response (this is Richards' version of the desire for representation, his "dream of communication"), and finding it somewhat wanting in the light of recent continental deconstructions of the speculative conception of unmediated "presence," Hartman returns once again to Richards' "psychoesthetic" regulative fiction, and takes his stand:

> At the end of this propaedeutic essay, I return therefore to the "psychoesthetic" ideal of perfect reciprocity, of giving and taking humanely balanced, and even of a psychic development that overcomes death, repression and discord by a "mighty working" able to subdue all things to itself. Here Richards, Freud and Wordsworth are of the same company. For invulnerability is the other side of pressure of demand. There should be something "from all internal injury exempt." Such anxiety myths as Balzac's *peau de chagrin*, a skin which magically shrinks itself and its owner's life every time a wish is consummated, is balanced by the dream the rabbis had of the righteous eating Leviathan in the world to come, without fear or satiety. A "consummation" devoutly to be wished! The word is useful here, in its ambiguity: Wordsworth calls his poems a "spousal verse" to anticipate a great and blissful "consummation"— a universally shared vision of Nature as recreated rather than consumed by the demands of consciousness. A consuming that does not consume but consummates: this is indeed the feast of the blessed.[25]

This passage is rather typical of Hartman's style of writing in his recent theoretical essays which—no matter how high the flights—always proceed from or develop a reading of specific texts, poetic or critical.

In the passage cited above, there is a panoramic display of major figures from different disciplines or "fields" of study ("Richards, Freud and Wordsworth"); there is the self-conscious reference to some recently revived, if unlikely, prefiguration of current critical concern on the continent ("Balzac's *peau de chagrin*"); there is, too, the deliberately predictable and rather mild sexual pun or two (on, for example, "consummation"); there is the renewed questioning of the impossible ideal of an unmediated and inexhaustible vision figured in terms suggestive of the mother-child nurturing experience ("a universally shared vision of Nature," etc.);[26] and finally there is a stylish conclusion whose flourishes remember many masters before centering on a gnomic formulation ("A consuming that does not consume but consummates: this is indeed the feast of the blessed"). Thus Hartman's metaphorical style preserves even as it purifies the particular structure of romance under consideration, Richards' "dream of communication," by self-consciously producing a play of figures that frustrates any easy appropriation or reduction of that dream by the hasty reader. In place of the notoriously unreliable narrator of modernist fiction, Hartman puts this figure of the critic a seductively digressive, only potentially "unreliable," mediator.

Unlike Harold Bloom, however, whose brooding, neo-Gothic self-seductions of style climax in an uncontrollable séance, in which the medium is all garbled or absurd message, spectre after spectre of many dead writers rising up and speaking at once in a scene of pandemonium and a world of Babel, Hartman writes always, even when most playful, with mastery. However loose or elliptical his style at times seems, Hartman always has the many master-figures he is alluding to, conspicuously or not, under control.

For purposes of comparison, let us look briefly at Bloom's practice in *The Anxiety of Influence*, from the chapter entitled ominously "Kenosis Or Repetition And Discontinuity":

> Critics, in their secret hearts, love continuities, but he who lives with continuity alone cannot be a poet. The God of poets is not

Apollo, who lives in the rhythm of recurrence, but the bald gnome
Error, who lives at the back of a cave; and skulks forth only at
irregular intervals, to feast upon the mighty dead, in the dark of the
moon. Error's little cousins, Swerve and Completion, never come
into his cave, but they harbor dim memories of having been born
there, and they live in the half-apprehension that they will rest at
last by coming home to the cave to die. Meanwhile, they too love
continuity, for only there have they scope. Except for desperate
poets, only the Ideal or Truly Common reader loves discontinuity,
and such a reader still waits to be born.[27]

Keats, Spenser, Wordsworth, Milton, Arnold, and I, think,
Dwight Frye's Renfield from the original film version of
Dracula, (re-)appear here in an unhappy, unwittingly self-
parodic "allegory" of the critic's own process of "misreading"
himself. (Could anyone seriously intend to appear so absurd?)
Compared to Hartman's sensible and sense-making "play,"
Bloom's satanic mimicry seems silly. Bloom's figures all serve to
focus the reader's attention exclusively on his effort (one might
say "strain") to represent himself in his text.

All the figures in Hartman's text, however, converge on the
trace ("a consuming that does not consume") of a single famous
master:

> At midnight on the Emperor's pavement flit
> Flames that no faggot feeds, nor steel has lit,
> Nor storm disturbs, flames begotten of flame,
> Where blood-begotten spirits come
> And all complexities of fury leave,
> Dying into a dance,
> An agony of trance,
> An agony of flame that cannot singe a sleeve.[28]

Like the "aesthetic poetry" Walter Pater praised, Hartman's critical writing (perhaps like Pater's own at its best) "renews on a
more delicate type" the writing of a past age,[29] but it does so
without being confounded with that past writing and so without
becoming either an "impure" parody of it (and so of its own
pretensions) or a "pure" style à la the tea table (and so a betrayal
of all serious critical aspirations). I think that this is the case
because Hartman is so much the scholar of the language—with

an understanding like Pater's: "Product of a myriad various minds and contending tongues, compact of obscure and minute associations, a language has its own abundant and often recondite laws, in the habitual and summary recognition of which scholarship consists."[30] Yet unlike the Pater of "Style" (1889), Hartman is not afraid to "contaminate" his prose with the purely colloquial: "We can't eat the breast and have it too."[31]

Whatever the reasons for the differences in style between Bloom and Hartman, the result for the reader is that he wants to know more about the mind revealed in Hartman's quietly powerful style. As Hartman says of Richards, so one could say of him: "Elements are repeated in his texts till the mind behind them becomes clear through iteration and aggregation, rather than absolute logical schemes on the one hand or artistic inventiveness on the other."[32] Which is not to say that Hartman does not invent and is illogical. Rather it is to suggest that he practices a patience before, a hermeneutic hesitation between, extremes. Hartman's positions, like his prose, do not rest on either a positivistic reduction of criticism to a science (however "human" its name) or a "purple" inflation of the critic's "possible sublimity." (Both monsters currently stalk the land.)

We can see Hartman's strategy of "wise passiveness" brilliantly in action in his review of Bloom's "severe poem," *The Anxiety of Influence* (1973), "a theory of poetry" which combines the worst features of both critical tendencies. Hartman's major point of contention with Bloom is that Bloom has become a literalist of Freud's imagination by transferring the master's idea of family romance from the realm of natural priority (father/son) to that of spiritual authority (precursor/ephebe) in a manner calculated to reduce the effectiveness of the poet's defenses (through their exposure), even as the critic thereby appropriates for himself more of the poet's claim of original creative power. (Power necessarily purchased, for Bloom, by the loss of self-knowledge.) Bloom has fixed what Freud termed "Bedeutungswandel," that wandering of signification characteristic of the primary (unconscious) processes, into one, admittedly elaborate, tragic portrait.

Bloom collapses Freud's binary structuration of life—childhood/
adolescence, mother/wife, father/husband—into a single baleful
figure, an ironic metaphor, that of the Covering Cherub, just the
way (I would contend) Yeats' speaker collapses love and death,
origin and end, at the opening of "Sailing to Byzantium" into—
"Those dying generations at their song—."[33] So Hartman sensi-
bly asks:

> Where is the joyous franchise of art? Hermeneutic freedom be-
> comes misinterpretation, the wit of poetry a compulsive "swerving"
> from identity, and family romance the nightmare of always walking
> into parents. . . . Thus Bloom's overcondensing of Freud takes
> away the second chance of sublimation: literary history is for him
> like human life, a polymorphous quest-romance collapsing always
> into one tragic recognition. Flight from the precursor leads to him
> by fatal prolepsis, [such] nature always defeats imagination, history
> is repetition of "one story and one story only."[34]

So much for Bloom right?

I think not. For I would argue that while Hartman's critique is
truly devastating, and surely Bloom's style, as we have seen,
cannot be favorably compared to Hartman's, Bloom's picture of
literary history as one vast visionary tragedy from Milton (at
least) to the poets of his generation and even to himself and his
critical contemporaries appears more persuasive to me as a representation, however exaggerated its gloomy emphasis, of the reductive, ideological implications of romance within our culture
today. In short, if Pater can stand for the critical past (at its best)
that cries to be recognized, and Hartman represents the future of
the profession, then Bloom—heir of Pater, Frye, and Nietzsche—
is certainly the present that demands to be transformed.

In any event, one can see that Hartman's strategic stylistic
difference from Bloom represents an important theoretical difference as well. Despite Bloom's "Gnosticism," all one comes to
know in his scheme of things is the necessity of one's repeated
ignorance—those sublime moments of producing yet more monumental lies against time of one's own. For Hartman, however,
the wandering between "first love" and final catastrophic self-
recognition (as dramatized in Joyce's "Araby," for instance) gen-

erates for the critic an authentically human knowledge worthy of a Keats. The critic concerned with effacing himself in his early prose is compelled to enter his own favorite fictions, to penetrate and to expose them, in his later texts, even at the risk of becoming "a form that seems to be him but is increasingly empty"[35] of all determinant meaning until, perhaps, he finds fulfillment in a perpetually delaying autumnal vision of his own creation. In short, Hartman believes that one can learn from the time spent attempting to do critical justice to the texts one interprets.

It is, in fact, this question of timing that explains Hartman's style. Like Keats in "To Autumn," for example, Hartman would prolong the play of signification amidst various possible points of view, various possible points of fixation, and so interrupt, for as long as he can, the violent oscillation between torpor and frenzy so characteristic of modern culture, and so fill the interval thus stretched out with a purifying attention to the particulars of our world, natural and cultural. In this, Hartman follows also Wordsworth, Pater and Valéry, the other great masters in the aesthetic tradition.

It is precisely because of his commitment to the aesthetic tradition from Schiller to Richards and Frye that Hartman finds Derrida (like Bloom in this one regard) such a challenging questioner of the literary critic's operating assumptions. The idea that "aesthetic education," that the knowledgeable appreciation of beauty in all its forms, can make a real difference in how we live our lives requires that Hartman, the most brilliant explicator of Derrida we have (no one else could possibly match the exorbitant wit of the great Jacques), become an equally challenging questioner of Derrida's operating assumptions, in a kind of Sphinx to Sphinx network.

Derrida, you will recall, sets as his goal the deconstruction of the edifice of Western metaphysics by revivifying—to the acute embarrassment of the academy—every "dead" metaphor in the "text" of the history of philosophy, upon whose back, as it were, every abstract principle has been raised. In this ironic manner, Derrida exposes the coercive, narcissistic desire for presence ("auto-affection") lying behind both the privileging of the philosopher's (or critic's) "logic," or "reality" and the poet's (or critic's) counter-privileging of "poetry," "madness," or "artifice." In either of these cases, the aim is a representation in writing of the phantasm or dream or illusion of an unmediated, face to face, vision of Being at one with itself. I quote, for convenience, a recent critic of Derrida summarizing his project of deconstruction:

> Here, then, is one fundamental sense of deconstruction: a kind of analysis which dismantles not only the programmatic statement of philosophical intention (Cartesian, Kantian, phenomenological, etc.) but also the corresponding canonical reading which accepts at face value the claim of the programmatic statement. . . . What Derrida's deconstruction tends to uncover beneath the apparently unique philosophical program and its residence in the unique historical locale of its birth—locale and program exist in a symbiotic relationship in traditional historicism—is a much longer and larger historical context, one governing all of these "unique" programs, through a set of rules for thinking that colors, compromises, qualifies, even subverts the philosopher's "unique" intention, and by so doing binds it over to the larger institutional enterprise of Western thought.[36]

To invoke the Yeats of "High Talk" for further clarification here: "All metaphor, Malachi, stilts and all."[37] But, as Michel Foucault and Edward Said have recently shown,[38] such metaphors, whether recognized as such or not, shape materially the life-and-death policy decisions within and between cultures.

But Hartman's question to Derrida is simpler than all this airy speculation might suggest, and much more inescapable for teachers of literature today, as they face once again those "tolerable conditions" in university classrooms Donoghue alluded so smugly to:

> Even if we do not seek to monumentalize our nothingness in the form of some permanent double [ironically called God, Reason, Nature, Self, etc.] . . . even if we understand the need for sacrifice [of such sublime doubles] and [their playful, witty] dissemination, must we spend our intellectual lives decomposing the vanity of the monumentalists: the writers, artists, philosophers, and theologians among us?[39]

With this "monumental" question in mind we approach the point of Hartman's concern for the subject of style, and so arrive at the threshold of *Criticism in the Wilderness: The Study of Literature Today.*

"Wanted: A Hero of Consciousness"

It was the dream itself enchanted me:
Character isolated by a deed
To engross the present and dominate memory.
                    Yeats, "The Circus Animals' Desertion"

In a 1973 essay, "Reflections on Romanticism in France," Hartman clarifies the persistent intention behind his interest in the question of "style." He contends, rightly I think, that literary critics today in America, even after Lévi-Strauss, Derrida, and Foucault, still dream the old humanistic dream of generating "the communal from the individual, . . . from within self-consciousness," by finding "the way from selfhood to a purified self."[40] Hartman goes on to put the issue even more forcefully:

How is the acculturated person, standing genuinely within his time, to sight all this cultural wealth and gather it into a synoptic frame? The situation is, once more, mythogenetic: the comprehensive forms or guiding myths come from the depth of the individual mind.[41]

In other words, Hartman, too, recognizes the same problem that Harold Bloom's criticism enacts (rather than corrects), the problem of cultural unity that has afflicted the West at least since the end of the eighteenth century, this problem which Romanticism and modernism in the arts attempted to solve by generating from within inspired individuals, acting willingly in concert, a new set of coordinating myths—a new "religious" or "ideological" system that would incorporate the best of the old as it would give a single if complex perspective on the world to the bewildered populace. (These attempts, of course, always fail.)

Yet, as Hartman remarks in "Toward Literary History," the artist today and his work inspire not awe or even respect, but, among the intellectually alive, only suspicion, suspicion of the possible elitist origins of the very forms the artist uses, or suspicion of the very idea of aesthetic illusion as an ideological reflex of late capitalism or of the metaphysics of presence, an authoritarian reflex that needs to be exposed and demystified as such. ("Would that all God's people were prophets!") Consequently, the artist has to become his own enemy in an attempt to purge his art of the grounds for suspicion, and the literary critic must attempt to provide "a new defence of art" that would "defend the artist from himself as well as against his detractors" by "expanding the notion of form until it cannot be narrowly linked to the concerns of a priestly culture or its mid-cult imitations."[42]

What is needed, therefore, is another less courtly Sidney or less imperious Shelley to arise and to demonstrate that the "perfection" of style need not mean the textual (re-)production of the bourgeois *subject*, but can mean the generation of a more mobile and playful *site* of poetic thinking—a *text* as challenging and free of ideological constraints as Joyce's *Finnegans Wake*. "Wanted: a hero of consciousness. . . . The hero of consciousness . . . is a solitary" who, by virtue of his critical self-consciousness, "is haunted by vast conceptions in which he cannot participate." Yet this hero must attempt to retain his poetic touch amidst the myriad forms of Western culture that demand *transformation:* "To keep in touch with imagination is an increasingly heroic task."[43]

In a very real sense, then, Harold Bloom's criticism is representative of the present state of affairs among the leading critics and poets of his generation. The aspirations to the sublime, the anxiety over the competition with the great modernist and Romantic masters, the suspicion of one's own motives and of the underlying formative assumptions of poetry since the rise of the bourgeoisie (i.e., since Milton)—all these features of Bloom's criticism make it representative of the fix the critic finds himself in when he looks to the major figures in the literary establishment. The trouble with Bloom, as we have seen, is that he makes the problem worst by simultaneously emulating and "de-idealizing" the literary giants. As a result, he neither emulates nor successfully critiques the past; rather, he becomes the ape of his own tarnished ideal, as he cynically admits in his recent "gnostic fantasy," *The Flight to Lucifer* (1979): "A degraded godhead,' he [Valentinus] said slowly. 'And a degraded heresiarch to celebrate it'."[44] Bloom is the prime example of what happens when the literary critic attempts to compete with the poet. Where Joyce, for example, has succeeded in producing classic expressions of the baleful influence of the romance of interpretation on the lives of people, Bloom would put his ersatz Yeatsianisms.

Hartman turns away from Bloom's course. Like Wordsworth, Hartman believes that the critic must invent a different style, a style of difference, and so inaugurate a different mode of consciousness that recognizes the joyous franchise of art. Yet Hartman does not embark on a vain flight from the past with grandiose assertions of making it all new. Like Wordsworth, again, Hartman refuses the temptation to an apocalyptic fervor that would isolate the critical imagination even further from his world. In fact, the critic must confront that world with the threat of apocalyptic thinking exposed as such, if the tradition of humane letters is to survive the various forces that could put an end to the liberal arts in our time. It is the purification of the Romantic quest for purification that we now need, and so the critic must carefully encourage the desire for a selective "contamination" of popular and academic cultures, a topic discussed further below.

The critic, however, cannot begin to offer such encouragement while the reigning assumptions of critical discourse remain intact, those neoclassical rules of critical decorum which would eliminate almost entirely the personality of the critic and the polemical bite of his position, as both are produced in his writing, and constantly revised and renewed there:

> To restate the Keatsian paradox: lack of identity characterizes the poet [and the critic]. The New Criticism interpreted this paradox in

its own way. The identity lack was associated with flexibility of
spirit, with the testing of premature statements through such de-
vices as irony, ambiguity, and the creation of dramatic personae.
The writer's "tolerance" of "no identity" reappeared at the level of
the sign or 'written character' as a masterful handling of ambiguities and made them incremental forms of rhetorical mastery
within an enlarged conception of poetics. Literary language was to
be distinguished from non-literary in terms of this special poetic
logic.[45]

For Hartman, then, New Criticism was, ironically enough, "a
parallel development to ego psychology."[46] The recognition of
the poet's lack of a fixed identity becomes, thanks to the dialectical irony of revisionism, a sign of the poet's self-mastery. For the
New Criticism, according to Hartman, the pressure of archaic
survivals in the psyche, the formative influence of the "overdetermined qualities of symbolic expression,"[47] must be kept in
the service of the old ego—a more complicated but nonetheless
still recognizably stable old ego. The project of the New Criticism—its resistance to the seduction of imitative form as far as
the critic's own discourse was concerned and its dialectical recuperation of self-mastery on behalf of the poet—this double-
edged project, perhaps useful or necessary once, can no longer be
countenanced as the end-all and be-all of literary study.

For Hartman "the scandal of theological" and "archaic" survivals within the psyche and at large in our romance culture is
potentially "a saving scandal."[48] This is especially true now that
the whole notion of reality-mastery, in any form, is a dream that,
thanks to Derrida, Lacan, and Heidegger, we can no longer afford to keep alive. For as Vietnam has shown (some of us at
least), that dream betrays "a desire for reality-mastery as aggressive and fatal as Freud's death-instinct."[49] Thus, Hartman's call
for a textual revolution which would creatively contaminate poetry and criticism with philosophical speculation and popular
concerns. The old principle of decorum must die, if the study of
literature is to survive as "humane letters."

What the productions of this textual revolution might look like
can best be suggested by examining the argument of *Criticism in*

the Wilderness. One can point, naturally, to precursor texts like Barthes' *S/Z* and *A Lover's Discourse,* Derrida's *Glas* or Borges' *Ficcones,* or even Carlyle's *Sartor Resartus* and Nabokov's *Pale Fire.* And in Hartman's most recent book, *Saving The Text: Literature/Derrida/Philosophy,* Hartman represents in the last chapter the kind of work he envisions in *Criticism in the Wilderness.* (My own candidate for a precursor-text will be presented later.)

In *Criticism in the Wilderness,*[50] Geoffrey Hartman makes it clear that what interests him in contemporary criticism is the critic's representation of the sublime, that is, the critic's desire for representation itself, inscribed in a text of his own that would serve to answer the inventive extravagance of a Joyce or a Yeats or a Pynchon. "The spectacle of the critic's mind disoriented, bewildered, caught in some wild surmise," concerning the text being read, and struggling to adjust to its unprecedented demand," is not that one of the interests critical writings has for us?" (*CW,* p. 20). In this "drama of reading," (*CW,* p. 50) the critic resembles a latter-day version of Wordsworth as he represents himself both at Simplon Pass when he suddenly discovered he and his companions had already crossed the Alps, and in the act of writing, long after the event, when he finally responds with his famous recognition of the Imagination's power (that "Unfathered vapor"), to propound visions far in excess of the conscious mind's capacities to discover or to contain. By means of a similar exorbitant response recognizing the authority of romance, the critic would make us "formally aware of the bewildering character of fiction." Thanks to the critic, we learn once again that "Books are our second Fall, the reenactment of a seduction that is also a coming to knowledge" (*CW,* p. 21). Thus, in a paradoxical humanistic turnabout, Hartman claims that "each work of art, and each work of reading, is potentially a demonstration of freedom: of the capacity we have for making sense by a mode of expression that is our own, despite political, religious, or psychological interference" (*CW,* p. 2). The ritual of style, the quest for that kind of perfection, becomes all, in the critic's attempt to preserve a natuaralistic visionary kind of writing in this

postmodern age: "perhaps *the* question when it comes to understanding poetry" today or contemporary American criticism
(*CW,* p. 33).

For Hartman, then, the critical spirit "does not automatically
place itself on the side of" reason, or enlightenment, or demystification (*CW,* p. 40). (The response of the most rigorous
critical nihilist, his constantly fading Cheshire cat grin, can become a reductive manner of demystification as habitual or formulaic as any traditionally fixed humanistic or religious
position.) Consequently, Hartman's own method of reading in
Criticism in the Wilderness is highly complex and very flexible, yet
possessed of a discipline all its own. Here is how Hartman described his method: "I allow a formal idea within critical theory
to elicit the analysis of a poem, and vice-versa; my shuttling
between, on the one hand two critical traditions [Anglo-Ameri-
can and continental], and, on the other, works of art and works of
reading, should be deliberate enough to suggest that criticism is
within literature" (*CW,* p. 5). Which is to say, I think, that criticism must be practiced now as a self-conscious craft or strategy,
an art that, unlike the ancient classics, but like many modernist
favorites, intentionally "fails" to hide its artifice.

It is because of this foregrounding of the reflexive artifice of
the critic, which discloses his desire for representation as some
sublime figure essentially different from all others, that Hartman
makes his extraordinary (if precedented) claim for the literary
quality of criticism today:

> Literary criticism is now crossing over into literature. For in the
> period that may be said to begin with Arnold—a period character-
> ized by increasing fears that the critical would jeopardize the cre-
> ative spirit, and self-consciousness the energies of art—literary
> criticism is acknowledged at the price of being denied literary status
> and assigned a clearly subordinate, service function. There is no
> mysticism, only irony, in the fact that literary commentary today is
> creating texts—a literature—of its own. (*CW,* p. 213)

It is because of Hartman's sense that criticism is transgressing
the boundary between its service function as commentary and
literature proper that he stresses, here, and elsewhere in the

book, the fascinated, virtually criminal delight the literary critic takes in enacting this transgression in his own texts, by making his readings self-conscious, ironic reflections on his desire for sublimity.[51] The literary critic today is producing texts which make him a precursor to himself, playing Moses to his potential Josuah.

Yet Hartman is not simply claiming, despite the revisionary use of Arnold's famous prophetic trope for the critic's activity from "The Function of Criticism at the Present Time," that literary criticism now is the *same* thing as poetry. Hartman clearly stipulates the radically indeterminate status of contemporary criticism. Strictly speaking, it is neither science nor fiction:

> One thing we have learned: whatever style of critical inquiry may be evolving today, criticism cannot be identified as a branch of science or as a branch of fiction. Science is strongest when it pursues a fixed paradigm or point of reference, however subtly modified, however self-transformed. Fiction is strongest as paraprophetic discourse, as prophecy after the event—an event constituted or reconstituted by it, and haunted by the idea of traumatic causation ("A sudden blow," "A shudder in the loins"). But contemporary criticism aims at a hermeneutics of indeterminacy. It proposes a type of analysis that had renounced the ambition to master or demystify its subject (text, psyche) by technocratic, predictive, or authoritarian formulas. (*CW,* pp. 40–41)

What criticism might become, however, is another matter, and Hartman's remarks, following Lukács' lead from his 1910 meditation on the ironic form of the critical essay ("The Nature and Form of the Essay"), suggests that criticism has an open future, especially if one thinks of the critical essay's potential affinities with Pascal's *pensées*, Nietzsche's aphorisms, or Kafka's and Borges' parables (*CW,* p. 82).

Thus Hartman's goal is still that of aesthetic humanism: to insure, by an increased knowledge of the various factors—ideological, psychological, and linguistic—conditioning our interpretive responses, that the preservation of our imaginative powers remains a viable possibility with which to conjure ourselves into existence: "The reflective persona has to avoid being a mere reflex of others; a bundle of inherited intentions, a mediated rather than mediating will" (*CW*, pp. 282–283). But to maintain this view now, in the face of the Derridean suspicion of every commentary's determination by the "buried" metaphors underlying all Western conceptual discourse, requires that the literary critic in America also recognize the romance structures haunting, like a barely repressed phantasm of some trauma, his sublime textual formations. (For the romance of interpretation is the sublime mode in which the metaphysics of presence manifests itself within the discourse of literary criticism.) To begin to recognize this situation is one of the things which constitutes the "extraordinary language movement" of modern "philosophical" criticism:

> The issue of language has now reached criticism itself, which becomes aware how much it has given up or repressed. Criticism is haunted by an archaic debt, by the eccentric riches of allegorical exegesis in all its curiously learned, or enthusiastic and insubordinate modes. We have no *Wundehorn* for critics. Yet the digressive essays of Coleridge, the freakish style of Carlyle and Nietzsche, Benjamin's packed prose, Bloom's and Burke's conquering chariot of tropical splendors, the outrageous verbalism of Derrida, or the "ridiculous terminology" (Artaud) of psychoanalysis, even the temperate taxonomic inventiveness of Northrop Frye—these amount to an *extraordinary language* movement within modern criticism. We cannot distinguish in this movement the vernacular energies from an artificial rage, but perhaps that has always been a defining condition of literariness. Criticism is freed from a neoclassical decorum that, over the space of three centuries, created an enlightened but also over-accommodated prose. (*CW*, p. 85)

The twentieth-century version of this neoclassical critical style, the managerial or communications model of effective prose, its blunt, chaste, sanitized surfaces, can no longer serve as *the* standard from which all else is measured as failure or forbidden deviation. If the critic would become authentically and creatively engaged in his role as mediator of the extravagant texts of the last two centuries or so, then he or she must begin to devise a style which could address a pluralistic society and be answerable to the literature and humanistic values he would promote.

So what Hartman proposes as the beginning of an answer to this question of critical style is "a hermeneutics of indeterminacy," a resolute exploration of the "free-play" of figuration within and between texts. Such a "revisionary" response must be considered, of course, a hermeneutics of Romantic irony: "Indeterminacy' is not a word to insist on. 'Irony' if its history [before the New Criticism] were kept in mind would be preferable." (*CW*, p. 278). But what exactly does Hartman mean by "a hermeneutics of indeterminacy" (or irony)? After all, Paul de Man makes much of "irony," as does Harold Bloom (it is the first of his "revisionary ratios": clinamen or the primal swerve). For an answer to that question, let us turn to Hartman's brilliant reading of Yeats' "Leda and the Swan," which becomes one of Hartman's own touchstones upon which the argument of *Criticism in the Wilderness* centrally and repeatedly builds.

First, to refresh our memories, the poem itself:

> A sudden blow: the great wings beating still
> Above the staggering girl, her thighs caressed
> By the dark webs, her nape caught in his bill,
> He holds her helpless breast upon his breast.
>
> How can those terrified vague fingers push
> The feathered glory from her loosening thighs?
> And how can body, laid in that white rush,
> But feel the strange heart beating where it lies?
>
> A shudder in the loins engenders there
> The broken wall, the burning roof and tower
> And Agamemnon dead.
>   Being so caught up,
> So mastered by the brute blood of the air,
> Did she put on his knowledge with his power
> Before the indifferent beak could let her drop?[52]

And now, to dazzle us even more, Hartman's "reading."

For Hartman, "Leda and the Swan" becomes a modern version of an Annunciation myth, an annunciation of Hartman's own powerful speculation on the violent indeterminacy at the heart of any writer's defensive schematizations of the sublime. The visionary phantasm of productive union with an overwhelming, unknown, and unknowable Other floods Yeats' classic poem (who could dare write a sonnet on "love" after it and hope to compete successfully?), and periodically interrupts Hartman's own text as he again and again in the middle of some other point in his argument must return to some aspect of "Leda and the Swan." Yeats' final "rhetorical" question is (re-)made in this eccentric way by Hartman into a radically open self-interrogation. It is not written off as just the "poetic license" of the silly old visionary. It is "written up," as it were, into the inspiration for the critic's theoretical speculations.

> The ultimate indeterminacy, then, centers on this face that cannot be imagined. Face or mask, human or inhuman stare: the indistinctness cannot be resolved, and is roused by no more than an intonation, a questioning and quasimusical statement. . . . for who could bear that visionary knowledge of final causality. . . . that *AND?* Only a non-person, a god, or a woman metamorphosed into divine impassibility. Or . . . the poet. . . . Is the poet, then, the last of Leda's brood, the last of these births that are also vastations? . . . If Leda did put on the god's knowledge, what then? We begin to understand the reserve of that question, and that Yeats wants us to intuit the psychic reality of crazies like Cassandra, or mythic figures vastated by seeing too much and who are mad, divine, or both. A myth of origins is made to yield a clue to the origins of myth. (*CW,* p. 35)

Hartman's concluding "analysis" here betrays the critic's inexhaustible desire to represent himself by means of a sublime mimicry of the poetic language and stance of the text he would interpret. When Hartman asks his own ironically open "rhetorical" question ("Is the poet, then, the last of Leda's brood, the last of these births that are also vastations?"), I think we are meant to hear an echo of Yeats' own final question from the poem, and we are meant to entertain the notion, as one possible answer to Hartman's question, that the critic now is truly the last of Leda's brood. Similarly, when Hartman begins his sentence "We begin to understand the reserve of that question," we are meant to read both a reference to Yeats' "Leda and the Swan" and a self-conscious allusion to the last question we have actually read, the critic's own.

Finally, with regard to this same sentence, I suspect we are meant to hear the opening of another famous formulaic pronouncement from Yeats' *Autobiography:* "We begin to live when we conceive life as tragedy."[53] And so on, until all the great Yeatsian originals underlying, as in a palimpsest, are brought to light in Hartman's revisionary representations. Except that if one would attempt to do so, not only would echoes and allusions to other texts and authors begin to emerge, no single dominant structure of revision (pace Bloom) would be (re-)produced. For Hartman, I believe, has intentionally refused to reduce the play of intertextual figuration to one, reductive scheme or set of schema based upon one pseudoscientific discourse, whether psychoanalytic, philosophical, anthropological, rhetorical, linguistic or a sublime mixture of all these modes. Quite deliberately, for the reader of Hartman's text, as for the reader of Yeats', "The ultimate indeterminacy" does indeed center "on this face that cannot be imagined." In this self-consciously ironic manner, Hartman would refuse the baleful destiny of an identity and so would preserve the *question* of visionary writing in a postmodern age. *This* is what he means, I think, by "a hermeneutics of indeterminacy."

Ironically enough, however, Hartman intends that this hermeneutics of irony become an informing and shaping critical practice within the day to day business of the profession. His hope is for a revitalized "aesthetic humanism" appropriate for the 1980s. For Hartman contends that "humanists" of the kind he hopes to see on the horizon must be involved in the formation and execution of educational policy (shades of Matthew Arnold close round the playful hermeneutic). Unlike, perhaps, their colleagues from economics or physics, literary intellectuals "will not easily sacrifice anything to anything else: they take their time, and ponder—often elaborately—whether a new step does not entail an exclusion rather than an advantageous change or transformation" (*CW,* p. 300). The critic's power of inventing novel tractics for delaying all final decisions, his knowledgeable temporizing, makes him the most representative figure within the academic community of all that it should stand for in the world at large, and so it is the critic whose desire for representation should be encouraged, both in his production of texts and his workplace. For the critic, Hartman goes on, is "incurably a redeemer. . . . His active life is spent in uncovering and preserving traces of the contemplative life—those symbols and inscriptions—buried in layers of change. Like Wordsworth's poet the humanist recalls forgotten voices, arguments, artifacts, 'things silently gone out of mind and things violently destroyed'" (*CW*, p. 301). It is in such acts of reinscription as Hartman conducted on Yeats' "Leda" that aesthetic humanism materializes the traces of culture and gives us some sense, however fitful and faint, of our imaginative genealogies, the secret hiding places of the imaginative power fueling our own romances of interpretation: "our life remains a feast of mortuary riddles and jokes that must be answered. In the shape of that answer everyone participates who takes time to think about time" (*CW*, p. 303). Or, to have Yeats revise Hartman:

> What youthful mother, a shape upon her lap
> ·
> A shape with lion body and the head of a man[54]

Such do seem to be two of the "choices."

Until this point I have resisted the urge to offer a critique of Hartman's position, believing that in his case at least a more "neutral" and "descriptive," a more "reflective" characterization is in order. Hartman is the most "reflective" writer among the Yale group of critics, and deserves a response in kind. I have made this strategic decision, however, not because there is no serious critique that could be mounted. I could ask, for example, isn't Hartman's position, despite its contemplative polish, still representative of much that is wrong with advanced literary studies in America today? Isn't Hartman, like Bloom, embarked on a romance of interpretation, a critical quest, as open to the pitfalls or revisionism as any of the quests exploded by Nietzsche or parodied by Joyce? Doesn't Hartman, like Bloom, also attempt to reenact the dialectical spiral of interpretation by making a double movement that would rescue the Romantics and visionary writing in general from reductive modernist critiques, even as it conjures up a more fundamental suspicion of the romance-structure of all such ventures at rescue? And doesn't Hartman, like Bloom, also because of his self-conscious foregrounding of the critic's artifice, seem to require of his readers that we make a variation on the New Critical (and ultimately Romantic) dialectical move, a move that would celebrate the problem of irony as the solution of the problem, with wound welcoming knife for more and more of what Yeats "self-victimage"? Are not Hartman's readers supposed to revise his "sublime" (mis-)representations of the critic's essential impotence in this society into a masterful subversion of the only apparent strength of the culture? Doesn't the "eternally" recurring cycle of interpretive activity require, despite the suavest and most poignant or genial of "hermeneutics of indeterminacy," that the interpreter provide a new faceless idol to substitute for the (last) one just overturned? Mustn't the critic of Yeats displace Yeats, or at least attempt futilely to do so? But do we really want another candidate for eventual "martyrdom"?

On this issue, Nietzsche, once again, proves his authority, when he writes that as "martyrs" all proponents of "new truths" in the history of religion, philosophy, science, etc., even the truth that there is or can be no definitive "truth," have "compromised their own deed" of redemption by adopting, unwittingly, or self-consciously for "practical reasons," the "poses, sacrifices, heroic resolution"—in essence, the very forms of representation—of their opponents.[55] And so these would-be "heroes" also became what they apparently beheld. But today we want no more "heroes" or "martyrs," or even "scapegoats." And I only hope that Geoffrey Hartman, despite the "redemptive" sound of *Saving the Text* (whether taken in its scientific sense of "saving the appearances" or in light of its obvious religious overtones), continues strongly to resist the Romantic charms of the scaffold. As Coleridge put it about a similar temptation to extreme solutions: "It is among the miseries of the present age that it recognizes no medium between literal and metaphorical."[56] And courting the abyss to reproduce one's own sublime image there does not seem to be promising, especially now as the profession

lurches into the icy waters of the mid-1980s. In short, I hope
that, following Coleridge's instructive complaint, Hartman's
"hermeneutics of indeterminacy" remain as indeterminate as
possible.

Concluding this section on a brighter note, I offer my own
candidate for a precursor-text of the coming "philosophical" or
"poetic" criticism. I offer it, however, intact—no commentary of
mine will enter this text—and merely as some food for thought,
for that time when we scholars of language and representatives of
the Republic of Letters want to begin (again) to speculate on the
creative possibilities of the critical sublime:

> Some things, nino, some things are like this,
> That instantly and in themselves they are gay
> And you and I are such things, O most miserable . . .
>
> For a moment they are gay and are a part
> Of an element, the exactest element for us,
> In which we pronounce joy like a word of our own.
>
> It is there, being imperfect, and with these things
> And erudite in happiness, with nothing learned,
> That we are joyously ourselves and we think
>
> Without the labor of thought, in that element,
> And we feel in a way apart, for a moment, as if
> There was a bright *scienza* outside of ourselves,
>
> A gaiety that is being, not merely knowing,
> The will to be and to be total in belief,
> Provoking a laughter, an agreement, by surprise.[57]

Critical Romance: A Retrospective Exhibition

> We do not converse with each other, because we know too much—;
> we exchange silences; we smile at each other through our knowl-
> edge.
>
> Nietzsche, *Thus Spoke Zarathustra*

Since the appearance in 1957 of Northrop's Frye's *Anatomy of
Criticism*, which rediscovered the significance of genre studies
for literary criticism, critical theorists in America have in-

creasingly turned their attention to romance, one of Frye's most impressively treated narrative modes. They have done so, in part, because romance, having its own distinctive rules and conventions (the sense of a world in crisis, a saving and suffering hero, an apocalyptic separation of good and evil, a highly stylized melodramatic plot) has become the most influential kind of narrative structure, informing sophisticated and ironic, as well as naive and popular cultural forms. From George Lucas' *Star Wars* (1977) and all those gothic novels and Harlequin romances at the supermarket checkout counter, to the poetry of A. R. Ammons and John Ashbery—even, some would say, to that unaging all-American boy from out of the west currently occupying the White House—the forms of romance appear to be everywhere.

More than anyone else, Harold Bloom has brought the mystique of romance into literary criticism. In *Anxiety of Influence* (1973) an in many other works, he has persuasively argued and relentlessly demonstrated how poetic and even critical careers can be seen as instances of the internalization of quest-romance, "a life of allegory" in Keats' fine phrase. Bloom's belated interpreter, be he poet or critic, struggles anxiously, in text after text, against the precursor-dragon (Emerson, Milton, the tradition itself, God, etc.) and attempts to form his own style by such struggles and so achieve a unique personal stance. Yet the precursor is so strong, generally, that, with a few swishes of his sublime tail, he can forever block access to those secret hiding places of creative power (past works), whose treasure is largely a rueful self-awakening ("Why, yes, even that could be me if only . . ."). Such ironic self-recognition, when repressed once more, becomes the stimulus to the futher revisionary work so necessary for the repeated securing of an imaginative identity, strong enough in its turn, to promise, in this age of shrill unbelief, some measure of symbolic immortality. For Bloom, critical romance takes the form of a ceaseless dialectical contest between a potentially paralyzing self-knowledge and a potentially creative self-forgetfulness, between cynical disillusionment and an ennobling if madness-tempting identification with the sublime figures of one's own revisionary interpretations.

Where Frye discovered the motive for romance in "the search of the libido or desiring self for a fulfillment that will deliver it from the anxieties of reality *but will still contain that reality*," it has been left to Bloom to show how the critic himself possesses (or is possessed by) his own phantasmagoria. In this way, Bloom has opened the critic's discourse to some of those anxieties referred so generally to by Frye and termed by Bloom "the sufferings of history." Thanks to Bloom, we now see how every significant interpretive act results in a text that represents not so much an escape from the anxiety felt over one's belated status in cultural history as "an achieved anxiety" or a revisionary work of repression.[58] In short, Bloom has shown us the cost in human terms that misreading the past exacts.

Given this context, it is not surprising to find Geoffrey Hartman in his recent theoretical works, and especially in *Saving The Text,* addressing this pervasive aesthetic phenomenon of romance directly and in a sustained fashion as it appears in critical discourse. After all, Hartman is a colleague of Bloom's at Yale, and has studied Frye's work long and hard, having written what is still the best short essay on him. But more importantly, I think, Hartman is self-consciously working within a certain cultural paradigm that the Romantic artists and philosophers established, modernists writers and critics ironically exploded and so, paradoxically, refined, and all of us—apparently—are now exhausting and/or parodying in this twilight time of late capitalism.

The reason for the pervasive recurrence of romance is not too difficult to discover. In a time of acute and prolonged cultural conflicts—religious, political, economic, literary—people who have been taught to aspire to and yet have increasingly grown suspicious of and disillusioned by the values of the ruling elites—such people turn to romance. That is, they turn to the fictional staging of the ideology of romance, for that impossible deliverance from the contradictions and anxieties of reality which will still contain (at least some) reality, albeit largely reshaped according to the designs of our greatest desires. But as Harold Bloom's work demonstrates, such a vision of an impossible resolution must be provisional and very fragile, temporizing, and so more and more open to the inescapable ironic perception of those "sufferings of history" from which there can be no escape: what oft was unthought but ne'er so well repressed. Yet such a development becomes dangerous precisely when illusion is seen to be such. Then romance can become virulent, nihilistic, alternatively authoritarian and self-destructive. An example from Nietzsche, a figure central to Hartman's argument about Derrida's work (especially *Glas*, and that work's place in the world of romance) will clarify what I mean by these last remarks.

Consider how in the following note composed shortly before his final collapse on the streets of Turin early in January 1889, Nietzsche revises a famous religious and literary archetype by ironically renewing a nineteenth-century philosophical commonplace in terms of the most extreme formulation of his own notion of the übermensch:

> The Revolution made Napoleon possible: that is its justification. For the sake of a similar prize one would have to desire the anarchical collapse of our entire civilization. Napoleon made nationalism possible: that is its excuse.
>
> The value of a man (apart from his morality or immorality, naturally; for with these concepts the value of a man is not even touched) does not reside in his utility; for it would continue to exist even if there were no one to whom he could be of any use. And why could not precisely that man who produced the most disastrous effects be the pinnacle of the whole species of man: so high, so superior that everything would perish from envy of him?[59]

Like the hosts of rebellious angels in Milton's *Paradise Lost* (book 5) when shown by God the Father his only-begotten Son, all the rest of mankind perishes, falling away in self-destructive "envy" or *ressentiment* from the emerging spectacle of Nietzsche's daimonic offspring. Nietzsche's repetitive, ironic hyperbole thereby explodes, even as it relies on, the then current, Hegelian idea of the great man (Napoleon) as a creative force in history, whose transfiguring if tragic sublimity justifies existence—aesthetically at least—by redeeming the waste, sad time in between his uncanny, volcanic (re-)appearances.

But where Hegel blandly accepts the death of the hero of world history (say, Socrates or Christ) as educationally necessary, in order to impress on the minds of men the new principle of evaluation that the hero represents, Nietzsche demands the Last Judgment, the self-martyrdom of the entire species, as the prerequisite for seeing his Anti-Christ, his self-evaluating, Dionysian reincarnation of the Classical Ideal, stride out upon the stage of world history—to dance all alone, no doubt, but hardly in the style of Blake's "Glad Day"; perhaps more in the style of Mallarmé's Herodias. As a whole, then, the above passage projects the image of an impossible future (the end of the species), based upon a sublime vision derived from the cultural past (the Second Coming) that would require the complete sacrifice of the possibilities for a humane life in the present, in a terrible parody of traditional patterns of belief. Such is the extreme form that critical romance takes in Nietzsche. It was not accidental that one of his favorite quotations from Plato was: "Each one of us would like to be master over all men, if possible, and best of all God." Nor that one of the most poignant expressions of his madness was: "'I' is every name in history."[60]

Such is the attraction of romance, these days, the spell of the sublime, that this ironic dialectic of revisionism is, I contend, fast becoming the most representative form of interpretation in America: in short, Nietzsche's kind of critical romance is our kind now, too. The contemporary literary critic, isolated from popular culture by his elitist training and from the powers that be by his marginal and practically useless position in the academy, retaliates by producing what might be called "fables of solitude," sublime idealizations of the interpretive will to authority, that compose for each critic his own romance of interpretation or self-conscious phantasmagoria, a kind of bitterly ironic dream that is known to be only a dream even as it quickly becomes an inescapable nightmare.

The critic's drive for representation is such that he desires to appear, even within the diminished and splintered contemporary context, as powerful and unavoidable an influence as any of the great literary classics from Homer to Joyce has been in the (re-)formation of the cultural past. Both apologists for Western culture (those few tired religious and secular humanists that are still left) and oppositional critics of the culture (all those "scientific" semiologists, deconstructive or merely "professional" anti-humanists) must practice, however reflexively and "strategically," this romance of interpretation, if they want to make a mark in American theoretical circles. (There are, of course, many critics who practice this kind of critical romance without being quite aware of the fact.) After all, all of us have been taught to idolize as representatives of "the grand style" certain portions of the cultural past and have been led to identify, usually early and blindly, profoundly, and exclusively, with all such representations of the sublime as the sole guarantor of the basis for "a name to come." (Each of us, like a poor-man's Matthew Arnold, has a head full of personal touchstones by which we judge the writings of others and those that we dare produce.) This romance of interpretation, part of the larger ideology of romance currently abroad in the land and enshrined by the Gipper on the Potomac, is thus a reproduction in a shriller tone of the American literary critic's perception of his or her strained relationship to what seems to be the decaying institutions of our culture.

Fortunately, for his readers, Geoffrey Hartman does not brood obsessively over the spectacle of the self-martyrdom of Nietzsche's critical intelligence in the final days of his sanity. Rather, in *Saving the Text,* he uses Nietzsche's theory of interpretation as the major cultural form of will to power, in order to develop the notion of a "will-to-write,"[61] a comprehensive motivation for understanding and characterizing Derrida's deconstructive play that avoids the purely negative determinations of the latter's simplistic detractors. In Hartman's generous view of Derrida, this "will-to-write" is a radical will to an unstable, open, hermeneutic identity, which ironically refuses to see itself reflected either in the written signature that society imposes on each of us as the (repressive) sign of a purely formal identity-unit in the apparatus of the State, or in the rebellious quest for a wholly "specular" name that is generated in the individual psyche by the archaic survivals of family romance. As such, Derrida's hermeneutic identity is an ironic identity of inscription with erasure, an act of identification with différance that is perilously close to the self-abnegation of the would-be saint or sage and yet is carried off by Derrida in a wholly "humorous" manner. Thus, Nietzsche is for Hartman here not so much a sublime figure for placing Derrida or for wrestling with him, as he is a lever for Hartman to use to pry open and expose the playful, silenic, cold autos-da-fé of Derrida's *Glas*.

In *Saving the Text*, Hartman begins by paradoxically recognizing the spell of the sublime in one of the most ironic and self-deconstructing of philosophers, Jacques Derrida, whose major text, *Glas*, aims to stage and show up, via a mock face-to-face debate between Hegel and Jean Genét (with Derrida's own incisive commentary ironically cut in the margins), all such self-mystifications of critical romance. The problem is clearly one of identity and difference: "How can mind accept rather than subvert or overlook . . . . the language of great writers, both in philosophy and literature?" (*ST,* p. xv). For Hartman, Derrida's solution is a project of critical suspicion that in its rigorous play may be applauded for the virtuosity of its evasions but finally cannot be seen as completely satisfactory as an exemplum for authentic literary criticism: "If Don Quixote, if Emma Bovary, die into the world of Romance, if Freud dies into the world of the Dream (making it as textual as life itself), then this quixotic, romantic, and Freudian thinker dies into the world of Philosophy. He returns it, as in *Glas*, to the status of a *coup de des* (Mallarmé), of *Gerede* (Heidegger), or *remarquesu* or *Zettel* (Wittgenstein). Between these lapsed forms of a still rigorous discourse, his language teeters, as extraordinary as it is ordinary" (*ST,* pp: xxvi–xxvii).

Despite the praise of Derrida here and elsewhere in *Saving the Text*, this passage also shows that Hartman realizes that for all its "aphoristic energy" the achievement of the incredible Jacques, that Dionysian tightrope walker, must be sui generis. For Hartman, all writing, that "joyful wandering of the written word," must begin, "if anywhere, in Romance" (*ST,* p. 49), the illusions of the sublime. And, as Hartman knows from the examples of Frye and Bloom, "any strong *artistic* achievement," even that of a deconstructive critic of all such metaphors of presence, must depend on the "sacrificial scattering of the burden of tradition or imagination" (*ST,* p. 56). Derrida's *Glas* is just such a "sacrificial" dissemination, a monumental and unsurpassable decapitation and decapitalization, executed as much by as on Hegel and Genét, that risks "the danger" of literature and criticism "getting lost, running amok or running scared" after Joyce's *Wake* and now Derrida's *Glas* (*ST,* p. 79). This is why Derrida cannot finally become exemplary or paradigmatic for literary criticism. Can the critic of such (self-)martyrdom even hope to top such an act as *Glas*? Should, after *Glas*, one try, or even bother to conceive of literary criticism in such terms as critical romance and the seductions of the sublime?

Yet Derrida has had and will continue to have an influence, and so the question of the sublime, or critical romance, will not so easily go away. The prospect of the critic's repeated identification and confrontation with the influential figures of the cultural tradition leads inexorably to another, more personally painful question for Hartman: that of the possibility of writing about literary or cultural history without falling into the deterministic traps of historicism—the scholar's last-ditch defense against (and instance of) the sublime: "With so much historical knowledge, how can we avoid historicism, or the staging of history as a dream in which epiphanic raptures are replaced by epistemic ruptures? . . . Can a history be written that does not turn into something monumental and preemptive in its turn?" (*ST,* p. xx). The problem is one of unity: how to unify the historical field under survey in a way that will not be either coercive and reductive or pointless and piecemeal. Whether one subscribes to the "organic" great man theory of history or to some more mechanistic or "discursive" formulation, the problem can only be solved if one is not misled by the conceptualized metaphors embedded in one's critical discourse and does not practice a self-suspicion so severe as to constitute a new rite of asceticism, which in its deconstruction of all those monumentalizations of our own nothingness (cultural works) becomes authoritative (if not totalitarian) in its turn— with free-floating terroristic imperatives appearing, as one writes, out of the blue, if not out of the abyss: "avoid talking about origins," "put everything under erasure," "pun unmercifully to show you're (self-)conscious of what you're doing," "be ironic, yet politically acute."

This is no merely theoretical problem to Hartman, who, like his late colleague Paul de Man, has not been able to deliver the promised literary history of Romanticism that he had once hoped to supply. Unlike Bloom, who turned opportunistically to the schematics of his own literary theory as a short-cut to such a history, or M. H. Abrams who has put his trust too easily (and, once too often) in the representative status of a very limited number of philosophical commonplaces, Hartman, like de Man in this way too, recognizes "the scandal of theological survivals in the most secularized of discourses" (*ST,* p. 99) and yet has resisted successfully the temptation to form, like Frye, a visionary "system" or "anti-natural" "secular scripture" out of his own favorite "touchstones." This resistance could be as much a testament to Hartman's critical impotence as it is to his "heroic" good sense, although I suspect that it is more likely to be the latter than the former case. For Hartman does accept the notion that literature (and criticism) has the shape of a would-be romance, in which the writer is repeatedly seduced to pursue the quest of the "specular name," that unique idealized form of identity that emerges out of childhood fantasies of the family romance ("Rumplestiltskin is my name"), to deny our socially acceptable and given "signature." (Hartman's repeated meditations on the critical fables of Benjamin rehearse this simple theme both here and in *Criticism in the Wilderness.*) Hartman also can see, in this light, how literature can appear to be, at least implicitly, what Genét's texts enact explicitly: a symbolic tearing up of "the proper name" (via irony) and an imaginative reassembling from the resulting pieces of some mythic version of that original fantasized identity—"a superhuman, mirror-resembling dream," Yeats' phrase for symbolic art ruthlessly composed out of the shards of a life (*ST*, p. 111). Yet while accepting and seeing such things, Hartman has steadfastly refused to give in to the seductive temptations to become what he beholds.

Hartman does not care to reduce the possibilities of literature and criticism to the saga of the "wounded name" (*ST*, p. 59). The perpetually fascinating, splintering, and witty recombinations of the details of the last two hundred years in the history of literature and philosophy that is presented in Derrida's *Glas* argues, to Hartman, against such a narrow perspective and in favor of the "new decorum" of this "joycing" kind of critical writing. For such writing resists the monumental "glassification" (*ST*, p. 28), the reification of our various desires in our own separate world of textual mirrors, each of which deceptively responds with, "Why, you are, of course, the fairest one of them all." Derrida's antimimetic slant insures against taking literally the possible Father Tyrants and Mother-Vamps (*ST*, p. 106) generated by the play of signifiers in a text. All origins are indeed questions, and so are metaphorical, self-divided, fictional constructs seen as such. Hartman, like Derrida, maintains his balance, his passionate cool, before the antithetical reversals of religious or occult paradigms staged in the texts of such writers as Genét:

> Genét's mirror image of the Holy Family, then expresses a reversal rather than a transvaluation of values. Given the conservative character of the institution of language, it is doubtful that there could be transvaluation. We can reverse or trope catachrestically, we can deploy all the subversive flowers in the anthology of speech, or we can reverse in another sense, by deconstruction, and expose the fallacy that every great artist's mind passes on itself—the result remains a secret recognition scene. (*ST*, p. 109)

Yet while Hartman clearly profits from his term in Derrida's school of suspicion, he does not become a disciple. That would be to identify with one determination of literary imagination, however mobile and impressive, rather than with the (admittedly unknowable) underlying principle of all such "creative" (self-)determinations.

After spending most of the book "translating" and "accommodating" Derrida for an American context—which is largely defined by the democratic celebrations and reactionary subversions of the native strain of the Romantic sublime—Hartman responds to the demands of Derridean deconstruction (in the brilliant final chapter,"Words and Wounds"), with the nearest thing to a critical credo this most ironically supple of writers is ever likely to produce. Hartman understands that Derrida's ironic "two-handed engine" of satanic deconstruction, his contagiously reflexive allusiveness, cuts down the great monuments of the past and conflates their ruins (as I have done with Milton's *Lycidas* and *Paradise Lost*), at the same time that it cuts the ground out from under the critic himself, and so is in danger of cutting off the future of criticism:

> Derrida's engine does not, of course, have the strength to smite once and for all. Its two-handedness remains symbolic of its impotence: it reproduces itself merely, giving us doubles that make us see more doubles still. The result for our time may be a factional split between simplifying types of reading that call themselves humanistic and indefinitizing kinds that call themselves scientific. The fate of reading is in the balance. In a clasroom darkly. (*ST*, pp. 52–56)

The problem with Derrida's anti-mimetic critique is precisely that in turning against itself, and of promoting the turning against itself of the critical community, his critique becomes perhaps the most acute representation of the marginal situation of the contemporary American critic, albeit an allegorical rather than purely historical one, as he has lived if not expressed that situation. So the problem again, is one of identity and difference, of the insidious whisper of unintended words within our words (*ST*, pp. 18–129), of the ridiculous effects of the sublime, which mock even our strengths: the most chaste and self-effacing of critical styles. Whose words are these? No one's, for no one possesses his own language. And this is as it should be.

Hartman insightfully locates the course of this ironic situation in the recurrent demand of the literary critic for much more than literature can ever hope to deliver, despite the most grandiose of its illusions, that of apotheosis of the poetic genius, or "daimon":

> Supposing the psyche demands to be cursed or blessed—that it cannot be satisfied, that it cannot even exist as a namable and conscious entity—as ego or self—except when defined by direct speech of that kind, then we have a situation where the absence of a blessing wounds, where the presence of a curse, also wounds, but at least defines. . . . Blessing and curse, euphemism and slander, praise and blame undermine statement. However neutral or objective words seeem to be, there is always a tilt of this kind, produced by the very effort to speak. There are those who must curse in order to speak: some interlard their words with obscenities, some kill them with kindness expressions. There are the extreme cases that suggest how close we are to muteness: to not speaking at all unless we untangle these contrary modes. . . . How thoroughly the human condition is a verbal condition! (*ST,* pp. 131, 132, 133)

To turn to literature or to any other field of discourse for the exclusive or major focus of one's identity, no matter how unillusioned and reasonable, is repeatedly to court the wounding of the "conscious ear," which, always expecting from language and its obsessively worked texts that definitive revelation of one's "specular name," can only hear the piercing words of a denial that frustrates such desire and so wounds afresh the ego's primal narcissism. At the worst, like Lear before Cordelia or Oedipus before Tiresias and the Messenger, what we get is a "nothing" or an "everything" so terrible in its beauty as to force the self-blinding gesture of tragic overreaction. At the best, we learn to laugh at the "posthumous" clownish tones of Beckett's ubiquitous *ne faire rien, ne faire rien,* that literature presents us with, when we ask it to supply us with "a name to come," we writers of ill-fortune all. Unless one tries to untangle these self-destructive desires for blessing and curse, one runs the risk of becoming nothing more than the place where language's always imminent "confusion of tongues" (*ST,* p. 140) occasionally happens to occur.

Consider, in illustration, as Hartman does, Walter Pater's characterization of the fundamental vulnerability to this disease that afflicted and inspired Prosper Mérimée's ironic art:

> The fear of committing a solecism is probably worse than the fact, but it should not be dismissed because it is too trivial a cause for language-sensitivity. Walter Pater reports in his essay on Prosper Merimée: "Gossiping friends, indeed, linked what was constitutional in him and in the age with an incident of his earliest years. Corrected for some childish fault, in passionate distress, he overhears a half pitying laugh at his expense, and has determined, in a moment never again to give credit—to be forever on his guard" (*Miscellaneous Studies*). The collocation of gossip, overhearing, a (perhaps) imagined slight of embarrassment, is very distressing: the reaction seems so extreme, and one wonders why *Pater* gave credit to it. Was it really the solecism or a similar fault, a mere *faux pas*, that explains it? (*ST*, p. 143)

Well, the answer is, of course, yes and no. It wasn't so much the incident that accounts for Mérimée's artistic quest, as it was the fact that its representation in language (that of correction and of laughter) offends the young Mérimée's sense of identity, and he determines to restore his good name, as it were, by perfecting in his art the exposure of similar faults and incidents, so as to gain the recognition, in his mind at least, of the great dead. As Pater puts it: "In each age, the number of the dead, that dark society, acts on the living with the force of an increasing majority working out is affirmations, asserting its preferences ever more and more distinctly, and with more completely universal assent" (*ST*, p. 67). *The Waste Land* is the great monument to the kind of ironic art Mérimée practiced as his defense against and solicitation of the approval of this "dark society."

But unlike modernism's saving Coleridgean fiction of the harmonius juggling act of "myth and irony, visionary figures of speech and verbal refinement" (*ST*, p. 145), moral value and aesthetic autonomy, and other such hollow rings and cheap crockery, Hartman's theory, following Pater's example, acknowledges the illusion involved in all "organic" conceptions of the formal order of literature. His theory embraces the inescapably contradictory aspects of aesthetic experience, all those built-in preconditions for such lacerating solecisms—since we invariably expect from literature, in this fractured world, an impossible dream of resolution that always segues to the usual disasters of reality. Stay tuned for "Film at eleven."

In *Saving the Text,* Geoffrey Hartman composes a psycho-aesthetic account of literary response that recognizes the deeply embedded desire of the critic for a kind of coistral refuge from such reality, whether it is founded on the level of the text, the tradition, the archetypes of the verbal universe, or language itself. Such refuge must ultimately become just another prison-house of formalist closure. The romance of interpretation, in which the critic pursues the traces of his earliest seductions by the sublime, so as to shore up an identity out of these ruins, must itself be cut short, before it becomes a labyrinth of threads, by the work of the critical intelligence. This is a work like that of Freud's conception of mourning—what Heidegger calls "sacred mourning"—in which the loved object is finally incorporated as memory, all its bounding outlines restored intact, rather than its history being endlessly (because unconsciously) reenacted and elaborated, obsessive phantasmagoria crystalizing into "systematic" ravings—"images that yet fresh images beget."

> The ideal act of criticism would circle back, in that case, to the design (the partial or complete [aesthetic] object) that stimulated it; and this circling back would take on a form of its own, closed enough to be recognizable as form, open enough to be extended. In this manner the form of interpretation rather than a positive content would respect the sense of closure associated with art. . . . The circle of art, like that of interpretation described above, limits the word as the subject of endless brooding. Closure formally seals that brooding (whether it is in the service of separation or recuperation); it sets a limit to brooding, or makes that limit coincide with imagining it. (*ST,* p. 150)

The work of art must be imagined, then, as a separate design, with its own vibrant closure, so that the ideal critical act may be saved from a sublime closure of self-identification (that is the same thing as an ironically apocalyptic openness). For such closure would be too difficult to tell from the death of the imagination: "We do not converse with each other," says Nietzsche's Zarathustra presumably to his creator, "because we know too much—; we exchange silences; we smile at each other through our knowledge."[62] After such knowledge, what forgiveness, what experience, would be possible?

The alternative to an interpretive care, a hermeneutic hesitation, that respects the individual differences of literary texts, even as it recognized family resemblances of one (imagined) kind or another, is a critical presumption that knows all the answers in advance and will give up just about anything, including self-respect, to insure that its "prophetic" anticipations of the results of reading turn out to be correct, however grotesquely self-mocking the unintended consequences:

> We cannot *not* heed threat or oracle, yet should we take them literally? To take them literally is in a way, to bring them about, to live under their sway, or else to wish for a partial fulfillment that might be interpreted as satisfying, and so averting them. . . . By equivocation or figurative action we substitute for the dread words another meaning, in effect another set of words. . . . There is no going back, no stumbling through ghostly or psychoanalytic vaults: the "dread voice" exists as the poem or not at all. (*ST,* p. 157)

Geoffrey Hartman's *Saving the Text* is a brilliantly written and finely executed warning to all of those critics who, whatever their good or evil intentions or their critical systems or anti-systems, would sacrifice literature on the altars of the only deity modern man can still seem to recognize: Ananké, or their will to power dressed to kill. I hesitate to assert that this book is Hartman's theoretical summa, or that it is, therefore, "must" reading, only because it has taught me not to credit such assertions; in this sense, it represents an exemplary education in critical intelligence.

And yet, for all that, one senses in reading *Saving the Text,* the end of an era in American critical theory, one that begins in 1971 with Paul de Man's *Blindness and Insight,* goes on to see in the middle of the decade all those pitched battles between Bloom and everybody else (stage-managed by Bloom, of course), and which comes to a close with de Man's rather exhaustedly rigorous

Allegories of Reading in 1979 and to fruition in Hartman's two recent theoretical works. For the prospects that lie ahead are a steep descent to the plains of practical criticism (once again), of historical reassessment, and, perhaps, of political, even revolutionary action (the age of Foucault and Marx?); the most fitting inscription for the post-structuralist movement in America, then, as summed up in the work of its ablest and most humane practitioner, would be the following emblem drawn from our finest Poet of Nature:

> Stop here, or gently pass!
> . . . .
> No Nightingale did ever chaunt
> More welcome notes to weary bands
> Of travellers in some shady haunt,
> Among Arabian sands:
> A voice so thrilling ne'er was hard
> In spring time from the Cuckoo-bird,
> Breaking the silence of the seas
> Among the farthest Hebrides.
>
> . . . .
> The music in my heart I bore,
> Long after it was heard no more.[63]

CHAPTER FIVE

AGAINST NATURE: ON NORTHROP FRYE AND CRITICAL ROMANCE

'I must rush again to War, for the Virgin has frown'd & refus'd.'
her privates he, so to speak.

Discovery

NORTHROP FRYE begins from the Romantic visionary assumption that, as Blake puts it in *The Marriage of Heaven and Hell*, "Where man is not, nature is barren."[1] In *Creation and Recreation*, a monograph on the biblical metaphor of creation in its secular literary contexts, Frye summarizes his prophetic attitude to nature in a most interesting manner. He uses a characteristically nineteenth-century analogy to highlight the differences between living within the protective "envelope" of culture to living in, or at least perceiving, the fundamentally alien environment that surrounds us. The "cultural insulation that separates us from nature," Frye suggests, "is rather like (to use a figure that has haunted me from childhood) the windlow of a lit-up railway carriage." Most of the time this "cultural insulation" functions as "a mirror of our concerns." Culture is a reflexive symbolic medium that man produces to feel at home in the universe. It makes him feel as if he were its center, even though he knows he is actually on its periphery being driven by forces he ultimately cannot control. Now and again, for some apparently unknown reason, culture fails to perform its reflexive symbolic function and the mirror turns into "a real window" which displays to us our actual position in the scheme of things. It represents, in short, "only the vision of an indifferent nature that got along for untold aeons of time without us, seems to have produced us only by accident, and, if it were conscious, could only regret having done so."[2] On the face of it, Frye sounds here more like the pessimistic Schopenhauer than the visionary Blake.

But on second thought, given his origins in the prophetic line of English poetry that includes Spenser, Milton, and Shelley, Frye's view of an alien nature and a defensive culture possesses a certain inevitability if not complete credibility. Frye, of course, would ultimately like to reverse perspectives, and claim that this initial understanding of man's position in the universe is a "fallen" one which must be overcome by adopting the revisionary or revolutionary understanding of nature and culture as the slave and the master, respectively, in the ongoing drama of mankind's self-creation. But it is significant that Frye, throughout his career, must repeatedly begin from this point of departure, subsuming all that is not "vision" under the term "nature."[3]

The question that arises at this point is why doesn't the "cultural envelope" remain hermetically sealed, as it were. Or, to put it more positively, how is it that culture permits at times the existence of an alien nature to pass through the protective, self-mirroring shield of its various media. The answer appears to lie in Frye's recognition of the representational as well as the symbolic function of language and culture.

In making a similar assertion about the alien nature of the nature that underlies man's cultural creations, Frye in *The Educated Imagination* points to the mechanism he thinks allows this threatening vision to penetrate the protective cultural envelope or "hymenal" screen. Despite his intentions, the visionary writer's own figures of speech often compose what Frye in *The Critical Path* calls his "underthought."[4] This "underthought" is really a structure of metaphors and figures that stand in opposition to the explicit visionary argument, much as Frye's figure of the lit-up railway carriage (an example of man's already dominant cultural power) ironically undercuts from the beginning the visionary argument against the power of nature that he is going to make in the rest of *Creation and Recreation*. Similarly, Frye's language in the passage from *The Educated Imagination* about nature reveals his own obsessive "underthought": "We have to look at the figures of speech a writer uses, his images and symbols," Frye advises, "to realize that underneath all the complexity of human life that uneasy stare at an alien nature is still haunting us, and the problem of surmounting it still with us."[5]

Thus, whether we look at the larger "cultural envelope" that surrounds us most of the time and that mirrors most of our concerns, or look at the structure of a writer's "underthought" on which he bases his antithetical argument against nature, we find the same paradoxical situation facing us. Man appears to be caught between the naturalistic view of the world associated with modern science and his desire for a different vision of the world, one mythic and apocalyptic in dimension and intensity. The situation that haunts Frye appears to be that in which man, like a visionary foetus, is being protected and reassured by his nurturing cultural creation, until his artificial womb begins to be penetrated by the alien reality of an indifferent or hostile nature. The picture of man that emerges via the structures and language of his personal cultural "envelope" resembles then a struggle between two titanic women-figures. One is the chosen, invented Muse-Wife-Mother of the visionary being, "the total body" of a man's or a culture's creations.[6] The other is the Terrible Mother, the White Goddess, the Cruel Mistress—that "subconscious" deity *Natura* who, when she is not acting indifferent, craves the ritual spectacle of human sacrifice generation after generation.[7] In Frye's eyes, the issue is clear: A birth, via culture, into visionary identity, or a dying, via nature, into nonentity.[8]

Man resembles in this light one of Milton's "emblems of creation" from book 7 of *Paradise Lost*. "The lion . . . pawing to get his hinder parts free, is an eloquent emblem of creation," Frye remarks in *The Return to Eden*, his book on Milton's epics. For, like man, Milton's lion is essentially unfinished, in the process of becoming truly itself. This emblem thereby represents to Frye the emancipation of "energy by form." As such, this emblem discloses the operation of "the same power that reappears in human life as liberty, the ability to act which is possible only in a state of internal discipline."⁹ This power Frye identifies with the creative imagination of visionary writers.¹⁰

For Frye, then, as for Aristotle and Sidney, liberty, freedom to act, imaginative creation, are works of deliverance from a cruel nature by means of the incorporation of energy into form, a process that requires from the individual "a state of internal discipline" within "the total body of vision."¹¹ Man's struggle against nature is therefore an active struggle for incorporation into what he himself is creating out of and upon nature.¹² Whether we recall Blake's vision, at the end of *Jerusalem*, of Albion's reunion with his wayward emanation, a reunion which enables man (as symbolized by Albion's "Sons" the Four Zoas or Blake's giant forms) to begin rebuilding the city of culture; or whether we recall Yeats' vision in "Sailing to Byzantium" of the lyrical golden bird nestled between glittering boughs within his holy city of art; the aim of the visionary perspective on life that Frye clearly shares with both poets lies in the production of a completely transformed nature and a radically transfigured body. Like Yeats or Blake, Frye desires a resurrection into beatitude, a deliverance from the masculinely penetrating and seductively rapacious Nature.

Life lived in the context of nature or in that of a culture founded on natural religion or the secular worship of natural forces is clearly a life of absurdity. For it is a life of blind accident, cyclical violence, repeated bondage, and fatal destiny—a life, in short, without human shape. Consequently, in such a context, the formative power of art can only appear, Frye asserts in *The Stubborn Structure*, a collection of essays on literature and society, as a "counter-absurdity." That is, art and, more generally, culture itself, can only seem as "artfully" mad as the world it would displace and transform is "naturally" mad: "Real life does not start or stop; it never ties up loose ends; it never manifests meaning or purpose except by blind accident; it is never comic or tragic; ironic or romantic, or anything else that has a shape. Whatever gives form or pattern [to life] is absurd, and contradicts our sense of reality."[13]

Man in the context of nature can produce at best a noble culture of ritual sacrifice like that recalled in the cult of Diana and the myth of the Golden Bough or that of Dionysus represented dramatically in the tragedies of the Greeks or of Shakespeare.[14] There primitive rituals of our guilt culture all enact a sacrifice of the present to a demonically-experienced sense of the past that makes of the future nothing more than an eternal recurrence of the same perverse spectacle. "We notice," Frye claims in *The Fools of Time,* his study of Shakespearean tragedy, "that anyone who is forced [as the tragic hero is forced] to brood on the past and [dread] the future lives in a world where that which is not present is present, in other words, in a world of hallucination."[15] Man's culture, when based solely on nature and its patterns of birth and death, becomes as phantasmagoric and destructive as can be imagined, producing in individuals what Frye calls "the whole psychology of sacrifice." This obsessive-compulsive pattern of response repeatedly climaxes in a "magnificent vision of heroic energy" being "poured out" as expiation to the past conceived as a dead father whose wife (the muse of his lost potential) bears an uncanny if predictable resemblance to the White Goddess.[16]

One can begin to see how Frye needs this haunting, demonic image of nature for his visionary project. He must see Nature, Reality, Life, in this essentially nihilistic light, as empty of all human significance and value, in order for him then to see in Culture, Vision, and Art the source—the formal cause—of all genuine meaning. Frye's critical perspective requires that unadorned natural man seem to be at first nothing but "a psychotic ape in the mirror" of the tragic culture he produces directly from nature. For, then, Frye can make his romantic proposal that man transform himself and his world, and nature itself, into, respectively, a visionary creator who is building a City out of the waste-land. Shades of the Pilgrim's errand in the Wilderness hang around all such proposals.

Frye's curious dialectic of nihilism and idealism takes on a polemical, even prophetic intensity in his first book *Fearful Symmetry: A Study of William Blake*. This work contains the essential Frye. Its three-part structure of "The Argument," "The Development of the Symbolism," and " The Final Synthesis" enacts a revisionary progression that has affinities with both Hegelian mediation and the narrative pattern of romance schematized in later theoretical texts. Its division into twelve chapters alludes to the traditional form of the epic. Its dedication to Dr. Pelham Edgar, Frye's mentor, activates the mystique of spiritual preceptorship about which Frye, in "Expanding Eyes," speaks so eloquently as the necessary origin of all creative or critical work.[17] Its time of composition—the years of World War II and its immediate aftermath—adds to the historical resonance of Frye's many occasional remarks on freedom, justice, tyranny, and such matters.

In *Fearful Symmetry* Frye writes to redeem Blake's reputation (and so to establish his own). He hopes to rescue his chosen precursor in the visionary tradition from both the spiritualists who, after Yeats, claim Blake for themselves and make him into a cult figure, and the hardheaded ironic modernists who, after Eliot, disown him and make him into a curiosity piece in their metaphysical tower (or socialistic caravan) of art. Blake, for Frye, is no table-rapping mystic who retreats into the crystal cabinet of his visionary art at the first touch of actuality. Nor is he a homemade wonder who creates his private system of mythology because he is a barbarously provincial nonconformist who would have been constitutionally incapable of submitting to the vision of sweetness and light contained in the urbane, civilized beliefs of the Anglican communion or the Bloomsbury group.

Frye argues instead that Blake stands in the central visionary line of modern poetry—Protestant, Revolutionary, and Romantic—that includes all the major poets of the English Renaissance and the other Romantic poets as well. Neither prototype of Madame Blavatsky, nor of Joyce Cary, Blake in Frye's account is a prophet whose celebration of "the Real Man," "the Imagination," "the Human Form Divine," makes him a perfect candidate for spiritual preceptorship in a liberal, democratic, and individualistic culture:

> To Blake, the spiritual world was a continuous source of energy: he harnessed spiritual power as an engineer harnesses water power and used it to drive his inspiration: he was a spiritual utilitarian. He had the complete pragmaticism of the artist, who, as artist, believes nothing but is looking only for what he can use. If Blake gets into the rapt circle of mystics it is only as Mercury got into the Pantheon, elbowing his way through with cheerful Cockney assurance, his pockets bulging with paper, then producing his everlasting pencil and notebook and proceeding to draw rapid sketches of what his more reverent colleagues are no longer attempting to see.[18]

Frye elevates Blake and his schematic prophecies by transforming him and his poetry into paradigms of the poet himself and of imaginative creation itself. As I shall later argue, there is more than just elevation going on in all such idealizing passages. Even on the face of it, the portrait of Blake and "his everlasting pencil" presented here is an ambiguous idealization not so much of what Blake actually was, of course, as of how his critic needs him now to appear if Frye is to surpass the antithetical interpretations of Blake previously discussed.

Frye recreates Blake for more personal reasons as well. For in his portrait of Blake the visionary cockney artist, avatar of the thieving hermeneutic god Mercury, Frye—the spiritual utilitarian par excellence—attempts to make the scientist and the humanist in his own psyche ironically one. Blake thereby becomes a prophetic emblem of *his critic's* ongoing self-creation, as the reader begins to admire the sheer energy and ironic inventiveness of Frye's wit, and so confers on Frye a powerful imaginative reality and an authoritative identity he would not otherwise possess.

The price of Frye's (re-)visionary conception is, unfortunately, the symbolic exclusion and death of nature. The most revealing of all such passages in his work occurs in part 1 of *Fearful Symme-try* and concerns that dreaded phenomenon, the Female Will:

> In some places Leviathan is called Rahab by Blake, and Rahab is also the name of the harlot who received the spies of Joshua, and whose life was spared in the conquest of the Promised Land. It is difficult to see what these two Rahabs can have to do with one another until we come to the Apocalypse and find there a Great Whore sitting on the back of a red dragon referred to as "that old serpent which is called the Devil, and Satan, which deceiveth the whole world." This beast, a water-monster, is evidently the Cover-ing Cherub seen from inside Paradise, and two smaller monsters, corresponding to the Leviathan and Behemoth of Job, are offspring of his. The Great Whore's rich clothes and precious stones recall the gilded serpent; she represents all human tyranny, for her name is Babylon and she sits on the seven hills of Rome; she is all forms of state religion, for she is drunk with the blood of the saints; she is chaos, for she sits on many waters; and her whoredom represents the possessive love of the jealous Selfhood. She is, in short, the ultimate fallen form of nature or the "female," Enitharmon and Vala combined in the time-world. Apocalypse means revelation, and the Great Whore is the chief thing revelation comes to remove, which is Mystery, a word used by Paul to refer to another consolidation of evil in the somewhat different form of the Antichrist. The Great Whore of the Bible is the Medusa who turns men to stone, the *femme fatale* of the romantic poets whose kiss is death, whose love is annihilation, whose continual posing of the unanswerable riddle of life in this world is reflected in the mysterious female smiles of the Sphinx and Mona Lisa; and whose capacity for self-absorption has haunted art from ancient Crete to modern fashion magazines. The visionary sees nature as a veil (the sound-association with "Vala" should be noted) between himself and reality: the tearing of the veil of the mystery-temple by Jesus is therefore the first act in the apocalypse. As vision consolidates, nature takes the human form of a beautiful harlot. The Whore and her beast, then, are the obstacles blocking up the view of the unfallen world; and when the Whore is stripped and burned all the evils of the Selfhood go from the Abyss, the chaos underlying matter, into the permanent second death of nonexistence.[19]

So much, one wants to shrug, for Walter Pater, Oscar Wilde, W. B. Yeats and all their fellow-victims of the Romantic Agony.

After such a cavalier dismissal, however, one must return to the passage. For it clearly deserves more serious attention; it contains and consolidates all the sentiments that inform Frye's

visionary polemic against nature. That polemic and its per-
sistence in Frye derives its strength from a definite literary
source (about which more later). Nature functions here as a
gathering symbol for all the often contradictory things that Frye
opposes and would transcend. Nature is both a harlot and a
dragon, Sin and Satan, Worldly Success and a State Religion of
human sacrifice. Mystery, Medusa, femme fatale, spiteful collab-
orator, treacherous ally, stripped and burnt Witch—Nature is the
veil torn by the prophet-figure so that he can recover his vision.
She is the Covering Cherub standing guard at Eden's gates who
must be passed through, the sublime threshold to vision he must
transgress, if the visionary creator is to achieve his symbolic
immortality via the elaboration and refinement of his systematic
personal culture—of his own heterocosm or separate textual
world. To become free, imaginative, and self-creative, a man
must sacrifice Mother Nature to his visionary project of producing and then identifying himself fully with his invented muse, his
artificial emanation. If Blake as spiritual utilitarian represents
the apocalyptically idealized image of his critic, then this portrait
of the Female Will as the Great Whore presents the degraded and
demonic image of all that threatens Frye's revisionary critical
work with failure. I suspect that hovering over Frye's first
"extended critical essay in the Swinburne tradition" is—among
others—the ghostly presence of Frankenstein's monstrous Bride.

Operation

But in his most recent book, *The Great Code: The Bible and
Literature*, Frye contends otherwise. He claims that the attentive
readers of the Bible become thoroughly implicated in the symbolic action of the Messiah narrative. (Frye takes the entire Bible
to be telling us the myth of deliverance in a purely undisplaced
form that he has been theoretically rehearsing for years.)[20] As
they assimilate and understand what they are reading, as they
begin to form a conceptual unity out of the materials of their

reading to correspond to the imaginative unity of the text, these
readers (symbolically) repeat in their critical acts of interpretation the archetypal pattern of descent and return encoded in the
Messiah myth. As the Bible's readers absorb the text, Frye goes
on to claim, they become "a symbolically female body" being
addressed by "a symbolically male God," in what we can say
"officially" is for Frye a loving act of creative verbal expression,
a manner of expression which can itself be seen—by Frye at
least—as an "imaginative product" that he also considers to be
"symbolically female" or "the daughter of a Muse." Frye refers
to the symbolic process of reader identification and transformation by the term "the Apocalyptic Bride."[21]

For Frye, then, the Bible, the Ur-text in Western culture,
proves to be contagious. In involves the reader in a process of
aesthetic response and self-revision made possible by its mythic,
archetypal style and apocalyptic vision or kergyma. The reader,
in essence, plays Messiah to his own Apocalyptic Bride, in order
to repeat imaginatively that pattern of Christian conversion, of
dying to the old self or material man and of being born again as
the new Adam, of a new, internalized Eden—a process which is
recorded in the Gospels as a model to be imitated by Christians in
every action of their daily lives. Just as, for Frye, the New Testament completes the Old—and the Secular Scripture of visionary
romance from the Greeks to modern Harlequin Romances com-
plements the Bible—so the reader fulfills the apocalyptic prophecy of both scriptures by allowing himself to be driven back by
what he reads to the beginning of things, both in the life of his
culture and in his personal life. He speaks once again the "first"
creative word that will recreate that life and make all things new
within the ever allusive mythic structures of his own symbolic
heterocosm or separate textual world. In this way, the reader in
becoming the Apocalyptic Bride of the Divinely Human Logos
would give birth to himself.

To attain this status as the Apocalyptic Bride of the prophetic
text (and so, ideally, of one's best or sublime self), the reader
must be able to perceive "'the pattern behind the pattern'," that

is, the pattern of generic, conventional and archetypal myths underlying the individual pattern of a particular text.[22] The reader, in Frye's view, must assimilate each text as if it were written according to the prescriptions of Eliot's "mythical method." He should recall the total visionary form of literature, the total body of vision, and fit this particular work into the larger cultural organism, the way a biologist fits a particular species within a genus or an astronomer fits a new star within his chart of the heavens. In this way, the reader can transcend the work and achieve the authentic ecstacy of the sublime and so recover a sense of his lost identity, learning again the uncanny lesson of vision, that what was old is now new once more:

> What is high style? This is one of the oldest questions in criticism: it would almost be possible to translate the title of Longinus' treatise, *Peri Hypsous,* written near the beginning of the Christian era, by this question. As Longinus recognized, the question has, once again, at least two answers, one for literature and another for ordinary speech. In literature it may be correct to translate Longinus' title as "On the Sublime," and use great passages in Shakespeare or Milton for examples. We shall discuss this problem next. In ordinary speech high style is something else. I should say that it emerges whenever the middle style rises from communication to community, and achieves a vision of society which draws speaker and hearers together into a closer bond. It is the voice of the genuine individual reminding us of our genuine selves, and of our role as members of a society, in contrast to a mob. Such style has a peculiar quality of penetration about it: it elicits a shock of recognition, as it is called, which is the proof of its genuineness. High style in this sense is emphatically not the high-flown style: all ornate language in rhetoric belongs to the middle style, the language of society engaged in routine verbal ritual. Genuine high style is ordinary style, or even low style, in an exceptional situation which gives it exceptional authority. To go at once to the highest example of high style, the sentences of the Sermon on the Mount have nothing in them of the speech-maker's art: they seem to be coming from inside ourselves, as though the soul itself were remembering what it had been told so long ago.[23]

In these remarks self-consciously recalling Plato's doctrine of recollection, Frye describes his peculiar urbane sense of the sublime both in the texts he reads and, as here, in the ones he has himself composed.

Just as Jung transfers the mythology of alchemy to the psychological process of individuation, so Frye transfers the internalized romance structures of that process of individuation to the aesthetics of sublimity as practiced by the would-be critic of all the great classics in the Western tradition.[24] Composing texts that assimilate and transfer the traditional touchstones of sublimity to a new context that one has "discovered" for oneself becomes a work that promises the perfection of oneself as a sublime text. It is not surprising, therefore, that Frye has repeatedly endorsed Oscar Wilde's notion that criticism is as creative as imaginative literature, that it is a form of literature.[25]

Similarly, it should come as no surprise that Frye conjures forth this aesthetic ideal for criticism, with the critic assuming the role of the romantic poet-hero,[26] in terms of a muse figure through which he can give birth to himself as a creative writer. In *A Study of English Romanticism*, Frye gives a revealing portrait of his own style of writing under the guise of distinguishing Shelley's visionary thinking from the aggressive argumentative thinking of a Hobbes, a Locke, or a Pope:

> Aggressive thinking makes a great parade of "stubborn facts" and "hard and fast" distinctions, and other synonyms, to use a post-Shelleyan image, of the domineering male in erection. Poetic thinking, being mythical, does not distinguish or create antitheses: it goes on and on, linking analogy to analogy, identity to identity, and containing without trying to refute, all opposition and objection. This means, not that it is merely facile or liquid thinking without form, but that it is the dialectic of love: it treats whatever it encounters as another form of itself. By the same token it is never abstract: abstraction is the product of a repetition of experience without fresh thought.[27]

Frye's trope of "poetic thinking" refers to a style of writing as much as it does to a manner of mind. Frye's celebration and appropriation of the "feminine" and "mythical" uses of language in this passage written in 1968 owes something to the ideology of erotic liberation popularized at the time by Norman O. Brown and Herbert Marcuse. But it owes more, I think, to the long-standing opposition in the culture and in Frye's own psyche between empirical or utilitarian principles and romantic or scholarly attitudes.

Ironically, Frye's own style here seems to be more argumentative and masculine than usual. There is not present here that sentimental turn, that rising to a prophetic height, which appears in Frye's writing, and especially highlights his conclusions. This irony suggests to me that Frye is repressing the fact that what he calls "the dialectic of love" is founded in his own work at least upon the exclusion and death of nature, which is represented in this passage by the mask of "the domineering male in erection." This figure characterizing a certain kind of critical manner represents (in a radically displaced form) the ever-replaceable male companion of the nature goddess archetype, the hero as dying god. A shift from the realm of myth to one of textual performance has occurred here.[28] Meanwhile, of course, the dialectic of love stands for the (re-)visionary mode of culture that would assimilate and transform all that it can, seeing in everything else a prophetic idealizing mirror of itself and its own critical form of romance. The real woman must "die" if the Eternal Feminine is to live.

Only by building up a world out of such acts of self-creation can one achieve an imaginative identity and so be seen by others as "a permanent form as well as a continuous existence":

> The real man, therefore, is the total form of the creative acts and visions which he evolves in the course of his "Becoming" life. The latter exists in time and space, but his "Being" or real existence is a work of art, and exists, like the work of art, in that unity of time and space which is infinite or eternal. The imagination or Being, then, is immortal, a form constructed out of time but existing in what Paul calls the "fullness of time." We arrive at the conception of immortality as soon as we grasp the idea of a reality which is not merely part of an indefinite persistence of an indefinite extensive physical world. But for that very reason immortality cannot mean the indefinite survival of a "Becoming" life arrested at some point in its development (that is, not growing older forever, like Tithonus), as in most conceptions of an immortal personality. What is immortal about the man is the total form of his creative acts, and these total forms are the characters, or "identities," as Blake calls

them, of the men who made them, the isolating of what is eternally humane in them from the accidents of Becoming. Everyman in the morality play slinks into eternity with his "good deeds," a few pitiful bits of jetsam he has salvaged from the flood of time; but those good deeds are the eternal reality of Everyman's existence, the spiritual form of Everyman.[29]

The essential act of this visionary Everyman Frye would incarnate (and would see incarnated in his readers via the mediation of the Apocalyptic Bride) is an aesthetic response that initiates one in a quest for the perfection of a personal sublimity.

One can see how this quest informs the particulars of his career by turning now to one of Frye's more important performances, "Criticism, Visible and Invisible," a 1964 essay. "I recently saw a documentary movie of the rock-and-roll singer Paul Anka. The reporter pried one of the squealing little sexballs out of the audience and asked her what she found so ecstatic about listening to Anka. She said, still in a daze: 'He is *so sincere.*' The will to unite rhetorical and direct address is very clear here."[30] Frye's rather callow observation (he sounds like Paul Lynde in *Bye, Bye Birdie,* a film of the same year), is clearly the one false, even ridiculous note in an essay that will shortly conclude in a sublime crescendo. Should one simply dismiss this remark as a lapse in taste, the critic like Longinus being expected now and again to stumble, especially when he is getting a long running start for a leap to the heights? Or should one see it as an unsuccessful attempt to be topical and unacademic? Or, perhaps, one should understand it as an example of Frye's unconscious elitism and chauvinism, an unthinking expression of a stock response to modern teenage girls, rock and roll stars (especially when they are also Canadian), and such things, a kind of mental reflex-action conditioned and sanctioned by the ideology of the critical institution?

Before trying to answer any of these questions, I must make sense of Frye's remark by examining the context that the essay establishes in which it can stand out so sharply. The essay appears first in the October 1964 issue of *College English* and is reprinted without revision in *The Stubborn Structure* in 1970. In the essay, Frye presents a popularization of his system of visionary criticism which I shall briefly outline.

For Frye, there are five modes of representation in Western literature based on the power of the hero in each mode which ranges from that of a victim to that of a god. These modes are the ironic and satiric, low mimetic, high mimetic, romantic, and mythic. Frye associates each mode with a different period in literary history and a different dominant literary form (hence, his view on this topic constitutes a theory of historical criticism). Ours is, for example, an ironic age in which the dominant literary form appears to be works of prose fiction in which the hero possesses considerably less power than we usually feel we do; the practically anonymous heroes of Kafka's works are representative.

Similarly, for Frye, there are five forms of symbolic representation, one appropriate to each of the five modes for representing the hero. These five forms of symbolism Frye terms as the literal, descriptive, formal, archetypal and anagogic. Not only does this schema create a horizontal, historical point of reference, it also creates a vertical, ethical dimension for literary symbolism. (Hence, his view on this topic constitutes a theory of ethical criticism.) If Joseph K. in Kafka's *The Trial*, for example, is the modern hero or victim par excellence the primary phase of symbolism appropriate for him is that of the literal; by "literal" Frye means a restriction of the hero's vision to that of the letter, the surface formations of language. Hence the absurdly riddling quality of Kafka's own text, as well as the ironically appropriate choice of names for his major heroes, Joseph K. and simply K. in *The Castle*. The upper limit of the symbolic vision, that of the anagogic, enshrines a god-like perspective in which all of nature no longer appears as the containing form of the human race but as the thing contained within the body of a cosmic Man "who builds his cities out of the Milky Way,"[31] a consuming vision of things devoutly to be wished for—at least by a visionary critic like Frye.

Thus, historical and ethical criticism find their systematic justification in, respectively, a theory of the modes of representing the literary hero and a theory of the symbols by means of which the hero's vision or world (or "ethos") is represented in literature. Similarly, archetypal criticism finds its rationale in a theory of myths and rhetorical criticism in a theory of genres. In this ingenious fashion, Frye revises for our century Aristotle's conception of causality as divisible for analytic purposes into four kinds of causes (material, formal, efficient, and final).

Frye's theory of myths, which incorporates his theory of modes of action and levels of symbolic representation in a universal narrative structure, describes the four preliterary or archaic narrative patterns (the mythoi of Spring, Summer, Autumn and Winter) out of which comedy, romance, tragedy, and irony and satire have respectively emerged.[32] And the latter theory of genres attempts, less sucessfully I think, to account for the formal differences between the genres of epic, fictional and nonfictional prose, drama and lyric poetry, in terms of the differences in the informing rhythm of each genre. The four kinds of mythos and the four genres imply a necessary fifth encyclopedic mythos and genre which the sacred texts of different cultures usually embody. (The musical analogy here as elsewhere in Frye's *Anatomy* appears to be paramount.) In terms of the Kafka example, then, one could say that the archetypal pattern underlying *The Trial* is that of the scapegoat myth, and that the dominant rhythm is that of continuity, the defining rhythm for Frye of prose fiction.[33] For an example of a purely literary form of the sacred text, Frye points to *Finnegans Wake*. In a sense, then, Frye's *Anatomy* represents an approximation in criticism of "the dominant fifth," the encyclopedic form of a sacred text embodying wisdom.[34]

I return now to the text of "Criticism, Visible and Invisible." In this essay Frye assumes that his audience has a general familiarity with his system, which permits him to emphasize one of its key distinctions, which he plans to elaborate in the essay. This distinction concerns the two types of critical activity, that of objective analysis and moral evaluation (this is what he calls "criticism militant") and that of the personal appreciation of and possession by the creative power of literature (this is what he calls "criticism triumphant"). This distinction is central for Frye, and it explains the two forms of his work, a study of the literary universe as an "objective" phenomenon whose structures can compose an anatomy, an arrangement into useful categories or a system of schematic nature, and the application of the wisdom appropriated by means of the study of this comprehensive order to the social and cultural needs of a chaotic time.

This distinction between "criticism triumphant" and "criticism militant" makes one think of Matthew Arnold's analogy between the church and the critical establishment. I suppose the distinction parallels that between "high" and "low" versions of the Anglican Church. One wonders, then, where the Broad Church version fits. But the language Frye uses primarily refers, I think, to two of the three orders of Christendom: the church in heaven, or Church Triumphant, and the church on earth, or Church Militant. In other words, the "invisible" criticism of the cultivated mind of the critic, what Frye calls the possession of literature, the appropriation of its imaginative power for oneself, parallels the church in heaven. (Frye alludes here to Milton's notion of Eden, after the Fall, becoming an archetype for "the paradise within" the authentic Christian.) The "visible" criticism of teachers and reviewers, especially those trained in the methods of rhetorical and formal analysis, parallels the church on earth. The question that arises in this context, as in that provided by my allusion to Arnold, is where is the parallel to the third order of Christendom, its church in purgatory—in short, the Church Suffering.

I think a clue to the answer to this question lies in Frye's own performance in the essay, especially in light of the way he concludes his argument for the repeated transformations of "criticism militant" into "criticism triumphant" in the minds of each generation of students, teachers, and scholars. The essay as a whole, and particularly in its ironically allusive and poignantly sublime conclusion, represents a patient refining of Frye's critical vision so necessary for the achievement of his quest, for his sublime triumph: canonization among the other literary saints of Western culture. The essay does indeed conclude on a climactic note:

> We remember the discussion in Joyce's *Portrait* in which the charac-
> teristics of beauty are said to be *integritas, consonantia,* and *claritas;*
> unity, harmony, and radiance. Poet and critic alike struggle to unify
> and to relate; the critic, in particular, struggles to demonstrate the
> unity of the work of literature he is studying and to relate it to its
> context in literature. There remains the peculiar *claritas* or inten-
> sity, which cannot be demonstrated in either literature or criticism,
> though all literature and criticism point toward it. No darkness can
> comprehend any light; no ignorance or indifference can ever see any
> *claritas* in literature itself or in the criticism that attempts to convey
> it, just as no saint in ordinary life wears a visible gold plate around
> his head. All poet or critic can do is to hope that somehow, some-
> where, and for someone, the struggle to unify and to relate, because
> it is an honest struggle and not because of any success in what it
> does, may be touched with a radiance not its own.[35]

Frye performs here in typical fashion. He is explicitly self-effacing, extremely lucid, mildly witty, full of much good sense, the well-balanced, urbane author of a prose of the center, as Arnold might say. And yet the blandly ironic juxtaposition between the formally negative assertions strongly establishes a visionary context which "may be touched with a radiance not its own." For one begins to see the visible structure of juxtaposition and negation dissolve into an invisible presence affirming a sublime identity. That is, the ironic material structure of Frye's prose solicits this possible sublimity, this textual vision of the mythic archetype of the Paradise Within (that "radiance not its own") from the reader who smiles in recognition at the charm of the critic's subtle self-assertion and careful invention. It is as if a passage of Emersonian import were written by an Auden.

Frye's characterization of the poet's or the critic's general struggle to unify and to relate culture to society discloses a significant coordination of functions between these two figures. It assumes, in fact, the fulfillment of Oscar Wilde's vision of the critic as an artist in his own right. Frye's choice of infinitives, for example, alludes succinctly to the celebration of the creative imagination in Eliot, Arnold, Coleridge and Wordsworth, and appropriates them to the critic's project.[36] Finally, his recognition of the possible futility of the critic's struggle introduces a note of "suffering" into the essay from "the still sad music of humanity" that suggests in a concrete manner that such performances as Frye's own in this essay represent the absent "criticism suffering," the underlying "final" cause, after all, of the work of the institution to produce a secular literary version of the apocalyptic vision in the otherwise alienated mind of solitary readers. Finally, when in the last line of the essay, Frye invokes "a radiance not its own" the reader senses an allusion not so much to the *claritas* of Joyce's Stephen Dedalus, nor to that of Stephen's theological model Thomas Aquinas, that brilliant reviser of Aristotle, but to that of the medieval Doctor's poetic counterpart and Joyce's (rather than his character's) chosen literary precursor, Dante. The allusion appears to be (in the context) to Dante's sudden vision of Beatrice on Mount Purgatory after his pagan guide Virgil has led him in his quest for the divine love as far as the great epic poet's heroic human knowledge can take Dante. Only a more-than-human knowledge, only wisdom, will now do if Dante is to continue his ascent to Paradise.

In being asked to receive favorably the critic's struggle to unify and to relate, therefore, the reader is being asked to assume the role of Beatrice as the critic plays Dante. That is, the sympathetic reader becomes the visionary mistress, the Apocalyptic Bride, presiding over the creation of the critic's beatitude, by seeing the sublime affirmation of identity underlying the ironic juxtaposition of negations. The reader plays the muse to the critic's self-creation. It is precisely this kind of "seeing" that Eliot's *The Waste Land* and Joyce's *Ulysses* demand. Frye's criticism, in other words, depends on what Eliot terms "the mythical method" as much as does the major texts of literary modernism. In fact, Frye's relationship to the modernist and Romantic strains of modern criticism is similar to Auden's vis-à-vis modernist and Romantic poetry.

No wonder, then, that Frye's topical allusion to Paul Anka and the little sexballs that idolize him both stands out in this context and yet fits it perfectly. For it appears to function as the demonic parody of the critic's prophetic vision. But, as we have seen, more is involved than simply this self-serving distinction. Frye commits his faux pas as he is contrasting the ceaseless onslaught of kinetic stimulus on the minds of modern people with the critic's visionary therapy of educating everyone in the ways of resisting such an onslaught by persuading them to appreciate and assimilate knowledge of the formal powers of literary art, a knowledge which, for Frye, can change their lives. This is a goal of "conversion" (or "transference" and "sublimation") that revises and appropriates for the critic Wordsworth's view, in his famous *Preface*, of the poet's function to mediate and harmonize, with his healing influence, the excessive stimuli of urban life. The interests of the academy are, naturally, served well by such a self-aggrandizing assumption.

Even so, the most effective way to understand Frye's assumption here is in the context of the psychology of vision already outlined, since the institution is served only as a by-product of the critic's motive, his desire for personal sublimity. First one must understand the pervasive intricacies of the critic's self-deluding strategy of writing before one can see how the institution of literary study has been affected by the influence of critics such as Frye. Consider, for example, how the image of this particular teenage girl, lifted out of the contemporary world, stands as a representative of history, as the raw material, or opportune basis for Frye's display of Juvenal satire. In the same way all the particulars of literary and cultural history in his more comprehensive and sustained works become, once they have been assimilated to the archetype of the Female Will, the occasion for the critic's antithetical self-creation, a process of composition whose ideal interpreter is Frye's prophetic Muse-Mother of the critic as aesthetic redeemer.

In order for him to be inventive, then, the "natural" woman in Frye—actually, his representation of nature—must be dialectically transcended, that is, in good Hegelian fashion, cancelled as the Female Will, preserved as the reader's muse-function, and lifted up, as a repressed memory trace that has been sublimated as the exalted figure of the prophetic muse, the sublime mirror image of Frye's potential symbolic self and of our cultural-redemption. The Faustian cast of this pattern of critical romance appears to be as unintentional as it is inescapable. The production of second nature always requires—in however symbolic a form—the sacrificial death of primary nature, and so one can say that being for second nature always entails being against nature. As we shall see, this antithetical will derives from the essential nihilism of the ascetic ideal.

This analysis of his style suggests that Frye's theoretical system exists for the same reason that Yeats' *A Vision* does: as a portable personal tradition or cultural envelope which enables the writer to achieve for the informed reader sublime effects and connections that would otherwise be impossible even to conceive in our fragmented modern world. In addition, my analysis also suggests the appropriateness of some of Frye's remarks in *The Great Code* for understanding his critical romance, to which I shall now turn.

Near the end of the volume, Frye characterizes in the most explicit terms ever his understanding of the prophetic motive. It is, Frye says, to behold the sudden and complete transformation of the endlessly repetitive nature of "fallen" temporality into a single monumental image, a creative emblem of eternity. This visionary or revisionary intention involves a process of apocalyptic transformation, or a sublime representation of potentially world historical proportions, a kind of symbolic act which, ironically enough, would bring an end to all action:

> If we follow the narrative of the Bible or a sequence of events in human life, it becomes a series of ups and downs in which God's people periodically fall into bondage and are then rescued by a leader, while the great heathen empires rise and fall in the opposite rhythm. At a certain point this perspective goes into reverse, and what we see is something more like an epic or romantic hero descending to a lower world to rescue what is at the same time a single

bride and a large host of men and women. In this perspective the
sequence of captivities and redemptions disappears and is replaced
by a unique act of descent and return. But the act, if in itself
unique, has many symbolic settings.[37]

The New Testament gives a climactic shape and an ultimate significance to the Old Testament, which, perpetually deferring
final revelations, it otherwise would not have. In this perspective, then, coming late in the story, as if the final and formal
cause of it, is actually a virtue and not a sign of deprivation.

As at the conclusion of the Book of Job or of Revelation, Frye
argues, what we see in the Bible as a whole is a central character,
representative of a people or a community of believers, being
delivered by the power of divinity working through him from the
coils of personal or collective history. By giving that story a
comic, visionary ending (thanks to the deus ex machina of the
Judeo-Christian tradition), the character or hero is transformed
into a sublime image which no narrative line can contain:

> We may take the Book of Job, perhaps, as the epitome of the narra-
> tive of the Bible, as the Book of Revelation is the epitome of its
> imagery. . . . The narrative framework of the Bible is a part of its
> emphasis on the shape of history and the specific collision with
> temporal movement that its revelation is assumed to make. In a
> sense, therefore, the deliverance of Job is a deliverance from his
> own story, the movement in time that is transcended when we have
> no further need of time.[38]

Naturally, the story of the Messiah, as recorded in the passion
narratives of the Gospels, provides Frye with his model for this
apocalyptic pattern of descent and return which transforms historical sequence into the visionary form of symbolic action—a
sublime image that stands free of its actual context by imaginatively containing it.

One could argue, therefore, that Frye in his critical writing
and in the stance he takes to the tradition and to his reader is that
of "some synthetizing critical Messiah" whose vision of the past
would transcend it by making possible the revision of the reader's
future, along the lines of prophetic self-invention. This represents a radical displacement, internalization, and, ultimately,
trivialization of the process of religious conversion within the

confines of Frye's romance of interpretation. One could also argue that in Frye's texts the appearance of narrative sequence, of a developing argument, and of a systematic coherence must always give way in the end to the formation of this simultaneous structure of critical romance as represented by the production of sublime self-images.

Frye's own obsessive quest for a prophetic literary identity always lies behind the manifest rhythm of his latest fable of the sublime in other writers. That is, the manifestly typological movement of his work, in which the categories of his critical system attempt to fulfill by rationalizing for a secular modern audience the religious and romantic vision he finds in literature, depends upon and ultimately dissolves into the latent mythic cycle of the quest-romance. In the same way the ironic juxtaposition of negations in the earlier passage from "Criticism, Visible and Invisible" finally resolves itself in a structural pattern affirming Frye's identity as a latter-day critical saint, a critical revision of one of Yeats' sages from "Sailing to Byzantium," "standing in God's holy fire." Frye's theoretical perspective "reads" the tradition and repeats in his texts its underlying mythic or ideological structures, soliciting the reader to come and follow him.[39] When one speaks of the reader in Frye, then, one necessarily refers both to Frye as reader and to the reader of Frye at the same time. But who is it, ultimately, that constitutes the dialectic of the reader here? To answer this question, I will step back from Frye somewhat and examine his work in light of the genre to which it belongs. After all, it is only fair that one turn Frye's own methods against him, isn't it? Being against Frye's being against nature finally means, I suppose, being against *his* nature, that is, it means being against "visionary" criticism.

Recovery

In the *Anatomy of Criticism*, Frye describes the fundamental conventions of romance as a narrative genre expressive of the representative aesthetic attitude informing all literary creations.

Romance as narrative is nearest, Frye says, to the wish-fulfillment dream, and the wish that it expresses is that of the recovery
of one's "true" identity as a creator (rather than a victim) of one's
destiny. Romance, whatever its social dimensions, is primarily
the secular version of salvation history. It is designed essentially
for individuals. Usually, however, the ruling social or intellectual
classes in each age kidnap romance and attempt to use it to
rationalize their values and customs, imposing on it their anxieties and ideologies, even as they would impose the genre on
their cultures, attempting to make it the dominant mode of the
imaginary (in both the Lacanian and Althusserian senses). In
such cultures romance comes to represent to everyone how it is
with the imagination and its relations with the entire economic
and social worlds. One thinks, in this connection, of how romance is made to express the chivalric code of the aristocracy in
the Middle Ages, or, in a later day, the prophetic, even revolutionary, vision of the Romantic poets. Yet, precisely because of
its origins in an insatiable desire for the permanent recovery of a
lost and actually never possessed ideal identity, romance subjects
all structures of authority, institutional and ideological, to an
unrelenting form of critique, finally turning (as in Freud and
Nietzsche) back on itself. Through the pattern of its images and
the general outlines of its narrative, romance thus prophesies a
utopian desire for the apocalyptic recovery of identity to occur
for all, each individual becoming as in the twinkling of an eye a
lord or a lady over him or herself.[40] As we shall see in more detail,
this last implicit dimension of romance explains Frye's centrality
as a theorist even for some socially-minded critics.[41]

The basic episodes in what Frye sees as a potentially endless
narrative form are three in number: (a) the *agon* or "perilous
journey and preliminary minor adventure"; (b) the *pathos* or
"critical struggle" to the death with one's enemy or mimetic
rival; and (c) the *anagnorisis* or "recognition" and exaltation,
often even apotheosis, of the hero.[42] The hero of romance and the
mythical Messiah figure in sacred texts like the Bible are thus
secular and religious analogues of one another.[43] The difference

is that for the Messiah figure the third phase of romance only occurs along with his *sparagmos* or sacrificial tearing asunder. In this context, one of Frye's remarks about the genre sounds an ironic note, when he characterizes the quest-romance purely in psychological terms as "the search of the libido or desiring self for a fulfillment that will deliver it from the anxieties of reality but will still contain that reality."[44] For what this implies is that the reader of Romance internalizes all the conventions of the genre, including that of the sparagmos. Just imagine: in a form of literature where wish-fulfillment is the admitted end, one must also pay for one's imaginary satisfactions, perhaps even with a self-crucifixion.

Clearly, Frye's career can be viewed in terms of romance. I assume that he knows this, and, in fact, that he has attempted over the years to reenact this pattern in his work, self-consciously if subtly, thereby transforming his writing life into a continuous allegory of his quest for the recovery of lost identity. One could argue, for example, that *Fearful Symmetry* represents Frye's agon; that the *Anatomy of Criticism* and the many works following in its wake refining and applying its theoretical principles to the analysis of literature and culture, represent, especially in the context of the many competing crises of the last two decades, the pathos; and that *The Secular Scripture* and *The Great Code* (when the second volume finally appears) represent or at least are intended to represent, his final anagnorisis, an exalted recognition scene in which the old Odysseus, no longer forgotten and hidden in our midst, reveals himself—no preparatory to, but as, the final showdown. The three-text sequence of the last phase of Frye's critical romance recapitulates and sublimates, as it were, the basic phases of the genre, producing a double mirror effect, demonstrating Frye's sophisticated awareness and subtle enactment of the *mise en abime* so many others just indefinitely anticipate. In this ironically reflexive manner, Frye's work represents the first generally successful completion of the critical quest, an achievement worthy of the same kind of appreciation and study as one traditionally gives to poetic careers.

What I mean to suggest is that within the Anglo-American tradition of literary criticism Northrop Frye's work represents not simply the systematic turn to schematic theories of criticism alone, a major change from the domination of the tradition by the pragmatic orientation of poetic-critics, but as well the institution of the academic vocation of criticism as a form of romance. If people like Arnold, Pater, Richards, and Eliot help to establish the attitudes, methods, and rationalizations of the critical institution, it is Frye who formulates a coherent ideology for the study of literature as a quest for sublimity that the critic can realize in his scholarly career as a writer who perfects an influential theoretical style all his own. This view implies that the profession of literary criticism in America has kidnapped romance and has made it express in a symbolic manner the values, customs, anxieties and desires of the profession—what Harold Bloom ironically refers to in *A Map of Misreading* as "the sufferings of history."[45] Given this ideology of romance, the critic can shape his life as a tragic or comic quest. For in this light all the potential obstacles to doing one's work become manifestations of what Frye calls the demonic or accusing memory,[46] the natural man's only muse, that guilty reminder of all the vicissitudes of personal and collective history that must be repressed and transformed in the critic's hermeneutic art, because they remind him of his lack of authentic identity in a marginal profession that too often represents to him the absurdity of a life begun in accident, carried on in futility, and concluded only by death.

But since the pattern I have been tracing in Frye, the particular form of his romance of interpretation, entails that all that is not Vision be seen as Nature, even when it is really History, the critic can appear to himself at least as always in the process of becoming sublime—but only, at a price. Nature as the Great Whore must be stripped and burnt, so that the prophetic critic can produce from the ashes of this hermeneutic art the stark outlines of his ideal muse, who stands for his possible sublimity, his desired rebirth into symbolic immortality as a literary classic. The critic, in essence, becomes nothing more than a principle of textualization. I see this pattern of personal despair and impersonalizing compensation as symbolically representative of a revisionary style of critical writing that has its fugitive beginnings in Pater (and Wilde), achieves definitive if often ironic expression and systematic elaboration in Frye, and finds its decadent gloss in the work of (among others) Harold Bloom and Paul de Man, and its satiric impersonation and implicit critique in the work of Geoffrey Hartman and several younger critics.

The critic writes, therefore, under the illusion that he can escape the nightmare of history, the absurd scapegoat vision of life, what Frye in the *Anatomy* calls the existential projection of bondage, victimization, and despair found most eloquently crystalized in existentialism and the literature that both inspired it and that it inspired.[47] The escape is provided by the transport of one's own metaphors of interpenetrating archetypes, as Frye himself discloses in the most famous single passage in his theoretical masterwork.

> In the anagogic phase, literature imitates the total dream of man, and so imitates the thought of a human mind which is at the circumference and not at the center of its reality. We see here the completion of the imaginative revolution begun when we passed from the descriptive to the formal phase of symbolism. There, the imitation of nature shifted from a reflection of external nature of a formal organization of which nature was the content. But in the formal phase the poem is still contained by nature, and in the archetypal phase the whole of poetry is still contained within the limits of the natural, or plausible. When we pass into anagogy, nature becomes, not the container, but the thing contained, and the archetypal universal symbols, the city, the garden, the quest, the marriage, are no longer the desirable forms that man constructs inside nature, but are themselves the forms of nature. Nature is now inside the mind of an infinite man who builds his cities out of the Milky Way. This is not reality, but it is the conceivable of imaginative limit of desire, which is infinite, eternal, and hence apocalyptic. By an apocalypse I mean primarily the imaginative conception of the whole of nature as the content of an infinite and eternal living body which, if not human, is closer to being human than to being inanimate.[48]

The aim of discovering a center for all of literature, a center which enacts this vision of transcendent identity as a literary monument, requires that all the cultural past, the touchstones of the sublime, be recovered and composed according to the romantic designs of one's primal desire:

> The preoccupation of the humanities with the past is sometimes made a reproach against them by those who forget that we face the past: it may be shadowy, but it is all that is there. Plato draws a gloomy picture of man staring at the flickering shapes made on the wall of the objective world by a fire behind us like the sun. But the analogy breaks down when the shadows are those of the past, for the only light we can see them by is the Promethean fire within us. The substance of these shadows can only be in ourselves, and the goal of historical criticism, as our metaphors about it often indicate, is a kind of self-resurrection, the vision of a valley of dry bones that takes on the flesh and blood of our own vision. The culture of the past is not only the memory of mankind, but our own buried life, and study of its leads to a recognition scene, a discovery in which we see, not our past lives, but the total cultural form of our present life. It is not only the poet but his reader who is subject to the obligation to "make it new."[49]

One wishes, then, always to be at the center of things, no matter where one may be in the literary universe; one wants to feel that one can produce this vision of a world of total metaphor, an interpenetrating cosmos of ceaseless transformation that confirms one's more than human nature by virtue of one's imaginative repetition or revision of the past.[50] If the tradition needs anything, it needs an "ideal reader," as much as Joyce's *Wake* does:

> If I have read the last chapter of *Finnegans Wake* correctly, what happens there is that the dreamer, after spending the night in communion with a vast body of metaphorical identifications, wakens and goes about his business forgetting his dream, like Nebuchadnezzar, failing to use, or even to realize that he can use, the "keys to dreamland." What he fails to do is therefore left for the reader to do, the "ideal reader suffering from an ideal insomnia," as Joyce calls him, in other words the critic. Some such activity as this of reforging the broken links between creation and knowledge, art and science, myth and concept, is what I envisage for criticism. Once more, I am not speaking of a change of direction or activity in criticism: I mean only that if critics go on with their own business, this will appear to be, with increasing obviousness, the social and practical result of their labors.[51]

This vision of the critic's interpretive labor is a fine apocalypse, but what does it assume?

A passage from *The Well-Tempered Critic* may help clarify the question if not provide any easy answer:

> Literature, we say, neither reflects nor escapes from ordinary life: what it does reflect is the world as human imagination conceives it, in mythical, romantic, heroic and ironic as well as realistic and fantastic terms. This world is the universe in human form, stretching from the complete fulfillment of human desire to what human desire utterly repudiates, the *quo tendas* vision of reality that elsewhere I have called, for reasons rooted in my study of Blake, apocalyptic. In this world the difference between the two kinds of high style just mentioned disappears. Some religions assume that such a world exists, though only for gods; other religions, including those closer to us, identify it with a world man enters at death, the extremes of desire becoming its heavens and hells; revolutionary philosophies associate it with what man is to gain in the future; mystics call it the world of total or cosmic consciousness. A poet may accept any of these identifications without damage to his poetry; but for the literary critic, this larger world is the world that man exists and participates in through his imagination. It is the world in which our imaginations move and have their being while we are also living in the "real" world, where our imaginations find the ideals that they try to pass on to belief and action, where they find the vision which is the source of both the dignity and the joy of life. High style, whether demotic or hieratic, is the authentic speech of that world, the language which is neither impersonal nor spoken by this or that person, but the language of humanity itself.[52]

Here in miniature, Frye summarizes his position on the aim of vision. The visionary writer or revisionary critic produces in his texts a version of existence as human desire prefers it to appear by means of his sublime style. He thereby creates his own textual heterocosm that, via the larger structures of genre, convention, archetypes and myth, interpenetrates analogically with those produced by other individual creators within their respective traditions or discursive fields. These separate worlds of "second nature" compose the solar systems and imaginative constellations of culture within the verbal universe of man. No one person, Frye understandably claims here, can speak for this Human Logos, since it simply is "the language of humanity itself."

There are enormous problems with this grand vision. First of all, it assumes that there is a common *human* nature, a set of fundamental human needs and desires which Western literature and the Western literary critic has most fully articulated and that one of these desires is to transcend history, the natural and all-too-human world. Second, in the sentimental haze of Frye's language, one may miss the fact that this visionary world exists only in ironic, antithetical relation to ordinary experience. Frye's vision reminds one of what Hegel calls the unhappy consciousness of the German Romantic ironists, who were so perversely happy in their self-division, sublimely ecstatic, in fact, over their profound alienation from actual life. Third, and lastly, Frye reduces the religions of man purely to an aesthetic basis, making (like Pater) all values whatsoever depend on the question of style, and, more tellingly, on the style of the privileged Western literary critic.

Like his conception of Christ as the radiant focusing glass of the divine Father's infinite light,[53] a triumphantly ironic revision of the similar tropes of Emerson's transparent eyeball and of Pater's hard, gem-like flame, Frye conceives of the critic as a mediator of man's apocalyptic vision to the masses, what he calls in the low-mimetic mode of the *Anatomy,* "a cultural middleman" between the classics and the public. The critic teaches the public to substitute the visionary knowledge of theory for all the lures of kinetic stimuli—that is, to substitute gnosis for any impulse to praxis at all. But the model for this substitution is not Arnold or even Blake. It is, rather, Shelley in *Prometheus Unbound.* "Thus the equivalent of faith in Shelley is a *gnosis* which is therefore not an act in Milton's sense, nor a pseudo-act, nor a parody-act, but a withdrawal from action. It might be called an achievement of a state of nothingness or void in which reality appears."[54] As we have seen, Frye makes this same recommendation in "Criticism, Visible and Invisible."

Frye wants to save literature and the rest of man's cultural productions from all possible kinetic responses to them. He wants, that is, to enshrine his prophetic revision of the critical attitude of "disinterestedness." So to preserve the mark of the cultivated gentleman in these times, Frye ends up recommending the recovery of man's freedom lost since the exile from Eden by means of this secular form of critical romance. Thus Frye, the Arnoldian visionary, prefigures Bloom, the Gnostic revisionist. Frye's is a benevolent-seeming Gnosticism. But it actually involves the degradation and radical correction, via the critic's practice of the high style, of nature, history, temporality—in short, of becoming. All veiling, elusivenes, deception, and betrayal assume the shape that the unrevised figure of woman takes in Frye's cosmos and that he names (after Blake) Vala or the Female Will. In essence, therefore, being arises, for Frye, ony from the ashes of a perpetual revisionary *auto da fé*. A Bloom could assume no more sublimely reductive spectacle of critical self-torment.

But the greater irony of Frye's revisionary efforts, of his antithetical quest for the perfection of his style and the recovery of a fabulous literary identity, is that the ultimate goal of the quest must remain, even for Frye, as elusive, deceptively attractive, and in the process of becoming as his figure of the Female Will remains eternally the same—a fact he occasionally recognizes himself:

> A direct experience or apprehension of [the apocalyptic world] would be a microcosmic experience, an intelligence or imagination finding itself at the center of an intelligible or imaginable totality, and so experiencing, for however brief an instant, without any residue of alienation. It would thus also be an experience of finally attained or recovered identity. Most of us, at least, never reach it directly in experience, if it is attainable in experience at all, but only through one of the articulated analogies, of which literature is a central one. Whatever it is it represents the end of our critical path, though we have not yet traversed the path.[55]

One suspects that Frye's unmediated vision of general being becomes at some point the same as the experience of nothing in particular, an essentially indeterminate or radically absent-minded experience of the imagination's power to represent without there being anything specific to represent, not even, I am afraid, a coherent identity for the critic himself to envision.

At best, one recalls in this regard the conclusion to Kubrick's film *2001: A Space Odyssey,* where the aging, senile astronaut, a Ulysses in quest of the Blessed Isles, splits into the different facets of his personality before he is suddenly transformed (in the last frame) into a gigantic starry foetus who is about to enter the system of constellations, with the appropriately insipid seraphic smile on its face. At worst, one recalls the old Emerson unable to remember the meaning of his own words. Frye's scene of critical assumption resembles more Kubrick's stylized grandeur, at least in principle if not in all the details: "If one could live in [the visionary cosmos], of course, criticism would cease and the distinction between literature and life would disappear, because life itself would then be the continuous incarnation of the creative word."[56] Perpetual fiat lux, in other words. The final irony of Frye's position, however, is that it recommends the revision of what is really an experience of being at a loss and at the mercy of the infinite calculus of language, into an occasion for the aesthetic response of a self-betraying trope for divinity. One does not know whether to laugh at such a spectacle of sublime repression or not. After a lifetime of such willful forgetting one could even forget oneself.

But Frye's antithetical quest against nature and search for vision does primarily remind one both of Blake, of course, and of Desseintes or any other representative writer in the symboliste tradition. For Frye's quest is for an escape from all the conditions and necessities of the writing life. That is, it is a quest to transform the painful contradictions of the writer's alienating labor into a vision that will compensate him for a life of suffering and self-victimage, a vision of what Yeats in *The Tower* calls the "translunar Paradise," reflected from "the superhuman/mirror-resembling dream" of the perfected "artifice of eternity," a vision inspired by a repressed self-recognition of a heartsick, dying animal desperately ignorant of its actual situation.

A question has suddenly occurred to me. Could it be that just as Frye in *A Natural Perspective,* his book on Shakespeare's last romances, conjures out of them their informing genius and calls him Orpheus (much as Nietzsche does with Greek tragedy and Dionysus), so I have conjured out of his texts the spirit of romance that haunts them and that I am here naming it "Yeats"? If so, then, just as Frye in that work concludes by calling for the complete abolition of the spectator's world in a "dance of vanishing spirits, a revel that has no end"[57] (a recollection—in fact—of Hegel's final vision in the *Phenomenology of Spirit*), so I shall end this section on Frye's visionary project by calling for the total dissolution of his prophetic culture into what are now the many fiery tongues composing its (re-)visionary babble.

Overview

Frye's legacy looms large on the horizon of anyone's view of developments in American literary criticism since World War II. Its amplitude is shown by the testimonials to Frye's influence made by such notable critical historians as Murray Krieger, Geoffrey Hartman, A. Walton Litz, and Frank Lentricchia.[58] Each of these scholars singles out Frye's visionary criticism as the defining and still informing point of departure for all that has followed in its considerable wake. Litz's comment in this vein expresses best the general uneasy consensus:

> *Anatomy of Criticism* represents in many ways a profound interruption of the Anglo-American critical tradition. The customary functions of the great critics from Johnson to Eliot, "discrimination" and "judgment," are deliberately overturned. Frye is not interested in the qualities which make works of art different from each other, but in those qualities which make them look the same. Works of widely different value can live comfortably in the same sentence, because they share structural similarities. . . . If *Anatomy of Criticism* is a major work of enduring importance, as I believe it to be, then it is the first great work of English or American literary criticism not produced by a practicing artist, and signals a decisive turn toward the continental model. The critic is no longer the servant of the artist but a colleague, with his own special knowledge and powers. Northrop Frye is a writer of great humanity and culture, and these qualities shine through even the most schematic parts of the *Anatomy;* but he provides a system which tempts the critic to

interpose himself between the artist and the audience as an independent creative force. *Anatomy of Criticism* is itself a high work of the
organizing imagination. As Frank Kermode said in his 1958 review,
"it would be reasonable to treat this as a work of criticism which has
turned into literature, for it is centripetal, autonomous, and ethical
without, I think, being useful." Kermode is here employing
"useful" in the sense of the critic who patiently analyzes and explains, conscious of the individuality of the literary work and the
practical needs of the reader. Like every admirer of the *Anatomy,*
Kermode has been influenced by it, and his own recent work has
tended toward more "structural" interests. But the fact remains
that Frye made extravagant claims for criticism that were relatively
new to the Anglo-American tradition, and delivered a system
which—when manipulated by less subtle minds—tended to homog-
enize literature and give the critic a spurious authority.[59]

In other words, as Geoffrey Hartman shows in his fine essay on
Frye "Ghostlier Demarcations: The Sweet Science of Northrop
Frye," Frye not only sums up the Symboliste and modernist
strains in aesthetics but revises the Romantic tradition and
makes it available as ideology appropriate for use by critical theorists. In this fashion, Frye prepares the American scene for the
introduction of continental developments from structuralism to
the varieties of deconstruction.

Frank Lentricchia, the leading historian of these developments, goes so far as to see in Frye's neo-Kantian aestheticism
the real seeds of the Nietzschean deconstructive criticism recently forced into bloom at Yale and elsewhere. For him, such
things are only *apparently* transplanted in toto from European
sources to American soil and then stubbornly grafted to indige-
nous developments of our native literary culture:

> All of his distinctions and arrangements, and even the basic import
> and value of his literary universe, appear to be dissolved in the
> generalized Nietzschean illusionism which he announces in [the
> *Anatomy's*] final pages, as he anticipates the new Nietzschean rhet-
> oricians at Yale. The key to the "situation" of Frye's own discourse
> is his vision of an uncoerced self; it is a vision generated by a
> thoroughly despairing and alienated understanding of the pos-
> sibilities of historical life. For Frye actual history can be nothing
> but a theater of dehumanization, a place of bondage and torture. A
> number of contradictions aside, the move is spiritually coherent

from his neo-Kantian view of freedom [and its celebration of the creative mind] toward his prefiguring of the recent rhetorical interpretation of Nietzsche (and its celebration of nonmimetic figuration). For what is celebrated in both instances is a fantastical, utopian alternative to the perception of a degraded social existence: a human discoursing free of all contingency, independent of all external forces, a discoursing empowered by unconditioned human desire. The consistency of Frye's [utopia] is the consistency of an idealism in extremis. *Anatomy of Criticism* is poised crucially in 1957, looking at once backward to traditions in poetics of which it is the culmination, and forward to postmodernist responses to those traditions.[60]

Lentricchia's argument with Frye is a compelling one, but he fails to take into account how Frye himself has ironicaly prefigured even Lentricchia's own critique. Such prophetic irony, a hallmark of Frye's critical practice, cannot be as simply overcome as Lentricchia's remarks suppose.

Frye, as usual, has been eloquently self-effacing and ironically elusive on the question of his influence. In "The Search for Acceptable Worlds," for example, he impersonalizes the question by placing it in a general theoretical discussion of influence. Nonetheless, his response does possess significance both in itself and for what it suggests about the impact of his work. Frye in this essay compares the process of influence to a vagrant "seeding" of one writer's work by another's. Phrases and ideas, sublime in nature, stand a bit outside or above their context and are almost randomly swept up by currents of opinion in a culture. They are then deposited, like the sea's tribute, on the shores of some poetic Robinson Crusoe or other. He then seizes upon the influential concept to proceed with a project of his own, much as Yeats, knowing no French, perfected his early Symboliste manner out of a single line from *Axel's Castle* intoned in his essentially English ear by Arthur Symons: "As for living, our servants will do that for us."[61] This view of influence, when applied to Frye himself, makes everything much more safely impersonal and practically anonymous, with everything, as well, totally dependent on the genius of the isolated critic or writer.

One does not have to be a professional cynic to see Frye's rudimentary theory of influence as an idealistic and bourgeois illusion. And yet, it does have a certain charm and rhetorical effectiveness. In "Expanding Eyes," for instance, Frye responds to Angus Fletcher (a former disciple) by attempting to disarm his rebellious son with his impersonal theory of influence. It would have worked except for the essay's conclusion. There Frye betrays the actual workings of influence, by symbolically transforming all his "sons" who are at the time coming into their critical maturity into daughters of his memory, ironic "Muses," from whom "the human creator recovers his creations . . . and lives again, like Job, [with] a renewed presence" that is his alone.[62]

As can be seen from this conclusion, Frye's most significant bequest to contemporary critics is his revisionary style of writing. This assertion appears a bit strange, perhaps, only if one defines "style" in a superficial way as merely ornamental. For, whatever his conceptual inadequacies, Frye seems on the surface at least to be, in terms of his ability to communicate ideas, the absolute antithesis of some recent theorists such as Harold Bloom. But, as has been shown, in light of the textual strategy operative at the level of "deep structure," Frye is in his work as much a revisionary allegorist of the ironic processes of reading as Bloom or de Man. Frye, like Miller or Hartman, dissolves a writer's world of argument into its underlying matrix of figures, converting a movement of thought into a structure of images and symbols or "underthought" that he is "discovering" and "displacing" into a theoretical and rhetorical context of his own making.

Although Frye learns this method of reading from Yeats in "The Philosophy of Shelley's Poetry,"[63] his perfection of it rivals Jacques Derrida's subversive resurrection of dead metaphor in the texts of authors he is deconstructing.[64] Frye's stated aim is, of course, quite different from Derrida's. It resembles more closely, in its benevolent intention to discover a definitive center of conscious imaginative design, Georges Poulet's phenomenological method of reading first introduced into Anglo-American criticism by J. Hillis Miller.[65] Yet, as my analysis suggests, Frye uses his archetypal method of interpretation much as other critical writers use their particular theoretical schemas to revise a writer's world into the visionary reflection of what he needs that world to be then, which is—no matter what the current specific career vicissitude, no matter how difficult or resistant the text, and no matter who the author may be (classic figure or otherwise)—always another convenient womb to nurture a sublime conception of himself as always about to be born into vision.

This is an extraordinary claim but one that is quite justified. Consider the concluding sections of Frye's first and (so far) last books *Fearful Symmetry* and *The Great Code*. *Fearful Symmetry* ends like this:

> We have seen that in his relation to English literature Blake attaches himself to a certain unity of ideas held in the English Renaissance, most clearly illustrated in the first book of *The Faerie Queene* and *Areopagitica*. We traced this unity of ideas in the sixth chapter, and are now in a position to sum it up more briefly as the unity of the meanings belonging to "word" in the above paragraph. In its Renaissance context it was a combination of certain Protestant and humanist tendencies, of new ideas about the Word of God combined with new ideas about the words of man. If we understand that to Blake there are no puns or ambiguities or accidents in the range of the meaning of "word," but a single and comprehensible form, we have wound up all of his golden string and are standing in front of his gate. But gates are to be opened, and there is still much to be seen by the light of the vision Blake saw—perhaps the same light that broke in on the dying Falstaff when he babbled of green fields and played with flowers, and on his hostess when she told how he had gone into "Arthur's" bosom, and how he had talked of the Whore of Babylon.[66]

What sense are we to make of this curiously resonant set of allusions? First of all, we must recall Falstaff's important role as a silenus foil to Prince Hal's impersonation of a triumphant Dionysus. Hal must see through this figure at last, if he is to become Henry V and achieve symbolic immortality in English history as the type of redemptive political hero. In this light, one can argue that by transmitting Blake's "true" vision (as opposed to those promulgated for him by Yeats or Eliot), Frye aspires to the equivalent heroic status within our literary culture at a time of severe crises. Secondly, Frye would achieve it by sacrificing not a Falstaff alone but the Great Whore of Nature as well, for otherwise call all he might the apocalyptic vision will not come. But for whom or what are Falstaff and the Great Whore covering figures? Frye's return to Blake and his prophecies as the model of visionary and the model of poetic performance, respectively, would displace, I think, Yeats and his tragic vision, especially as enshrined in his last virulently anti-humanistic phase of "visionary madness" (as Reuben Brower has identified it). I am thinking in particular of some of Yeats' *Supernatural Songs* such as "What Magic Drum" and "Meru." In this setting, the purpose of Frye's allusion to the final scene of Falstaff's life from the *Merry Wives of Windsor* becomes clearer. He would subsume Yeats and his vision under the comic archetype of the *miles gloriosus* and the demonic image of the Great Whore. In this ironic manner, Frye would overcome Yeats' influence. The young Frye's revisionary intention is to make Yeats wear a strangely feminine Falstaffian mask, while he suddenly dons that of Henry V. Unfortunately, in Frye's case, the faces beneath these masks resemble more that of the speaker from Yeats' "Meditations in Time of Civil War" for whom "the abstract joy," the Urizensic study and manipulation of "daemonic images," appears to suffice all too well.[67]

Similarly, when we turn to the conclusion to volume 1 of *The Great Code*, we find the same strategy of rhetorical self-aggrandizement (and sublime belittlement) at work underneath the surface play of self-effacing allusiveness:

> Man is constantly building anxiety-structures, like geodesic domes, around his social and religious institutions. If Milton's view of the Bible as a manifesto of human freedom has anything to be said for it, one would expect it to be written in a language that would smash these structures beyond repair, and let some genuine air and light in. But of course anxiety is very skillful at distorting languages.
>   There is a sardonic Old English riddle (at least, I doubt if its progression of imagery is pure accident) that begins: An enemy deprived me of life, took away my strength, then soaked me in water,

then took me out again and put me in the sun, where I soon lost all my hair.

The answer is "book," specifically a Bible codex. The riddle obliquely describes the method of preparing a codex in the writer's day, and seeems to be referring also to the shearing of Samson in Judges 16:17–22. The normal human reaction to a great cultural achievement like the Bible is to do with it what the Philistines did to Samson: reduce it to impotence, then lock it in a mill to grind our aggressions and prejudices. But perhaps its hair, like Samson's, could grow again even there.[68]

This passage functions not only as an answer to all the secular critics of religious and romantic visions, but, as well, to all the many critics of Frye who would turn his Book of Vision into the basis for the elaboration of their own anxiety structures—all those, that is, who have attempted to grind Frye's powerful system down, by snipping off its visionary curls. One cannot help but see, I think, how this conclusion would portray a potential critic of Frye as a philistine Delilah who in the second volume of *The Great Code* will have to pay for the degradation of this theoretical Samson (so much for Frank Lentricchia, for example). Such a critic will suffer a last judgment passed upon him and his kind by the former victim, just as soon as his luxuriant locks begin to grow once again.

I think his critics are meant to succumb to the stylized Romantic glamor of Frye's conspicuously allusive manner. By figuring the demonically open secret out, one could forget in the process that Frye is no Samson, however speculatively conceived. Rather like a very minor Milton, he projects this tragically self-reflective figure for the critics to identify with and react to. As he works his seductive magic on them, Frye practices this kind of strategic irony, in order to overcome his tradition, by bringing it down all around us. The best defense against Frye, however, would not be a simple dismissal of his project of resurrecting and repeating the entire cultural past in schematic form as silly and futile. The best defense—I suspect the ony meaningful defense—is to work through all the coils of this dragon, even as one repeats for the last time (in one's own case at least) their contours in a satiric critique. The critic must work through Frye with a forked tongue in his cheek.

The issue does not depend on strategic questions alone, however. Nor is it simply a matter of Frye's reader suddenly discovering behind the mask of the scholar the leering face of the seducer whose greatest triumph lies in his enslavement of another's imaginative (rather than merely physical) responses. The issue is a more broadly social and moral one. Let us look, for example, at what Frye *does* in the following passage from "The Instruments of Mental Production," an essay that addresses the relation of a literary education to the practical and ethical interests of society:

> Ever since Adam was thrown out of Paradise and told to plough and till an accursed ground, the most important distinction in human life has been the distinction between labour and leisure. By labour, here, I mean the whole productive aspect of society, the accumulating and distributing of food and the means of shelter and the more specific wants of a settled social order. According to Veblen, Adam soon tires of tilling the ground and compels Eve to do it instead, confining his own activities to hunting and fishing and thereby beginning a "leisure class," the class that is defined as superior because it contributes nothing to social production. When leisure and labour become personified as an upper and a lower class, the conceptions of waste and alienation come into society: alienation for the worker, who is cheated out of nearly all the fruit of his own labour, and waste for the leisurely consumer, who can put nothing ot productive use. American democracy has blurred these social distinctions and has replaced the leisure class with the affluent society, but it has not thereby lessened the feelings of waste and alienation. The sense that society, considered in its producing and distributing aspect, is something cheap and ignoble, that it is not worth loyalty, that many of its products are absurdities and that operating its obsessively busy machinery is spiritually futile, is at least as strong as it ever was. And this time there is nobody to hate, no tyrants or silk-hatted capitalists or swaggering lords, no one essentially different from ourselves for whom we can relieve our feelings by abusing.[69]

Having learned very well the lessons of modernism, Frye ironically juxtaposes a mythic archetype (Adam) and what appears to be a modern reality (the enemy in us all), in order to create in the reader's mind a sublime identity of master and slave, owner and worker, that transcends historical differences and political critique the way the Incarnation is said to mediate between God and man estranged since the Fall. It is as if Frye were standing in a time and place beyond all times and all places, at the end of deliberate exploitation and ideological mystification, if not of de facto alienation and confusion. In fact, of course, Frye's closing representation of modern reality and the idea of the end of history it assumes are as fabulous and falsifying a set of figures of speech as those he invokes at the passage's opening.

Frye thereby achieves a god-like perspective on his text of the social world at the cost of his critical intelligence and, if we are wise, of our sympathy. A Stephen Dedalus he is; a Karl Marx, or William Blake, even a Matthew Arnold, he isn't. What type of critical intelligence do we need more these days?

In a way, one could argue that Frye has unwittingly become more like one of the characters of Cervantes or Flaubert who fall victim to a system of "private mythology" than the would-be anatomist of this "theoretical" disease of self-betrayal, a problem for Frye more profound than intentional evil: "Very few," Frye laments in an early review-essay, "have followed Cervantes in tackling the far deeper problem of private mythology, of how one's behavior is affected by a structure of ideas in which one thinks one believes. Flaubert (in *Madame Bovary*) was one such follower, and Dostoyevski (in *The Idiot*) was another; but the full exploitation of this field has yet to come. One hopes it will come soon, as the shallower fields are nearly exhausted."[70] One wonders what was lost when Frye was bewitched by Yeats' influence rather than being schooled by the works of that figure he unaccountably fails to mention here, James Joyce, whom Frye does recognize later as the modern master of the anatomy form.[71]

The question, in other words, is one of style in the largest sense. Who better than Frye could have provided us with a true *Anatomy of Criticism,* in which, as he himself defines the genre, obsessive mental attitudes that turn people into walking caricatures of their own professed intellectual ideals, are satirized by being reflected in the ironic mirror of the satirist's style as he exuberantly piles up "an enormous mass of erudition about his theme" and overwhelms his pedantic targets "with an avalanche of their own jargon?" Who better than Frye could have shown the dangers of reducing all of life to antithetical patterns of speculative possibilities and ridiculed with more subtle irony and pointed analysis the traditional butt of the satirist, the figure of the *philosophus gloriosus,* that enthusiastic dispenser of "maddened pedantry," which is the disease of the intellect that stands at the root of much of the evil and folly in society? One could even suggest that Frye did attempt to do something like this in his work, particularly in the polemical introduction to his *Anatomy of Criticism,* but that he failed to keep the necessary distance from the abyss of his own systematic creation.[72] That is, gazing into the universe of the *Anatomy of Criticism,* he became what he wished to behold there rather than what he and the profession really needed him to be.

Similarly, the critics following Frye, even those who would revise or overcome him, too often end up repeating in their own ways this self-betraying quest of the literary theorist.

As one representative instance, consider the curious case of Fredric Jameson. In *The Political Unconscious,* Jameson attempts to produce a Marxist *Anatomy of Criticism* appropriate for a radically revisionary age. Quite surprisingly at first, Jameson openly acknowledges Frye's influence and even privileges his views of romance as the displaced expression of a utopian desire for fundamental revolutionary changes. Jameson's project requires this understanding of the genre, and so Frye's theory of romance receives a dialectical endorsement. But where Frye goes wrong for Jameson is, of course, in the internalization and individualization of romance, as symbolized in Frye's famous ecstatic celebration of "the cosmic body" in the second essay of the *Anatomy.* Jameson sees this climactic vision as an essentially "privatized" fantasy of "the alienated intellectual."[73]

> Thus, not only does Frye's Blakean anagogy rejoin by a paradoxical movement that whole metaphysics of desire; the very concept of apocalypse as the end of history and the culminating struggle of the collectivity is here curiously redirected, rechanneled and indeed

recontained, by the image of Blakean absolute "man" and transfigured body projected out upon the universe. Yet equally paradoxically, the association lends Frye's metaphysic of desire a kind of collective and Utopian resonance which the more purely Freudian versions of the metaphysics lacked: when we come to it from the more purely anarchistic and individualizing limits of the left Freudians, this transfigured libidinal body glows and expands with all the political energies of a Blake engraving, and makes it clear that the program of libidinal revolution is political ony to the degree that it is itself the figure for social revolution. Yet this movement of figurality is precisely what from the other point of view the arrangement of Frye's allegorical levels recontains: for, being the final "phase" of the allegory, the image of the cosmic body cannot stand for anything further, for anything other than itself. Its figural and political momentum is broken, and the collective content of the image has been reprivatized in the henceforth purely individual terms of the isolated body and the merely personal ecstasy.[74]

So far so good. Yet where Jameson goes wrong for me[75] is, however, in his attempt to create a theoretical heterocosm of his own, one that, whatever his conscious aims, tends to enact in its narrative strategy and theoretical style of systematic elaboration and schematic refinement the drama of Jameson's own will to power over the field of contemporary criticism. That is, Jameson's text recontains or closes off the radical political elements of his argument on romance, within its formal, rhetorical structure even as it thereby reflects and appears to set "free" the sublime image of the transfigured theoretical critic who smiles his work to see—a creator at last with his own separate world to oversee.[76]

I agree in principle with Jameson's critique of Frye's "aestheticizing" textual strategy. It is only that I see it operating in *The Political Unconscious* as well.[77] Both writers would be hermeneutic gods, containing literary and cultural history within a theoretical apparatus that creates and then can repeatedly confirm their own unique critical identities. In other words, the form of both master-works, *Anatomy of Criticism* and *The Political Unconscious*, is essentially that of romance, only displaced to a theoretical context and dressed up with different rhetorics fit for each era. Ironically enough, for both the visionary Frye and the Marxist Jameson, history becomes the raw material, the inspiring muse or daughter of memory, for the solitary production of their respective god-images. Each self-conscious system-maker would become the ideal reader of himself, begetting sublime images of themselves in the lesser minds of their fascinated readers and fanatical critics.[78] Clio, the muse of history, in ancient myth, is always in danger of becoming (in Yeats' telling phrase) "that raving slut who keeps the till,"[79] when seen from the ultimately disillusioning perspective of critical romance.

However, Frye and Jameson are not wrong to point to romance as the most influential of modern narrative forms. One dominant form of discursive practice in critical writing for the last century or so has been what I call the romance of interpretation. It is a literary genre with its own set of conventions and style, one entirely appropriate for a revisionary culture of betrayal and self-deception. I shall conclude my study of Frye and critical romance now with a comparative analysis of the interpretive strategies of Frye and Nietzsche (in *The Anti-Christ*), both to suggest how pervasive this ideology of romance actually is and to clarify how, as Frank Lentricchia suggests, Frye prefigures current post-structuralist forms of critical practice. My hope is that contemporary critics do indeed come to recognize the origins of their celebration of Nietzschean perspectivism and deconstructive irony in the familiar, neo-Kantian, and archetypal approach of Frye, much the way I suppose Satan, surprised by Sin initially (as he would exit Hell's gates), came once again to see in her negative image the lineaments of a sublime story better left forgotten or, at least, one more suited for a work of disillusionment few can bear. In this way, the oppositional stance of today's theorists to all that they represent as traditional and superseded could be seen for what it is, as a self-serving gesture inspired and perpetuated primarily by the institution itself.

In those sections (28–38) of *The Anti-Christ* dealing with "the psychological type of the redeemer," Nietzsche rejects, out of hand, the notion that the Gospels contain, to any significant degree, accurate accounts of Christ's character or of his actions. The Gospels are for Nietzsche a pious fraud at best and at worst the cynical betrayal, by the most prominent and resentful true believers of the early Christian community, of the "glad tidings" of this supposed god-man. After suffering the death of the Cross, Christ must "repent" by being sacrificed to the need for power and influence of St. Paul and the rest over that community and over the greater Jewish and Roman cultures.

Similarly, Nietzsche rejects Renan's liberal, secular, and humanistic interpretation of Christ as a genuine hero on the world historical stage. Renan sees Christ as a man of genius, like Socrates, a master of irony, who uses his imaginative power to educate individuals in the perception of moral value. Nietzsche sees Christ as a character worthy of the psychological inventiveness of a Dostoyevski: a prince of idiots who suffers from a severe aversion to all vigorous stimuli, especially those of touch, because he is pathologically incapable of offering resistance to any stimulus at all.

Immersed entirely in a world of symbols and symbolic actions, seeing emblems everywhere, seeking to abolish or efface all sharp oppositions, however unprovocative in nature, as being too painful to bear, Christ, Nietzsche argues, attempts to elude all analysis and rational formulation, not out of self-conscious irony, nor because of his superhuman nature, but due to a physiological necessity—he has no core personality, no ruling instinct or will to disclose, except this will to nothingness, this negation of all will. Peace of God at all costs. According to Nietzsche's understanding of nihilism, this would make Christ the perfect decadent, the paradigm of self-destructive will.

> To make a *hero* of Jesus!—And what a worse misunderstanding is the word "genius"! Our whole concept, our cultural concept "spirit" had no meaning whatever in the world Jesus lived in. To speak with the precision of the physiologist a quite different word would rather be in place here: the word idiot. We recognize a condition of morbid susceptibility of the *sense of touch* which makes it shrink back in horror from every contact, every grasping of a firm object. Translate such a physiological *habitus* into its ultimate logic—as instinctive hatred of *every* reality, as flight into the "ungraspable," into the "inconceivable," as antipathy towards every form, every spacial and temporal concept, towards everything

firm, all that is custom, institution, Church, as being at home in a
world undisturbed by reality of any kind, a merely "inner word," a
"real" world, an "eternal" world. . . . "The kingdom of God *is*
within you". . . .[80]

Reality for such a being, Nietzsche goes on to say, is merely the
occasion for metaphor, since, for Nietzsche, to create metaphors
is to desire to be elsewhere. Christ's kergyma, consequently, is no
dogma or set of commandments, but simply the practice of his
"idiotic" life, a life lived in blessedness, or wholly symbolically.
Such a life, as Keats said of Shakespeare's, is a life of allegory, in
which all the particularities of the world are consumed in the
vision of the end of salvation history being realized in the person
of Jesus Christ. That is, Christ for Nietzsche, like Frye for us,
subsumes the diversity of experience and the differences of language under the sublime image of man's incipient divinity. It is
one of the crushing ironies of world history, Nietzsche concludes, that this delusion-system has been taken seriously.

Notice what Nietzsche has done here in *The Anti-Christ*. He
has discovered, beneath the Gospel narratives as we have them
and as antithetically interpreted by St. Paul and Renan, traces of
a different story, not that of the redeemer, nor that of the moral
reformer, but that of the decadent, nihilistic psychology of the
redeemer-type, that is, the psychology of the revisionist par excellence. Nietzsche has discovered the sublime image of all that
he must avoid or overcome, if he is to remain imaginatively
healthy.

Neurasthenic, autistic, amnesiac, hysterically reactive—such
are the features of the man of decadence as Nietzsche conceives
of him, a man who is unable to withstand the purposeless sufferings of existence and so seeks to escape this innocence of becoming by flight into an ideal, visionary world of symbols. For such a
world, with himself as both its center and containing form, is full
of purpose: it must perpetually reveal the god as in the final act
of a biblical narrative or an ancient play, and the irony of that
revelation is, of course, that the god is oneself. Such a visionary
world can stand as the measure of existence and the model for its

correction. Nature is only the medium for the construction of consoling phantasmagoria. The man of decadence, therefore, has his prototypes in Christ and St. Paul, Socrates and Plato, and his latest avatars in Wagner and Nietzsche himself earlier in his career.

What Nietzsche has done in *The Anti-Christ* is to use his theory of nihilism and decadence as a frame, within which he produces a portrait of Christ as *idiot symboliste*, the hidden god or "genius" of the gospel texts. In doing so, Nietzsche reinvents and revises his precursor, much as Christ (as seen by the early Christians) reinvented and revised the Old Testament, particularly the prophets, and particularly Isaiah. The figure of Christ Nietzsche produces appears in antithetical relation to the traditional religious interpretations and to the modern humanistic view. In addition, it represents the negative inversion of Nietzsche's avowedly "masculine" and tragic ideal derived from his understanding of Greek heroic culture. Consequently, "Christ," like "Blake" for Frye, or "Frye" for Jameson, functions for Nietzsche as a mirror image—whether demonically or apocalyptically conceived—of the revisionary critic's own specular or self-reflective mask or interpretive persona.

Let's return to Nietzsche's practice here. Just as Christ stands between traditional Jerusalem and imperial Rome, between Caiaphas and Pilate, so Nietzsche stands between ecclesiastical Rome and modern Paris, between the Pope and Renan. But, in Frye's terms, Christ and his story compose, for Nietzsche, the demonic image of a Dionysian revelation. That is, the Gospel constitutes Nietzsche's haunting "underthought," his anxiety that he, too, is only a decadent. Similarly, I would contend, Nietzsche and his story, as I am teasing it forth now, compose Frye's "underthought," and the "underthought" of every revisionary critic. For Nietzsche has revised the materials of tradition, in order to give birth to his precursor as a weak, decadent, mimetic rival for sublimity, as the feminine parody of his strongly antithetical self-image. In this fashion, Nietzsche stabilizes and controls the radical interplay of argument and figure in his revisionary interpretation, an interpretation that has for its informing intention the emasculation of his precursor, via the latter's confinement within a narrative of decadence and betrayal, and the exaltation, even the apotheosis of the author of this narrative. Every precursor becomes a demon to be expelled and incarcerated; and every latecomer would become his divine warden. Nietzsche spells out this sublime motive most clearly at the conclusion of *Ecce Home,* when he identifies himself not simply with the anti-Christ, but with a different, more powerful god altogether: "Have I been understood: *Dionysus versus the Crucified!*"[81]

There are considerable ironies in all this, to be sure, not least of which, given Nietzsche's imminent and virtually complete collapse, is the prophetic nature of his "deconstructive" characterization of Christ as an idiot. But there is another irony, more significant for my argument. Without his mimetic rival for sublimity, his demonically defective antagonist or ironic double, Nietzsche would not be able to govern the play in his text of mataphor and antithesis, argument and figure. His text would have no definite shape. It could have gone on indefinitely. He needs, in short, his alter ego.

The rhetorical necessities, the strategies of textual production dominant in the culture since the Romantics, require that Nietzsche impose on his reading of the Gospels the structure of a mimetic rivalry, that is, the structure of a tragic romance. This romance of interpretation has a strikingly Oedipal cast. The figure of Christ as an idiot symboliste provides Nietzsche with a curiously androgynous counterimage upon and through which, as Frye does repeatedly in his texts with emblems of fallen nature, Nietzsche can beget his "new" heroic ideal and so (he hopes) come to father a new epoch in human history, one in which mankind can be surpassed by the übermensch: "And one calculates *time* from the *dies nefastus* (unlucky day) on which this fatality (Christ's birth)—from the *first* day of Christianity!—*Why not rather from its last?—From today?* Revaluation of all values!"[82]

Nietzsche, then would use his projected image of Christ as a negative exemplum, for the production of his antithetical ideal. Christ, as decadent (as opposed to Frye's fallen) nature is the ironic muse of Nietzsche's self-invention as the heroic substitute for the murdered divine Father. And so the oedipal situation completes itself. An otherwise inexplicable remark in *The Anti-Christ* becomes understandable in light of this analysis:

> But it is potently obvious what is alluded to in the symbols "Father" and "Son"—not potently obvious to everyone I grant: in the word "Son" is expressed the *entry* into the collective feeling of the transfiguration of all things (blessedness), in the word "Father" *this feeling itself,* the feeling of perfection and eternity.[83]

In translating the Christian symbolism of "Father" and "Son" into his symbolism of "Dionysus" and "the Womb of Being" (from the *Birth of Tragedy*), Nietzsche finishes off the Christian God in accord with the oedipal impulses underlying the revisionary critic's romance of interpretation.

This rhetorical structure of mimetic rivalry, with this strongly oedipal aura, has become I find a paradigm for critical writing. As Harold Bloom notes for the poets, so, too, perhaps even more so for the critics: the precursor must be found wanting in some respect (or, as here, in all respects). This defect, whether represented as a lack of intelligence, strength, self-possession, imagination, common sense, or political acumen, is usually seen as a destructive influence that must somehow be overcome. In this fashion, the precursor is made over into a woman-figure conceived in the image of the White Goddess or Great Whore archetype, the ironic, degraded and degrading muse of a project of personal sublimity, which, usually imaged in terms of some ideal woman-figure, has for its goal the apotheosis of the revisionary writer:

> How the "Real World" at Last Became a Myth
> History of an Error
> 1. The real world, attainable to the wise, the pious, the virtuous man—he dwells in it, *he is it.*
>   (Oldest form of the idea, relatively sensible, simple, convincing, Transcription of the proposition "I, Plato, *am* the truth.")

2. The real world, unattainable for the moment, but promised to the wise, the pious, the virtuous man ("to the sinner who repents").

   (Progress of the idea: it grown more refined, more enticing, more incomprehensible—*it becomes a woman*, it becomes Christian . . .)

3. The real world, unattainable, undemonstrable, cannot be promised, but even when merely thought of a consolation, a duty, an imperative.

   (Fundamentally the same old sun, but shining through mist and scepticism; the idea grown sublime, pale, northerly, Konigsbergian.)

4. The real world—unattainable? Unattained, at any rate. And if unattained also *unknown*. Consequently also no consolation, no redemption, no duty: how could we have a duty towards something unknown?

   (The grey of dawn. First yearnings of reason. Cockcrow of positivism.)

5. The "real world"—an idea no longer of any use, not even a duty any longer—an idea grown useless, superfluous, *consequently* a refuted idea: let us abolish it!

   (Broad daylight; breakfast; return of cheerfulness and *bon sens;* Plato blushes for shame; all free spirits run riot.)

6. We have abolished the real world: what world is left? the apparent world perhaps? . . . But no! *with the real world we have also abolished the apparent world!*

   (Mid-day; moment of the shortst shadow; end of the longest error; zenith of mankind; INCIPIT ZARATHUSTRA.)[84]

Canonization among the other immortal classics within the Western tradition, becoming the next episode in its history—such is the end of the psychology of revisionism. The ideal reader of such texts as *The Anti-Christ* or *Twilight of the Idols* is transformed as well into the daughter of this perverse union between Nietzsche and his precursor; for it is the reader, as Frye knows when he calls her/him "The Apocalyptic Bride," who will carry on the writer's seductive quest, and so in turn potentially become both revisionary creator and ironic muse for yet another hungry generation.

Fables of the Sublime

Frye, of course, would probably respond to my characterization of him as the latest version of Nietzsche's revision of Christ the idiot *symboliste* by saying that I have caricatured him. Since I have taken my model of revisionary interpretation from Nietzsche, I have made a hollow idol out of what is essentially a demonic parody of Frye's humanely alien, Arnoldian vision of individualized apocalypse. But in response to such an objection I would counter that our age of mutual assured destruction, as Frye himself observes in his 1962 essay,[85] "The Imaginative and the Imaginary," makes it virtually impossible to distinguish between the visions of the prophet and the delusions of the madman. This question of distinguishing between vision and delusion is crucial, and deserves more attention.

The typical way that the question arises in Frye and is handled by him can be seen most revealingly in *The Great Code*. After charting the Messianic quest in the Bible as a cycle of descent and return that is worked out repeatedly in the Old Testament and, as a single unique act, structures the New Testament, Frye remarks: "It may seem inconsistent to show the Messianic quest as a cycle when the anti-cyclical bias of the Bible has been so stressed, but this is one more example of the fact that every apocalyptic image has a demonic parody or contrast, and vice versa."[86] What appears in works which Frye privileges to be an obsessive structure of recurrence turns out to be, as in Blake's "Mental Traveler," the demonic parody of vision. In other words, the continuing narrative form of a cycle functions in a purely rhetorical fashion in Frye and in the works he likes, and in a blindly literal-minded way in works and authors he does not like.

This distinction between apocalyptic vision and demonic parody reflects a larger opposition between two different hermeneutics, that of a future-oriented typological mode of interpretation with a past-directed cyclical mode. For the former, final causes exist and govern the realm of the human spirit and the productions of culture. That is, principles and conscious intentions mean something. For the latter, material causes are all-determining and they precede all their formal effects temporally and logically, which means material causes such as biological drives, economic structures, and the irrational play of language as inscription make cultures and their products derivative phenomena.

This conflict of interpretations is one between what Paul Ricoeur terms a hermeneutics of faith, whether it is openly religious or not, and a hermeneutics of suspicion, whether it is openly secular or not. While the former style of interpretation is dialectical and teleological (as in Hegel), the latter style is demystifying and genealogical (as in Nietzsche). If the fault of the hermeneutics of faith is sentimentality, then that of the hermeneutics of suspicion is cynicism. For Frye, who values the vision of deliverance in which the symbolic representation of individual transcendence suddenly appears to stand sublimely beyond the containing forms of personal and collective narratives, the hermeneutics of suspicion while, perhaps, a useful instrument for demystifying social ideologies of all sorts, must be interpretively overcome by a visionary faith in the genuinely creative power of the human imagination to realize one's self-ideal.

Consider, for example, Frye's position on Nietzsche in *The Great Code*, a classic statement of Frye's antipathy to Nietzsche: "The old tension between typological and cyclical views of time recurs in Nietzsche, who developed a conception of a 'Superman' surpassing the 'all-to-human' level of existence that we know—another of the diachronic conceptions suggested by evolution. But because of his preference for the synchronic deity Dionysus, Nietzsche was compelled to incorporate his Superman into a cyclical framework of identical recurrence, a framework that I should think would effectively destroy the dynamics of the conception for most of his readers."[87] Given Frye's own cyclical understanding of literary history, that an age of irony is giving way to an age of myth and so *Finnegans Wake* is our most representative work, his critique of Nietzsche could be applied to his own work, especially in light of the allure for him of the sublime image of visionary creator, a heroic or superhuman figure of the writer modeled on the image of the biblical Messiah. But one can see what Frye does not like here. It is not so much the proto-fascist vision of the übermensch, as it is the containment suffered by that visionary image within a cyclical narrative form of tragic resonance.[88] One of the ironies of Frye's position as a leading theorist of narrative is that not only does he privilege one narrative form, comic romance, over the others, but he ultimately privileges the sublime image over narrative form for the same reason that Nietzsche prefers the synchronic deity Dionysius, viz., its tremendous power to engross the reader's attention and so, apparently, to contain time itself in an eternal now, a privileged movement of vision.

My position is that this tension between conflicting forms of interpretations recurs in Frye's own texts; despite his attempts or those of his critics like Jameson to discover there the makings of a genuinely diachronic social criticism, the requirements of argument and the narrative form of Frye's critical history of the visionary tradition impose on him a synchronic rhetorical structure, discoverable in the interplay and "underthought" of his ruling metaphors, which gives his work the shape of a romance of (self-)interpretation. The primary underlying intention of this romance is the production of Frye's own fables of the sublime, in which the critic achieves and repeatedly rediscovers his identity as "some synthetizing critical Messiah,"[89] who, like Christ at the marriage feast at Canaan, must renounce the Female Will of Nature, in order to fulfill his mission of representing in this world the creative will of the absent Father, to whom his faithful Son will spiritually give birth during the miraculous course of his vocation. Frye's relation to Blake could be seen, for example, in these terms, with the inadequate critics of Blake serving as emanations of the Female Will, Frye as the beloved Son, and Blake, of course, as the hidden God of Frye's intended plot.

In short, the force of convention, of the genre of critical theory and narrative, what I am calling the romance of interpretation, shapes Frye's texts as belated imitations of the secularized romantic quest for apocalyptic vision, as seen in Blake or Hegel. Coming late in cultural history, for someone like Frye at least, becomes a virtue, because, for such a visionary critic, his work stands as the final cause that gives form and meaning, a recognizable human shape to what otherwise would be a vast panorama of brutality and anarchy that the history of our culture, that inadequate muse, must always seem to be to oppositional critics. Ironically enough, Frye becomes for an entire generation of literary theorists, the revisionary muse of various projects of "mad pedantry," that striving after the sublime, for which Nietzsche in *Daybreak* provides the perfect gloss:

> "How can one make oneself mad when one is not mad and does not dare appear so?"—almost all the significant men of ancient civilization have pursued this train of thought; a secret teaching of artifices and dietetic hints was propagated on this subject, together with the feeling that such reflections and purposes were innocent, indeed holy. The recipes for becoming a medicine-man among the Indians, a saint among the Christians of the Middle Ages, an angekok among Greenlanders, a pajee among Brazilians are essentially the same: Senseless fasting, perpetual sexual abstinence, going into the desert or ascending a mountain or a pillar, or "sitting in an aged willow tree which looks upon a lake" and thinking of nothing at all except what might bring on an ecstacy and mental disorder. Who would venture to take a look into the wilderness of bitterest and most superfluous agonies of soul in which probably the most fruitful men of all times have languished! To listen to the sighs of these solitary and agitated minds: "Ah, give me madness, you heavenly powers! Madness, that I may at last believe in myself! Give deliriums and convulsions, sudden lights and darkness, terrify me with frost and fire such as no mortal has ever felt, with deafening din and prowling figures, make me howl and whine and crawl like a beast: so that I may only come to believe in myself! I am consumed by doubt, I have killed the law, the law anguishes me as a corpse does a living man: if I am not more than the law I am the vilest of all men. The new spirit which is in me, whence is it if it is not from you? Prove to me that I am yours; madness alone can prove it." And only too often this fervour achieved its goal all too well: in that age in which Christianity proved most fruitful in saints and desert solitaries, and thought it was proving itself by this fruitfulness, there were in Jerusalem vast madhouses for abortive saints, for those who had surrendered to it their last grain of salt.[90]

It should come as no surprise, I suppose, that the philosopher of the antithetical will and the theoretician of romance reveal in their revisionary textual strategies this apparently inescapable structure of critical romance. For both writers strive to achieve the most comprehensive perspective possible on whatever it is they are reading—a text, an author, a genre or an entire cultural history. Both writers dissolve and reassemble the elements of whatever it is they are reading according to a systemic framework of their own devising, which isolates for analytic representation the "underthought" or metaphorical (as opposed to argumentative) embodiment of the will or desire informing the narrative under consideration. Both writers, finally, produce their own textual world out of the debris of those worlds they have imperiously made use of for their own sublime purposes. As Frye remarks about Revelation, in words that could apply with equal justice to his or any other writer's Bible of hell, "It has been described as a book that either finds a man mad or else leaves him so."[91]

Consider, as one illustration of what Frye means, the following famous passage from the *Anatomy*, in which Frye so applies his archetypal approach to a series of cultural works that they all dissolve into the outlines of his own will to dominate cultural history:

> In looking at a picture, we may stand close to it and analyze the details of brush work and palette knife. This corresponds roughly to the rhetorical analysis of the new critics in literature. At a little distance back, the design comes into clearer view, and we study rather the content represented: this is the best distance for realistic Dutch pictures, for example, where we are in a sense reading the picture. The further back we go, the more conscious we are of the organizing design. At a great distance from, say, a Madonna, we can see nothing but the archetype of the Madonna, a large centripetal blue mass with a contrasting point of interest at its center. In the criticism of literature, too, we often have to "stand back" from the poem to see its archetypal organization. If we "stand back" from Spenser's *Mutabilitie Cantoes*, we see a background of ordered circular light and a sinister black mass thrusting up into the lower foreground—much the same archetypal shape that we see in the

opening of the book of Job. If we "stand back" from the beginning
of the fifth act of *Hamlet,* we see a grave opening on the stage, the
hero, his enemy, and the heroine descending into it, followed by a
fatal struggle in the upper world. If we "stand back" from a realistic
novel such as Tolstoy's *Resurrection* or Zola's *Germinal,* we can see
the mythopoeic designs indicated by those titles. Other examples
will be given in what follows.[92]

If we do indeed stand back far enough from such revisionary
practices as those discovered in Frye's or Nietzsche's late texts,
then at the center of the critic's own readings there suddenly
appears his favorite archetype, that story of divine meta-
morphosis or desired incarnation as the redeemer of his own lost
and representative imaginative potential. "Pages of illustra-
tions," as Stevens puts it.

The finest statement of this visionary aim appears in Frye's
retelling of the Gnostic "Hymn of the Soul" in *The Secular Scripture:*

> Suddenly, in the middle of these dreary anxieties, there comes a
> great trumpet call from a very different imaginative world, the
> "Hymn of the Soul" in the Acts of Thomas. The Soul says that
> when he was a child in the palace of his father, his parents provided
> him with money and jewels and sent him down to Egypt, where he
> was to find a pearl in the sea guarded by a serpent, and come back to
> his original state again. He also has a brother who remained in the
> upper world. The Soul disguises himself and descends, but his
> disguise is penetrated and he is persuaded to eat the food of the
> lower world, like Proserpine before him. This causes him to forget
> both his origin and his mission, and fall into a deep sleep. His
> parents send a "letter" to him, the lowerworld oracle that we have
> met before; the Soul reads it, and as he reads his memory comes
> back. He puts the serpent to sleep, seizes the pearl, and starts back
> again. At the beginning of his quest he had been clothed in a gar-
> ment which is clearly the form of his original identity. He meets this
> garment again and realizes that it is, in fact, his real self. He sees it
> "as it had been in a mirror," and it is brought him by twins: "Two,
> yet one shape was upon both." Putting it on, he makes his way back
> to his own world. Like Apuleius' story, this is a story of the "Soul";
> in other words it is the story of ourselves. Crucial to it is the role of
> the letter or message, which not only awakens him but is what
> draws him upward to his self-recognition. It seems that one be-
> comes the ultimate hero of the great quest of man, not so much by
> virtue of what one does, as by virtue of what and how one reads.

> In traditional romance, including Dante, the upward journey is
> the journey of a creature returning to its creator. In most modern
> writers, from Blake on, it is the creative power in man that is
> returning to its original awareness. The secular scripture tells us
> that we are the creators; other scriptures tell us that we are actors in
> a drama of divine creation and redemption. Even Alice is troubled
> by the thought that her dram may not have been hers but the Red
> King's. Identity and self-recognition begin when we realize tht this
> is not an either-or question, when the grat twins of divine creation
> and human recreation have merged into one, and we can see that the
> same shape is upon both.[93]

Despite their superficial differences (Nietzsche's "nihilism,"
Frye's "idealism"), Frye, prophetic critic of the romantic Soul
and Nietzsche, tragic philosopher of *homo natura*, are, as Yeats
claims Daimon and Beloved are, antithetical masks of the same
sublime quest for identity. That is, they are clearly marked with
"the same shape upon both." "Where nature is not, man is all
manner," as a Joyce could have said.

Thus, Frye's antithetical quest for identity, much like Emerson's in *Nature*, transforms all that stands beyond his imagination
into a composite figure of opposition, Natura, against which he
can strive and through which he can give birth to his ideal muse
and so, in turn, to himself as the fulfillment of Oscar Wilde's
prophecy of the critic as artist:

> Poets do not write, like Swift's spider, "out of their own bowels, and
> in a restricted compass." The poet is taken over by a mythical and
> metaphorical organism, with its historical roots in the Bible, and
> the integrity of that organism is his Muse, the mother that brings to
> life a being separate both from herself and from him.[94]

The only problem, of course, is that, as disclosed by the metaphorical structure that composes his symbolic identity, Frye in
the process of self-transfiguration would not so much displace
and transform Nature as become her in a revised form—or, at
least, become "her privates he," as he, in fact, did by playing the
role of Mother, the ironic revisionary muse, to a generation of
similarly constituted literary theorists:

> As with other products of divine activity, the father of a poem is
> much more difficult to identify than the mother. That the mother is

always nature, the realm of the objective considered as a field of communication, no serious criticism can ever deny. But as long as the father of a poem is assumed to be the poet himself, we have once again failed to distinguish literature from discurssive verbal structures. The discursive writer writes as an act of conscious will, and that conscious will, along with the symbolic system he employs for it, is set over against the body of things he is describing. But the poet, who writes creatively rather than deliberately, is not the father of his poem; he is at best a midwife, or, more accurately still, the womb of Mother Nature herself: her privates he, so to speak. The fact that revision is possible, that a poet can make changes in a poem not because he likes them better but because they are better, shows clearly that the poet has to give birth to the poem as it passes through his mind. He is responsible for delivering it in as uninjured a state as possible, and if the poem is alive, it is equally anxious to be rid of him, and screams to be cut loose from all the navel-strings and feeding-tubes of his ego.[95]

The one conspicuous word we need alter here to discover Frye's underlying revisionary nature and motive should now be as clear as is the epithet for all such defensive critical operations of self-recovery enacted against nature: *Contra Naturam,* the critic indeed is.

CHAPTER SIX

PAUL DE MAN: NIETZSCHE'S TEACHER

Good teachers yearn to be obliterated.
Time

NIETZSCHE'S TEACHER, really, is Zarathustra, his own creation. This is the case in several senses of the word "teacher." Zarathustra is a new law-giver (as well as an old law-breaker, as suits the Messianic type). "Can you give yourself your own good and evil and hang your own will over yourself as a law,"[1] Zarathustra asks in "Of the Way of the Creator" from part 1 of his book. (Prophetic figures always seem to propose laws via rhetorical questions declaimed in an imperative tone, don't they?) In addition, Zarathustra as the hero of this work, which Nietzsche deemed his most instructive, cannot help but become instructive in turn to his readers, if only, at times, in a way not intended by his author. For we wonder, at times, why Nietzsche felt so positive that this text was his masterpiece. "'Are you visiting woman,'" a little old crone asks Zarathustra, and then answers her own question with a "wise" Nietzsche exclamation: "Do not forget your whip!"[2] It is clear, however, that Zarathustra is also a "teacher" in the common sense of the term. He announces the new trinity of doctrines: that the übermensch or over-man will be the meaning of the earth, that the eternal recurrence of all things will be seen as the underlying principle of the cosmos, and that the will to power, the ceaseless process of self-overcoming by all living things will inspire a new nobility of select thinkers and writers in the coming centuries to produce works of culture to rival those of the ancients. But, finally, Zarathustra is Nietzsche's teacher in a more poignant sense. For Nietzsche learns from the invention of this teacher figure, and what he learns appears to be how to live alone, how to bear his incredibly torturous solitude. Zarathustra, in short, allows Nietzsche to laugh at his own prophetic pretentions.[3]

One of the episodes from the "Prologue" to *Thus Spoke Zarathustra* can be read as Nietzsche's comic parable of the relationship between a teacher and his teachers, or, perhaps, it would be more accurate to say, the relationship between students who would be teachers. An experienced tightrope walker, while performing his act before a marketplace crowd in the village called "The Motley Cow," suddenly becomes intimidated by the spectacle of a buffoon who, coming up behind him on the high wire, leaps over him as an act of provocation. At the sight of his rival's triumph with the crowd, the older man loses his nerve, fails to meet the challenge, and plunges with his pole into the scattering mass of people; as "a vortex of legs and arms," he stands out, briefly, against a background like that of a sea "in a storm."[4] Only Zarathustra bothers to offer the dying man some words of consolation. He says, ironically enough, that the older man's exemplary life of courage now dies along with his body, and, as well, his soul with his body. The dying man appears to smile at this. Zarathustra takes up his corpse, carries it for three days and nights, and buries it upright in a hollow tree, safe from prowling wolves. Zarathustra realizes in a moment of sudden insight that the smile of his now dead companion has taught him a significant lesson. Most men, on hearing his doctrine of the superman, must perceive Zarathustra as a weird cross between an overleaping buffoon and a burdensome corpse, an all-too-literal embodiment of the Spirit of Gravity, his enemy. Zarathustra concludes, therefore, that he needs living companions who could be educated as he has just been educated.

What Zarathustra realizes here is that most men have been taught to think metaphorically in a habitual fashion, to invent in a reflexlike manner a single entity, no matter how hilariously or banally monstrous, out of the strongest and most diverse of chance juxtapositions. Most men need, therefore, to unlearn this manner of thinking, to break this dubious mode of self-deluding essentialist thought by practicing a form of Romantic irony like Zarathustra's own, in which such chance juxtapositions between a buffoon, a corpse, and a would-be prophet do not automatically suggest an absurd, fateful hybrid but merely suggest more possible masks for the will to overcome oneself to adopt—however self-overcoming may be conceived. Such mask-play composes the discipline of irony for Nietzsche's Zarathustra and his studious reader. With this Nietzschean "wisdom" in mind, let us turn to Paul de Man.

Of the several recent critiques of his work offered by liberal humanists, sociologically minded, anti-humanistic historians of the critical institution, deconstructive scholars of the abyss of intertextuality, et al., the late Paul de Man chose to respond only to one of them, Stanley Corngold's comprehensive critique "Error in Paul de Man."[5] There appear to be reasons for this unexpected event that go beyond the incisiveness of Corngold's critical argument. First of all, Corngold is a former student of de Man. The old teacher must attempt to put his rebellious boy back in his place if possible. Second, the essay appears in *Critical Inquiry*, a leading journal of literary theory. It is included as well in a new volume on the Yale critics, the first, no doubt, of many. Finally, Corngold's critique mimics de Man's own style. This is no small feat, since de Man's style, at its best, is an imposing amalgam of philological nicety and philosophical sophistication delivered in an ex cathedra manner reflexively structured to highlight the irony of its own considerable tendencies to reductive overstatement, exorbitant overreading, and theoretical overkill. There are, then, personal, institutional, and rhetorical reasons aplenty to help explain de Man's decision to answer, of all his recent critics, Stanley Corngold.[6]

On top of these "contextual" explanations, there is naturally Corngold's argument with de Man itself. And it is a telling one.

For it concerns the epistemology of reading articulated by de Man in major performances over the years. Corngold is, in fact, the only one of de Man's critics to trace convincingly the underlying continuity, virtually an ascetic or neo-Pascalian one, between the Sartrean and Derridean phases in de Man's work.[7] In de Man, for Corngold, there is a consistent strain of skepticism about our ability to know, with philosophical certainty, anything beyond the categories (whether rational, linguistic, or rhetorical) that we ourselves have made—if we can know anything definite about these. This essentially radical, post-Kantian position is, Corngold finds, given an intonation of sublime pathos in essay after essay, from such a famous early piece as "Intentional Structure of the Romantic Image" (1960) to a baroquely virtuoso performance, "Shelley Disfigured" (1979). This identifiable if paradoxical tone reminds one of Heidegger or Schopenhauer or, perhaps, Rousseau in one of his frequent, romantically self-lacerating imitations of Augustine.

Specifically, Corngold argues that de Man, so good at distinguishing in the work of others between *error* and *mistake,* cannot distinguish between the categories when it comes to practicing his hermeneutic art, and especially in Nietzsche's case. For Corngold, error is a blind misreading, due to purely methodological considerations, of another writer's work that nonetheless produces impersonal insights into the particular problem under discussion; and mistake is a sophistical distortion, for pragmatic advantage, barren of any further interpretive value, except in the subjective context of the scholar's own psychology or career opportunities.

One result of this failing, according to Corngold, is that when in one of the chapters on Nietzsche in *Allegories of Reading* ("Genesis and Genealogy") de Man reads some ancillary notes to *The Birth of Tragedy,* he mistakenly reads them as a prefiguration of Nietzsche's later ironic deconstruction of consciousness, a deconstruction that de Man insists also undermines all notions of the self—including Nietzsche's own highly touted biological conception of the self as an embodied will to power. All notions, that is, go, except a strategically textual notion. In this fashion, de Man can suggest that Nietzsche prefigures not only his later position but de Man's as well. Corngold knows that what de Man commits in this instance is really a self-serving mistake and not an inspiring error because he catches de Man in an obvious mistranslation.

While the philological details of the ensuing debate between de Man and Corngold over the proper translation of these notes are not entirely devoid of critical interest, only the conclusion seems sufficiently relevant to my argument to warrant extended discussion.[8] From the evidence Corngold presents, it seems clear that out of either a combination of hastiness and euphuistic enthusiasm (de Man's own excuse) or arrogant scorn for Nietzsche's intended biological perspectivism and disdain for his reader's expertise (Corngold's accusation), de Man does indeed mistranslate Nietzsche, in a way which brings him more in line with the purpose of the deconstructive argument. As Corngold in his response to de Man's "letter" dryly concludes apropos these possible explanations, neither one is very "auspicious."[9]

Ironically enough, then, Corngold, de Man's onetime student, corrects his teacher, that arch-deconstructor, on matters of philological accuracy that bear on the question of de Man's philosophical rigor and theoretical integrity. After all, de Man's lifelong critical project has been to articulate for literary study a post-Kantian epistemology of reading, a rhetorical theory of interpretation that would not be reducible to aesthetic, psychological, ethical, or historical models of human understanding, since, for de Man, all such post-Romantic models are dependent for their institutional authority upon specious analogies between cultural products and natural processes or objects. Such a theory, if successfully elaborated, could truly be called a rhetoric of understanding, and, in de Man's eyes, it would be radically subversive of all ideological stabilities, since it would expose the fundamental uncertainty at the heart of all our systems of representation. Such exposure would constitute an act of "betrayal," as it were, which would interrupt the habitual translation from rhetorical to aesthetic, historical, and other categories, that lies at the basis of Western man's making of history, with all its attendant disastrous effects. "It could, in principle," de Man claims in his preface to *Allegories of Reading*, "lead to a rhetoric of reading reaching toward the canonical principles of literary history."[10] Yet if de Man can only develop such a rhetoric of understanding (or "reading") by interpreting the rhetoric of other writers in a habitually Procrustean manner, then one has to ask some hard questions about the ultimate worth and usefulness of de Man's theory.

De Man's response to Corngold, while not one of his best performances, is nonetheless significant for what it discloses about his principles of critical reading. First of all, de Man assimilates Corngold's distinction between error and mistake to the philosophical opposition, respectively, of necessity and possibility. For Corngold, de Man claims, error is an instance of necessity and mistake an instance of possibility. To read creatively one must commit an error; but when one makes a mistake one need not have done so, and one may or may not inspire others by such mistakes. De Man then can claim that it is the purpose of deconstruction to demonstrate how such classical binary oppositions as this one between necessity and possibility (or contingency) that he has just adduced for Corngold's argument about error and mistake gets generated from the play of differences among the signs in a text by acts of metaphorical identification and simplification. These acts of identification of metaphorical thinking have as their end the coercive privileging of one side in the invented opposition over the other. By privileging error over mistake, self over the play of the signifier, Corngold, in de Man's eyes, is merely a polemical ideologue of the natural self, of the "will" taken more in a Schopenhauerian than Nietzschean sense. That is, de Man reads Corngold's privileging of the category of the self as Corngold's confession of belief in a unitary, extra-linguistic entity, a willing, desiring, individual being. Nietzsche, Corngold does indeed claim, "spoke . . . not on behalf of a pan-ironic, pan-textual conception of consciousness but on behalf of a deep self for whom irony was only a mask."[11]

Secondly, de Man argues that the mistake in his translation of the passage from Nietzsche which Corngold seizes on does not at all affect the conclusions he draws from it, since the passage is only one of several quoted, others could have been cited, and, besides, the next two chapters on Nietzsche in *Allegories of Reading* ("Rhetoric of Tropes" and "Rhetoric of Persuasion") argue even more persuasively, using less compromised, more literally translated passages, for de Man's deconstruction, following Nietzsche's lead, of the self. In short, then, de Man implicitly claims that he did not have to be that accurate or careful anyway.

Both forms of defense—revisionary philosophical one-upmanship and rhetorical pooh-poohing—appear (to serious readers of de Man) as logically ineffective as they are strongly familiar. One set of his remarks, however, does bear analysis and meditation:

> I take it that for Corngold the distinction between mistake and error is clear and that he can distinguish between them without fail. This accounts for his trenchant tone of accusation: only someone very certain to tell one from the other can denounce mistakes with such conviction. The tonality gets transposed to my own diction: I am said to *force* crises, to *devastate* horizons and perceptions, to *demolish* metaphors, and to *hate* genealogies, but all this sound and fury never allows me to move one jot beyond the benign and self-tolerating universe somewhat surprisingly attributed to Kant. I sound, in short, like a bully who also wants to play it safe. The pattern of defense is familiar coming from those who feel threatened by readings that lay claim neither to hostility, nor to tolerance, nor indeed to any easily presonifiable mode of relationship. With regard to concepts or to the fellow-critics I write about, I have never felt anything approaching hostility nor, for that matter, benignity; very different sets of terms would have to be used to designate a rapport that is a great deal less agonistic than that of forensic, familial, or erotic combat.[12]

De Man thus accuses Corngold of transposing to his diction the tonality of conviction actually emanating from the despairing commentator's own critical text. Kierkegaard has perfected this strategy of defense in *Stages on Life's Way*, a strategy that could be called the "you're another" defense when he says apropos of the crudest examples of the "higher" biblical criticism, that one cannot expect to see an apostle looking out of the mirror of Scripture when what is looking into that mirror in the first place is only an

ape. This defense suggests that de Man's understanding of his
own texts is an ironically reflective one. (Whether or not, he also
assumes that, like Scripture, they are "sacred" or "inspired" is
another question.) In addition, de Man's characterization of the
mode or style of his relationships with inherited concepts and
influential predecessors of "fellow-writers" is one that apparently
transcends the "agonistic" model of "forensic, familial, or erotic
combat" in a form of "rapport" that, precisely because of its
reflective and indeterminate nature, can be termed, somewhat
ironically, "spectral." It is spiritually illuminating or seductively
illusory—or perhaps, necessarily both at once: that is, "ghostly."

What interests me about this defense is de Man's simultaneous
evocation and evasion of a "personifiable" mode of relationship
with the subjects of his writing. For, by describing this relationship as a "rapport," beyond agonistic revisionism of any conventional kind, de Man indulges in, as he objects to, a psycho-
aesthetic or erotically repressed characterization of the writer's
relationship to his own rhetorical figures, textual strategies, and
intertextual relations. It is, therefore, not just a question here of
the teacher accusing the student of projecting Corngold motivation onto de Man texts. Rather, it is a question of the common
procedure of what I call critical romance, that self-betraying and
revisionary alignment of certain kinds of impersonal textual
strategies with certain forms of projected "intentions," whether
of a conscious or unconscious nature. As Harold Bloom has
shown, critical romance, or aesthetic revisionism, depends upon
analogies between textual structures and psychological constructs that are themselves based, ultimately, upon coercive analogies between the mind and nature. But the reading of one
writer's relations with another in terms of the Freudian model of
family romance, with the later writer playing the anxious son to
the earlier writer's castration-threatening papa, is, for de Man, a
method of interpretation of highly questionable epistemological
rigor. It is the kind of reading that de Man has always put into
question.[13]

For such "agonistic" forms of interpretation are based, finally,
either on a blind faith in or a cynically willful assertion of, meta-

phorical identities between textual, psychic, and natural processes. Yet, in the very manner of its articulation in the above passage, de Man's objection to such a procedure of critical reading implicitly acknowledges the practical impossibility of successfully avoiding the self-expressive characterization of rhetorical procedures that his objection is precisely meant to subvert. By thus openly enacting the critical reader's inescapable dilemma, by ironically embracing the "natural" fallacy he would condemn and evade, de Man hollows out his own rhetorical stance, transforming a common act of critical misrepresentation and self-expression into a reflective, antithetical mask or rhetorical persona. Thus, de Man becomes the stoical theorist and witty practitioner of the lie.[14] Such a transparent mask's ironically impersonal and artificial outlines suggest the underlying image of a face as uncannily familiar as its features are undecidably fixed.

My interest in this debate between de Man and Corngold, therefore, goes beyond the question of which one may be more correct or persuasive than the other with regard to the translations of Nietzsche's text. I am interested more in de Man's formulation of the relationship between one writer and another, and how this particular formulation is apparently provoked, ironically enough, by Corngold's stinging critique. I say "ironically enough" because the discourse of critical romance would automatically cast Corngold in the role of nervously defensive, hostile, errant son; and yet de Man's own deconstructive theory of the rhetoric of understanding requires that he resist the temptation to such easy psychologism. De Man's solution to this dilemma is to posit a more original form of relationship, between writers or ideas, a spectral "rapport." This kind of relationship would transcend even as it must enact the dilemma de Man faces in attempting to articulate a rhetoric of understanding via psycho-aesthetic language, however ironically subverted that language may be said to be.

In this complex fashion, the notion of a spectral "rapport," arising as it does out of this extremely agonistic form of critical encounter, is a key for understanding de Man's influential de-

constructive theory of interpretation as an ironic allegory of
irony, even if this idealistic notion of "rapport" also appears here
as a defensively motivated form of imaginative compensation and
a harsh act of exclusionary discipline keeping the unworthy out.
Two of de Man's most revealing and powerful essays, "The Literary Self As Origin: The Work of Georges Poulet" (1969) and
"Shelley Disfigured" (1979) read in the light of this rhetorical
conception of spectral rapport disclose the paradoxical coherence
of de Man's theoretical practice, a practice that nesessarily if
"erroneously" traces the pattern of critical romance even as it
negates its "mistaken" epistemological authority.

As a highly ironic defense of literature, delivered by an aus-
terely impersonal, yet still prophetic-sounding author whose
message is that criticism is as self-reflexively "fictional" as literature itself, the Poulet essay typifies de Man's work of the 1960s.
De Man answers the largely European critiques of the privileged
nature of "literature" as "an autonomous activity of the mind, a
distinctive way of being in the world to be understood in terms of
its own purposes and intentions,"[15] by accepting the critical insight of structuralism, deconstruction, and all the rest, into the
linguistic and ideological basis of this essentially bourgeois notion of the "literary." He then tries to demonstrate that the
source of such an insight is, ironically enough, the "rhetorical,"
that is to say, the inescapably "fictional" or "literary" play of
tropes in the texts of these other disciplines. As in the case of
Northrop Frye's literary conception of archetypes, so de Man's
literary conception of rhetorical figures can only be systemat-
ically put into question at the risk of undermining the epistemological claims and logical coherence of the disciplines that
would interrogate literature and literary study. If all the judges
are guilty of the same crime, how can literature be held responsible?

Another way of saying this is to say that literature as the reflexive interplay of rhetorical tropes, as "fiction," is not confined to
one field or discipline. Rather, it is everywhere, principally in the
form of the founding and unifying ideas of particular objects of

study, methods of procedure, and models of analysis and experimentation, in the human and natural sciences. For such ideas are, to de Man, essentially metaphorical in nature, convenient and effective "fictions," inventive generalizations drawn, speciously, from a welter of conflicting and confusing data.[16] De Man expresses this nominalistic attitude most succinctly in the following remarks on Nietzsche's "rhetoric of tropes" in "On Truth and Lie in an Extra-Moral Sense". "The critical deconstruction that leads to the discovery of the literary, rhetorical nature of the philosophical claim to truth is genuine enough and cannot be refuted: literature turns out to be the main topic of philosophy and the model for the kind of truth to which it aspires."[17] Similar arguments could be made for the disciplines of linguistics, structuralist anthropology, psychoanalysis, semiology, deconstruction, and so on. So if "literature" haunts the productions of these disciplines, why not, as well, the "work" of the literary critic and scholar of consciousness, Georges Poulet?

More specifically, the essay, first included in a festschrift for Poulet in 1969, seems designed as an answer to Jacques Derrida's "Structure, Sign, and Play in The Discourse of the Human Sciences." The implication of Derrida's piece—that the notion of a centered structure in the humanities, especially the notion of the self as center, is the disguised expression of a nostalgic desire for the deity—effectively neutralized Poulet's presence at the now famous Johns Hopkins conferences on the structuralist controversy in 1966 and 1967. Like all of his defenses of literature at this time, de Man not only admits the validity of such critiques as Derrida's, he rushes to push them even further, making them more comprehensive, rigorous, and reductive than they otherwise are. For de Man, the self in this essay, as in the rest of *Blindness and Insight*, cannot be said to appear unambiguously in the literary text as the visionary presence of a prophetic voice, without the critic betraying his bad faith, a willed blindness that produces no insightful error, only an embarrassing mistake. Nonetheless, by a sudden and subtle rhetorical move, de Man snatches victory for literature and literary study from the self-

defeating jaws of the abyss by strategically expanding the definition of the literary to include any text whose language stages its
own discursive and rhetorical strategies as an ironic allegory of
the reading of such rhetorical and discursive reflexiveness. That
is, de Man takes as his model of the literary text not so much the
great impersonal classics of the Western tradition as the various
"works" of his favorite critics as he "essays" their rhetoric in
Blindness and Insight, and especially, as he tries out and puts on
trial the phenomenological rhetoric of Poulet.

To insure his authority for making this move, de Man not only
admits the worst that can be said against the privileged notion of
a "purely" literary consciousness, he also adopts the familiar
stance of the informed expert on all matters continental and comparative since Rousseau. This stance of authority also allows de
Man to presume to speak, as he does at the essay's opening, from
the perspective of future historians of our own critical moment.

> A few years hence, the discussions that give to the literary studies of
> today such a controversial and didactic tone, will have faded before
> the intrinsic value of works that, in spite of being works of criti-
> cism, are nevertheless literary achievements in the fullest sense of
> the term. The case of poets or novelists that would occasionally
> write criticism is far from unusual; in modern French literature
> alone one can think of a long line that goes from Baudelaire to Butor
> and that includes Mallarmé, Valéry, and Blanchot. The nature of
> this double activity has often been wrongly understood. One as-
> sumes that these writers, out of dilletantism or out of necessity,
> have from time to time deserted the more important part of their
> work to express their opinion on the writings of their predecessors
> or contemporaries—a little in the manner of retired champions eval-
> uating the performance of younger athletes. But the reasons that
> prompted these writers to take up criticism have only a limited
> interest. What matters a great deal is that Baudelaire's *Essay on
> Laughter,* Mallarmé's *La Musique et les lettres,* or Blanchot's *Le Chant
> des Sireness* are more than equal in verbal and thematic complexity
> to a prose poem of the *Spleen de Paris,* a page of *Un Coup de Des* or a
> chapter of *Thomas l'obscur.* We are not suggesting that the poetic or
> novelistic parts of these works exist on the same level as the critical
> prose, and that both are simply interchangeable without making
> essential distinctions. The line that separates them marks out two
> worlds that are by no means identical or even complementary. The
> precise itinerary of such a line, however, would in most cases reveal

> a more subterranean path than one might originally have suspected
> and would indicate that the critical and the poetic components are
> so closely intertwined that it is impossible to touch the one without
> coming into contact with the other. It can be said of these works that
> they carry a constitutive critical element within themselves, exactly
> as Friedrich Schlegel, at the onset of the nineteenth century, char-
> acterized all "modern" literature by the ineluctable presence of a
> critical dimension. If this is true, then the opposite is just as likely,
> and critics can be granted the full authority of literary authorship.
> Some contemporary critics can already lay claim to such a distinc-
> tion.[18]

As future historian or critical prophet de Man can put the controversies and debates of the day in a longer perspective, usually an
ironic perspective, making relationships and creating paradoxical
reversals at will, controlling and elaborating, or cutting off,
where he wants to, all the while sounding impersonal, convinc-
ing, and unassailable: the visitor, not from another planet, but
from another era, observing with tolerant bemusement the various squabbles of our time, most of which will rightly go unsung.

It is within this defensive context that de Man develops and
refines his theory of the blindness and insight structure of critical
interpretations. The necessity for theoretical consistency and
methodological comprehensiveness forces upon critic after critic
a blindness to the very insights his systematic theory and methodological schemes make possible, a blindness that is necessary
since these insights subvert the very system or method that produces them.

> In all of them a paradoxical discrepancy appears between the gen-
> eral statements they make about the nature of literature (statements
> on which they base their critical methods) and the actual results of
> their interpretations. Their findings about the structure of texts
> contradict the general conception that they use as their mode.[19]

What this means in Poulet's case is that his avowed position as a
self-effacing critic of the creative writer's inaugural act of literary
consciousness (or *cogito*) produces, for de Man, in a sudden turnabout of great ingenuity, profound insights into the nature of
literary language and its constitutions of the literary self. These
insights thus testify to Poulet's genius as a practical reader of

texts, as his now neglected work dutifully fulfills the loud promises of some structuralist and deconstructive critics.

This is an extremely intricate strategy of defense, and deserves
further discussion. At the risk of violating de Man's avowedly
anti-revisionist "spectral rapport," I shall characterize this strategy in familial terms for purpose of clarification. Imagine a man,
husband and father, whose interchanges with his wife produce
the precisely opposite insights from those he would have pre-
dicted (or hoped for) and whose child always claims them as his
or her own, in a self-deluding act of overcoming or superseding
the father's authority and influence. De Man's criticism of the
critics he writes on highlights this "abysmal" pattern in their
texts, as if he were holding up a mirror to himself and his readers
precisely at the moment we are all going to repeat this ironic
pattern with respect to these critics or to him. Like Nietzsche in
the prologue to Zarathustra, de Man invents a parable or, to use
his word, an allegory, of such irony and expects us all to be
chastened or disciplined by it.

In this fashion de Man's essay on Poulet, like his other essays
in *Blindness and Insight,* also demonstrates "the self-reflecting
mirror effect" of the work of literature, its repeated fictionalization of the unsurpassable void at the heart of human understanding that can only be "figured" in terms recognized to be at once
inescapable and inadequate, i.e., "fictional." The Poulet essay,
like these other essays, describes an ironic circular structure that
in the course of its round repeatedly reflects critically on its own
unfathomable, "original" impulse and projects, perhaps blindly,
admittedly fictional images of that impulse in the essay. The
essay thus characteristically becomes an ironic allegory of its own
self-defeating strategies of reading and of the vagrantly "intentional" structure of its own highly suspect "romantic" images.

For example, Poulet, de Man's old colleague, onetime mentor,
and close friend, respresents what de Man would most wish to
be, a monumental critic of the history of literary consciousness, a
critical Rousseau who writes the confessions of the literary self,
and who, "in the course of a single article" can renew "entirely

the interpretation of a given author." He can do this because he sacrifices none of his own inventive power, since he views the work from the position of the author and not that of the mere reader, reaching as he does so into that "nearly inaccessible zone" where the very "possibility" of the literary work's necessary existence "is being decided."[20]

Poulet, as de Man represents him, possesses the unique imaginative power of "spectral rapport" with the subjects of his writings, of reaching into that nearly inaccessible zone where the literary work's very existence is being decided. De Man's representation of Poulet betrays de Man's own strategic assumption of or wish for just such a rapport with the power, found in Poulet's act of reading. It is as if Poulet, as de Man would have him, plays midwife to the original inspiration, and repeats or reenacts the birth of the particular work in his own texts. Yet, as we shall see, de Man's conception of Poulet, while relying upon the outlines of such genetic or "natural" metaphors for its articulation, persistently hollows them out with its ironic theoretical reflexiveness, thereby putting into question any literal belief in the "truth" of such figures. De Man's theory of the blindness and insight structure of interpretive understanding is an ingenious, at times almost compelling, defense of literature every bit as prophetic in its ironically touched pretenstion and wishes as Shelley's more famous defense is in its openly sublime stance.

De Man primarily focuses on passages from an early essay by Poulet, "A Propos du Bergonisme" (1924) and a late study "La pensée critique de Charles du Bos" (1965). In addition, he discusses several selections from the multivolume *Études sur le temps humain,* the 1968 book on Benjamin Constant, and *La Poule aux oeufs d'or,* Poulet's novel published originally in 1927 under the pseudonym Georges Thisbet. De Man's theme is the shift in Poulet's thinking from his *le point du departure* to *le instant de passage,* that is, from the literary cogito as the origin and center of the writer's career, to those dispersive moments of transition and reversal in a text or in the career which undermine or reanimate the literary self. Such a shift signals in Poulet a change from an obsession with conscious intentions as the origin of the text to a concern with how the text projects and revises the self. De Man's point in all this is to suggest that Poulet in his actual practice of reading (as opposed to his more official "position" papers) is extremely sensitive to the fragility of the literary self as it originates and repeatedly begins anew in confrontation with its own essentially linguistic and rhetorical status as a sign.

As de Man describes at some length in "The Rhetoric of Temporality" the self originates as an already divided structure in its encounter with language. The power of language to constitute the self as an empirical and an ontological entity is often represented in literature as a "fall" that at least produces occasional insight (if no eternal wisdom). Baudelaire's poetry, as his essay on the comic suggests, is representative in this respect, since, for de Man it tells the story of the impossibility of the self as sign coinciding with another anterior sign felt to be its unknown, unknowable and yet somehow authorizing source, which is itself implicated intertextually in a labyrinth of such signs.

> The meaning constituted by the allegorical sign can then consist only in the *repetition* (in the Kierkegaardian sense of the term) of a previous sign with which it can never coincide, since it is of the essence of this previous sign to be pure anteriority.[21]

This understanding of the self, of irony, and of allegory reminds one, as de Man notes, of the plight of Eros and Psyche. It is as if this were the literary writer's chronic plight, as well. Desiring and yet ever incapable of a rapport with the power that articulates his text, the writer repeatedly conjures up one after another "spectral" mask, asking of each, I suggest, the question Wallace Stevens asks of the solitary singing woman walking by the sea in "The Idea of Order at Key West": "Whose spirit is this?"

Better than anyone else's, for de Man, Poulet's work reveals this post-romantic ironic predicament:

> The originality of his approach stems from the fact that he does not content himself with merely receiving works as if they were gifts, but that he participates, much more than he claims to do, in the problematic possibility of their elaboration. . . . Poulet identifies himself with the project of its constitution; this is to say, his point of

view is not so much that of the critic—as he himself defines it—as that of the writer. Consequently, the entire problem of anteriority and origin is not met as in the substitutive scheme which calls upon another to intervene, but is experienced from the inside, as seen by a subject that has delegated none of its inventive power to anyone else. Poulet often succeeds, in the course of a single article, in renewing entirely the interpretation of a given author. He can do so because he reaches as by instinct into the nearly inaccessible zone where the possibility of a work's existence is being decided. His criticism allows us to take part in a process that, far from being the inexorable development of an impulse that none could resist, appears as extremely vulnerable, likely to go astray at any moment, always threatened with error and aberration, risking paralysis or self-destruction, and forever obliged to start again on the road that it had hoped to have covered. It succeeds best of all when it deals with writers who have felt this fragility most acutely. Poulet can reach the quality of genuine subjectivity because, in his criticism, he is willing to undermine the stability of the subject and because he refuses to borrow stability for the subject from outside sources.[22]

In a brilliant maneuver, de Man transfers this insight into the constitution of the literary work from his own reading of Poulet to Poulet's readings.

He credits Poulet with this sensitivity to the literary self's problematic relationship to its own language, a relationship that Poulet puts in the more subjective, less rhetorical terms of one writer's encounter with another writer's sublimity, in the self-effacing act of reading, an act in which the reader assumes a new self identical with an earlier, superior self somehow lost long ago and only now recovered.

But how are we to understand a movement which allows for a superior or "deeper" self to take the place of an actual self, in accordance with a scheme of which the encounter between author and critic was only the symbolical prefiguration? One can say, with Poulet, that between these two selves, "relationships are born, revelations carried over and a marvelous receptivity from mind to mind made to prevail." Nevertheless, this relationship exists first of all in the form of a radical questioning of the actual, given self, extending to the point of annihilation. And the medium within which and by means of which this questioning can take place can only be language, although Poulet hardly ever designates it explicitly by that name. What was here being described as a relationship between two subjects designates in fact the relationship between a subject and the literary language it produces.[23]

For de Man, then, Poulet discloses how the only self and world the literary writer possesses is the self as sign and the world as language. As in Proust, de Man argues, this problematic relationship defines the vocation of writing, a vocation that of all modern critics Poulet participates in most fully.

> A conception of literature as a language of authenticity, similar to what is found, for example, in some of Heidegger's texts after *Sein und Zeit* is not Poulet's. He remains far removed from any form of prophetic poeticism. The quest for the source, which we have found constantly operative in his thought, can never be separated from the concern for the self that is the carrier of this quest. Yet this self does not possess the power to engender its own duration. This power belongs to what Poulet calls "the moment," but "the moment" designates, in fact, the point in time at which the self accepts language as its sole mode of existence. Language, however, is not a source; it is the articulation of the self and language that acquires a degree of prospective power. Self and language are the two focal points around which the trajectory of the work originates, but neither can by itself find access to the status of source. Each is the anteriority of the other. If one confers upon language the power to originate, one runs the risk of hiding the self. This Poulet fears most of all, as when he asserts: "I want at all costs to save the subjectivity of literature." But if the subject is, in its turn, given the status of origin, one makes it coincide with Being in a self-consuming identity in which language is destroyed. Poulet rejects this alternative just as categorically as he rejects the other, although much less explicitly. The concern for language can be felt in the tone of anguish that inhabits the whole of his work and expresses a constant solicitude for literary survival. The subject that speaks in the criticism of Georges Poulet is a vulnerable and fragile subject whose voice can never become established as a presence. This is the very voice of literature, here incarnated in one of the major works of our time.[24]

In a homage sublimely expressive of his own desire, de Man speaks of the "Poulet" he would like to resemble, in an apparent instance of "spectral rapport" or critical romance astonishing to see in the text of the most ascetic of our contemporary masters of suspicion.

Rarely does Paul de Man forget himself so obviously, and overcome his reserve, if only for a moment and if only in a still highly ironic context. De Man thus allows himself to identify with this projected figure of an author he is writing on, to the point where he attributes to his "Poulet" his highest wish for himself: to be seen as a literary writer whose voice speaks as it were the very voice of literature itself. Usually, as in "Lyric and Modernity," de Man characterizes the relationship between one writer and another in more problematic terms, as being like that between Baudelaire and Mallarmé or like that between "soul" and "self" in Yeats' occult speculations, in which all the many surface echoes of the Other in Mallarmé's work, like all the many surface resemblances of the antithetical self or soul to the empirical ego's sublime projections, disguise the fact that no genetic, genealogical, or, more specifically, familial model of relationship can ever represent effectively, with philosophical certainty, "this dark zone" of Baudelaire "into which Mallarmé could never penetrate," or that "proper dark" into which the Yeatsian speaker in "The Statues" tragically peers to trace the lineaments of an impossibly idealized face.[25] Such peering, as if into an abyss of darkness, as Nietzsche comments in a famous passage in *The Birth of Tragedy,* produces bright spots of illumination as compensation, Apollonian masks of the Dionysian will, just as the attempt to peer at the sun produces as a protective healing device, dark spots before one's eyes, even when shut. Yet in his essay on Poulet, de Man seems to forget or repress this "tragic knowledge" for a moment, and identifies himself with this dark void of insightful blindness and calls it "Poulet."

To be spurred into evasive song appears to require that the writer project his originary darkness, in order then to name it repeatedly with one after another possible mask, whether it be "Poulet" or "Rousseau" or "Shelley."

> Poetic language names this void with ever-renewed understanding and . . . it never tires of naming it again. This persistent naming is what we call literature.[26]

At best, then, one writer can produce an ironic allegory of such impossible intertextual relations with another writer. As the representational dimension of a writer's language is exhausted by ironic subversion, this inaccessible, impenetrable zone of dark-

ness where the work's very existence is being decided is (re)pro-
duced in the reader in the form of an interrupted or suspended
dialectic, one of the aporias of understanding. The ironic interplay between blindness and insight, error and more error, that de
Man traces in the work of Husserl, Lukács, Blanchot, and the
rest produces just such an effect on even the most resistant of
readers.

All this sounds remarkably like a displaced form of religiosity
and mysticism, sort of like Meister Eckhart, with de Man's deity
being the void, the abyss, or the inaccessible zone of darkness.
The inability of language ever to represent, except ironically by
negation, this self-created rhetorical principle, also sounds familiar. In this connection at least, I think Harold Bloom in *Kabbalah
and Criticism,* following Hans Jonas' speculations on the relations
between existentialism and Gnosticism in *The Gnostic Religion,* is
right on the mark. According to one version of the Gnostic gospel, the female principle or Gnostic Sophia, in a solitary effort to
"know" the father, the unknowable Alien God himself, conceives
a thought of her own and brings forth an abortion that starts the
catastrophe of creation—our temporal cosmos—from which we
must be saved by Gnostic enlightenment, which ironically consists in recognizing the impossibility of all such intimate knowing. Similarly, for de Man, the attempt to know the other writer,
to have a "spectral rapport," produces a blindness or error that is
also creative and insightful, even if what is created is seen as an
elaboration of error and all that we can know is this insight into
the impossibility of knowing unambiguously the "truth" about
such principles. Whether the Gnostic analogy proves useful or
not, the irony of knowing that certain knowledge is impossible
does pervade de Man's work.

Consider, for example, the conclusion to the Poulet essay once
again. There are several self-betraying ironies here, all of which
make knowledge and judgment virtually impossible. First of all,
the later Heidegger's alleged prophetic "poeticism" strikes one as
the antithetical image of de Man's own, more modest prophetic
stance enacted at the essay's opening. Is it that de Man is accus-

ing Heidegger here of a crime he himself has already committed, in a different context and idiom, admittedly, but, nonetheless, in ironic imitation of his philosophical master? Is de Man's figure of Poulet's work as "the very voice of literature" any less prophetically poetic than Heidegger's celebration of poetry as the presencing of Being? Similarly, is de Man's abrupt "discovery" of Poulet as a critic of language rather than a critic of the conscious self not a mask of his own wish to become, in that future projected at the beginning of the essay, just such a critic as he describes Poulet as already having been all these many years? Doesn't the argument of the essay repeatedly enact this ever narrowing dialectical spiral which has de Man as its focal point, just as the opening paragraph anticipates nicely just such a form of argument? Isn't it, finally, de Man's own love of anguish that we hear animating Poulet's "constant solicitude for literary survival," a solicitude and anguish that inspires de Man's opening stance as the prophetic source of a definitive if projected historical center from which one can pass a last judgment on our own era as it fails even to appreciate, not to say, live up to, the example of Poulet in his creative criticism? In short, isn't it de Man in the writing of this essay on Poulet who produces the literary self as origin of the work he revises and reads as that of Poulet? Just as in the case of Baudelaire and Mallarmé, the figures of Poulet and de Man as alien god and his prophetic disciple, respectively, allegorizes that impenetrable zone of darkness out of which spring the fictional reflections of de Man's own work of "spectral rapport."

De Man's interpretive practice demonstrates that the situation of the critical reader can be compared to that of the idiot, increasingly hysterical, questioner in Blake's "Tyger." The fabulous, unfathomable darkness that the speaker projects as the Other (or nature in this poem) is progressively discovered to possess a kind of fierce order, as symbolized by the fearful symmetry of the tyger, a central figure or mask of the speaker's own repressed creative will which suggests a Cosmic Author and Plutonic Blacksmith behind all of the sublime creation, and which authorizes the tyger's existence. De Man's criticism does not so much blindly enact this pattern of response as ironically betray it at work informing the critical insights of others. In this sense, his position can be compared to that of the implied author of Blake's poem, and not to that of the speaker. Yet when in response to the Derridean challenge he privileges Rousseau and Nietzsche in his essays on their self-deconstructed nature, de Man comes close to monumentalizing them as blindly as Blake's speaker monumentalizes the tyger. As we shall see, this question of the inescapably monumental dimension of critical romance informs the conception of spectral rapport in "Shelley Disfigured."

Giving a local habitation and a sublime name to the void of willful forgetfulness, that dark impenetrable zone of repression, characterizes the modern writer's quest for his own difference from the past. This quest, as de Man points out in his meditation on Nietzsche's "Use and Abuse of History" in "Literary Modernity and Literary History" destroys itself as soon as it is seen to be such and so demonstrates its own impossibility of completion. "When they assert their own modernity, they are bound to discover their dependence on similar assertions made by their literary predecessors; their claim to being a new beginning turns out to be the repetition of a claim that has always already been made."[27] Thus, the act of writing or revisionary reading is founded and founders upon the absurd nature of human understanding as disclosed in the study of literature.

The literary imagination, the "source," if you will, of this absurdity, is for de Man a self-constitutive and self-deconstructing rhetorical figure or master trope:

> this "imagination" has little in common with the faculty that produces natural images born "as flowers originate." It marks instead a possibility for consciousness to exist entirely by and for itself, independently of all relationship with the outside world, without being moved by an intent aimed at a part of this world. . . . We are only beginning to understand how this oscillation in the status of the image is linked to the crisis that leaves the poetry of today under a steady threat of extinction, although, on the other hand, it remains the depository of hopes that no other activity of the mind seems able to offer.[28]

De Man indicates that the aim of writing is to produce and that of reading to reproduce this post-enlightenment, symbolic imagination and its anti-natural, alien images, images that transcend by ironic subversion all natural categories and all discourses based upon specious anologies with such categories. It follows, then, that the revisionary interpreter's quest becomes a quest for a greater understanding of his own radical difference from and inescapable implicataion in the signifying networks of all such ultimately deterministic "natural" categories. For, as de Man suggests here, the future of literature now depends upon the critics and not upon the poets. The nearly inaccessible zone where the very existence of the literary work is being decided; the impenetrable zone of darkness that one writer must become for another if literary history is to go on; the paradox of enacting even as one puts into question the aesthetics of "spectral rapport" or "critical romance"; and, as I shall suggest, the various aporias of deconstructive criticism represented in "Shelley Disfigured," are all allegorical figures of this ironic situation, the post-romantic predicament of the revisionary writer.

What de Man identifies in this early passage as the anti-natural imagination of Romantic or modern texts, the ironic ground of the intentional structure of their Romantic images, cast here in terms of Sartre's conceptions of Being as the *en soi*, the in-itself alone, reappears in later essays as all these other paradoxes, dilemmas, predicaments, ironies, and deconstructive aporias. As I see it, therefore, de Man's criticism is an allegory that has as its often barely discernible hero, who is given different names and masks to wear but who is always caught in situations of excruciating irony, this antithetical conception of the human imagination. Such a conception is radically anti-humanistic, not to say anti-human. No reproducible critical method or educational program, which has for its end the knowledge or perfection of man as the rational animal, the measure of all things, could ever emerge from such a conception of the literary imagination. Just what kind of critical practice or mode of teaching is implied by such a conception remains to be seen.

The reason, then, that Stanley Corngold's critique elicited from de Man the defense of his spectral rapport with other writers is that it threatened to expose the fact that de Man's criticism is what could fairly be called a Gnostic allegory—an allegory of his desire for an ironic, antithetical imagination, self-moving and unmoved by the world, self-determining and self-subverting. Corngold's critique suggests that de Man needs to find figures of such an imagination reflected back at him from his own haunting interpretations of the work of a Nietzsche, a Yeats, a Poulet, a Rousseau . . . or a Shelley.

If the Poulet essay as a paradoxical defense of literature and literary study represents most fully the prophetic manner of de Man's radically phenomenological work of critical history in the 1960s, then "Shelley Disfigured" (1979) can fairly stand for his later deconstructive criticism. It also represents, I contend, the nihilistic culmination of his writing career. This is not to say that "Shelley Disfigured" precludes the possibility of further deconstruction in other essays, whether by de Man or now by his heirs. Rather, I suggest that it undermines and undoes, prophetically betrays, as it were, all of the possible perspectives on the question of the relationship of history and form, especially that of literary history and literary form, and so any further writing on the subject by de Man or later deconstructors can only repeat and refine some feature or other of its forbiddenly systematic deconstruction of all principles of coherence, including, of course, those of a purely rhetorical nature. Every principle of coherence—philosophical, ethical, historical, aesthetic, psychological, linguistic and even rhetorical—succumbs to the "randomness," what de Man also terms the "madness" of words—to the arbitrary and inexorable power of verbal acts simultaneously to posit and subvert both the representational and reflexive or allegorical dimensions of texts. In other words, "Shelley Disfigured" enacts and valorizes a kind of irony (or "permanent parabasis")[29] which could be called "absolute" or "Romantic" but which I prefer to dub "sublime irony," since the power of language as characterized by de Man pervades his texts with the uncanny, dreadful calm or "lucid madness" associated with that recognition of some greater than human—all-too-human force, passion, or intention which has traditionally been identified with a daemonic conception of divinity.[30]

In "Shelley Disfigured," then, de Man faces the most general form of the question posed by critical romance or spectral rapport as a discipline of style. Assume that the literary critic in his attempt to characterize the intertextual relations between writers and their writings must employ a "naturalizing" discourse of aesthetic, historical, and ethical or psychological categories and metaphors, a discourse of interpretation or reading known to be in "error" or "fictional," or "revisionary" but nonetheless inescapable. Then how, except by means of a relentlessly self-deconstructive or radically revisionary irony of the type de Man discovers in Shelley's *Triumph of Life,* can the critic hope to subvert the tendency of his own words to monumentalize the authors on which he is writing for the expressed purpose of putting into question, as their own texts did before him, this very process of monumentalization. Like Byron's tipsy narrator in the preface to *Don Juan* the literary critic, heir to Aristotle and Longinus both, wants a hero but cannot afford to allow himself to take one without a large grain of self-mocking parody. Or, rather, the critic, if he is being honest, can only report that his own language enacts this ironic work of monumentalization and disfigurement simultaneously, in a perfect example of "permanent parabasis," whenever he begins to write, whether he intends it to or not.

In this respect, de Man's "Shelley Disfigured" performs what he claims the texts of Rousseau and, especially, of Nietzsche disclose to him and his readers.

> From a historical point of view, it is instructive to see a genetic narrative function as a step leading to insights that destroy the claims on which the genetic continuity was founded, but that could not have been formulated if the fallacy had not been allowed to unfold. This may well turn out to be an exemplary model in trying to understand the aberrant interpretation of Romanticism that shapes the genealogy of our present-day historical consciousness. Moreover, bearing in mind the analogy that operates, in *The Birth of*

> *Tragedy*, between genetic movements in history, and semiological
> relationships in language, the rhetorically self-conscious reading
> puts into question the authority of metaphors as a paradigm of
> poetic language. For if genetic models are only one instance of
> rhetorical mystification among others, and if the relationship be-
> tween the figural and the proper meaning of a metaphor is con-
> ceived, as in this text, in genetic terms, then metaphor becomes a
> blind metonymy and the entire set of values that figures so promi-
> nently in *The Birth of Tragedy*—a melocentric theory of language,
> the pan-tragic consciousness of the self, and the genetic vision of
> history—are made to appear hollow when they are exposed to the
> clarity of a new ironic light.[31]

De Man makes several important points in this densely packed
conclusion to his essay on Nietzsche's *Birth of Tragedy*. First of
all, he clarifies and refines in the first sentence his theory of
interpretation as a structure of blindness and insight. An analogy
may help. The narrative line of Joyce's *Ulysses*, despite all the
structural complications, appears to be leading, as the Homeric
myth would require, to a reconciliation between Bloom-Ulysses
and Stephens-Telemachus ony to result in the dramatization of
the impossibility of such happy climaxes. Similarly, *The Birth of
Tragedy*, for de Man, as a representative of ironic modern texts,
reaches some necessary conclusions that call into question the
method by which they were made possible, thereby calling into
question the genetic model of narrative organization for literary
and cultural history, even as they demonstrate the fruitfulness of
such error. A rapport between Nietzsche and his writing or between Nietzsche's critic and his reading of Nietzsche, such identification and such understanding, which underlies and
underwrites the conventional forms of literary history, can only
be, as in the case of Stephen and Bloom, "spectral."

Nonetheless, de Man goes on to claim that what he calls "the
aberrant interpretation of Romanticism" forgets or represses
such knowledge of epistemological uncertainty in the name of a
view of Romanticism as the secularization and internalization of
the Judeo-Christian deity's relation to his creation, expressed in
terms of a subject-object dichotomy dialectically sublimated by
an organic conception of the poetic imagination. Reading

Nietzsche the way he does recalls what Abrams, Frye, Bate, and Bloom would blindly forget: "all metaphor, Malachi. . . ." Finally, de Man concludes that Nietzsche's text discloses how ironic juxtapositions become transformed into sublime identities only to be deconstructed in their turn when metaphors reduce themselves back into metonymies. An example is the way the apparently univocal oratorical voice in *The Birth of Tragedy* turns into two competing voices, neither one of which can establish its authority without the appeal to a god-figure (Wagner) as its deus ex machina—a conventional strategy that betrays by its very means the unconventional end being sought.[32]

Consequently, for de Man, all theories of language as representational, all views of the self as expressive or phenomenological, and all visions of history as genetically or genealogically conceived, stand exposed as hollow idols in "the clarity of a new ironic light"—provided by, of course, de Man's own far from "sunny" reading. Thus, for de Man, the blindness and insight structure of interpretation takes the form, with regard to Romantic and "post-Romantic" works, of a naively historicist understanding of such works. This understanding is founded on specious, unquestioned analogies with and conceptions of nature, that major examples of Romanticism such as Nietzsche's *Birth of Tragedy* put repeatedly into question as inadequate theoretical formulations of textual processes and events. I suggest that de Man's own reading of Shelley's *Triumph* enacts most fully this vision of modern or Romantic texts.

The best overview of de Man's argument, strategy, and motive in "Shelley Disfigured" occurs in Jonathan Arac's recent masterful essay, "To Regress from the Rigor of Shelley: Figures of History in American Deconstructive Criticism," which analyzes *Deconstruction and Criticism* and *Textual Strategies*. Rather than attempting to replicate perfection, I will now quote extensively from Arac:

> Paul de Man's "Shelley Disfigured" stages a history so horrid as to scare us back into the text. Through reading *The Triumph of Life*, de Man argues that we are deluded when we think that events can be

linked in a historical continuity, whether narrative or causal or
both. For the "decisive textual articulation" of the poem is "its
reduction to the status of a fragment brought about by the actual
death and subsequent disfigurement of Shelley's body, burned after
his boat capsized and he drowned off the coast of Lerici." Moreover, "this mutilated textual model exposes the wound of a fracture
that lies hidden in all texts," and the final test of a reading will be
"how one disposes of Shelley's body." Thus, when de Man "claims"
for Shelley an exemplary "rigor," above all the stiffness of death is
imaged: *"The Triumph of Life* warns us that nothing, whether deed,
word, thought or text, ever happens in relation, positive or negative, to anything that precedes, follows, or exists elsewhere, but
only as a random event whose power, like the power of death, is due
to the randomness of its occurrence." This deep truth is imageless,
but inevitably we lapse into "recuperation," constructing "images
or narratives," as does de Man in this figuring of disfiguration as a
mutilated corpse. But why choose to figure history in the rigor of a
corpse? . . . *The Triumph of Life* can be said to reduce all of Shelley's
previous work "to nought." That is to say, reading "rigor" as a
wish, the power of de Man's reading would be greater if the rest of
Shelley's corpus were annihilated. More crucially, the power beyond
image and sequence that de Man calls the "positing power of language" occupies the place in his argument that the moment of inspiration does in Shelley's "Defense of Poetry." The famous image
of the fading coal catches the discontinuity Shelley poses between
the moment of power, of "original purity and force," and whatever
else there is. De Man and Shelley both set a gap between two states,
one powerful and timeless, the other human: it is only in the "intervals" between inspiration that "a poet becomes a man." For de Man
being a man means only the possibility of exhibiting an exemplary
rigor, while Shelley, as we have seen, hoped for more from human
life, at times. De Man has not misread Shelley, but he has decisively
chosen one alternative over the other. Has he chosen the more open
and flexible?[33]

The only thing I would add to this summary of de Man's deconstructive theory, practice, and influence is to claim that, as in
the Poulet essay, what de Man claims for his chosen author he
wishes for himself and enacts in his own text and that the primary
object of de Man's disfiguration of Shelley is not Shelley or any of
his precursors or disciples, poetic or critical. Rather the work
de Man's text would culminate by reducing to nought, the statue
that he would erect and deface, the critical romance he would
enact and climax, the ironically reflecting mask he would make

of Shelley only to pull it away again to expose the dark vacancy are: de Man's work, de Man's monument, de Man's romance, and de Man's mask.

I realize that my little addition commits the fallacy of attributing to an author as a source features of his text over which de Man claims no author has control:

> And to read is to understand, to question, to know, to forget, to erase, to deface, to repeat—that is to say, the endless prosopopoeia by which the dead are made to have a face and a voice which tells the allegory of their demise and allows us to apostrophize them in our turn. No degree of knowledge can ever stop this madness, for it is the madness of words. What *would* be naive is to believe that this strategy, which is *not* our strategy as subjects, since we are its product rather than its agent, can be a source of value and has to be celebrated or denounced accordingly.[34]

I also realize that de Man explicitly admits the repetition of this "madness" of monumentalization in his own text. It appears there in the guise of "the assertion of methodological claims made all the more pious by their denial . . . beyond good and evil . . . of piety."[35] So it hardly seems fair to place on de Man's shoulders the responsibility for a predicament that he argues persuasively has impersonal, linguistic bases. Yet, I would nevertheless contend tht de Man's conclusion demonstrates his text's reflexive complicity with the rhetorical structure of corrosive irony it discovers in Shelley's *Triumph of Life:*

> If it is true and unavoidable that any reading is a monumentalization of sorts, the way in which Rousseu is read and disfigured in *The Triumph of Life* puts Shelley among the few readers who "guessed whose statue those fragments had composed." To monumentalize this observation into a *method* of reading would be to regress from the rigor exhibited by Shelley which is exemplary precisely because it refuses to be generalized into a system.[36]

Coming as it does in an essay intended to be a rigorous example of deconstructive reading and originally written for a collection of such essays that cannot help but seem to be a manifesto for the Yale critics, such a conclusion must be for his own work and for the work of deconstruction in America what de Man claims Shelley's poem is for Shelley's career: a reduction of "all previous work to nought."[37] Thus de Man's position in "Shelley Disfigured" seems to enshrine nihilism as the principle of critical activity in our culture at this time. After all, "Shelley Disfigured" puts de Man among the few readers who, like Hardy in "Barbara of the House of Grebe," "'guessed whose statue those fragments had composed'" with regard to Shelley. And so this now defaced figure of Shelley in de Man's reading of *The Triumph of Life* "prophetically" places our critic among those who, like Yeats in "The Statues," it is presumed, are some of Shelley's "closest readers and disciples."[38]

Yet, despite my previous remarks, the relationship between de Man and his figure of Shelley is not simply a repetition of his relationship to Poulet or of Shelley's apparent relationship to Rousseau, in which the older figure stands as the source of a knowledge or wisdom that the younger figure aspires to possess despite all the sacrifices involved. De Man in the opening sections of the essay clearly attacks "the recuperation of a failing energy by means of an increased awareness," that rhetorical strategy—familiar from a reading in Wordsworth and his critical heirs—which underlies the humanistic conception of education in our culture. (After all, is not practical wisdom also said to be the end of education?) At the risk of sounding perversely paradoxical, I would say that de Man stands in relation to his Shelley and Shelley's Rousseau the way Zarathustra stands in relation to his corpse and buffoon:[39] that is, as the belated teacher of a prophetic irony discovered in and imposed upon the works of his predecessors, even as such irony undermines this rhetorical stance by exposing its projective, fictional, and self-defeating logic—its status as "error." As de Man implicitly suggests here at the conclusion of "Shelley Disfigured" and explicitly argues in "Rhetoric of Blindness" for Rousseau,[40] such sublime irony, in which the genealogical conception of relations between writers is subverted and shown to be "spectral," in "error," functions to enable a belated writer to assume the status of an earlier writer's ideal reader—his "Socratic" teacher, in effect. Such sublime irony can only compose an eccentric, provisional style incapable of being formulated into a program or method and thus passed on to others, without travesty.

In short, de Man would become the perfect ironist, whose steps, like that of the seducer in Kierkegaard's *Either/Or* (vol. 1), leave traces that begin to erase themselves as they are being made. The error (or is it mistake?) that de Man's critics have repeatedly made involves not only their failure to perceive this intention in de Man's texts, but, as well, its generally successful enactment there. In this connection, one should recall de Man's response to a student in the audience of English and Comparative literature people at Columbia University, when he first delivered "Shelley Disfigured" in the fall of 1978. The student naively but correctly asked, "Where is Shelley here?" De Man's only response was to smile, for him, rather broadly. "This impossible position is precisely the figure, the trope, metaphor as a violent—and not as a dark—light, a deadly Apollo."[41] Such may have been the words of enlightenment that de Man's smile deceptively masked and mistakenly assumed: "A shape all light,/ . . . as if she were the dawn."[42]

Notes

1. Visionary Criticism: An Introduction

1. See my "Revisionary Madness: The Prospects of American Literary Theory at the Present Time," *Critical Inquiry* (June 1983), 9(4):726–742.

2. See my "The Romance of Interpretation: A 'Post-modern' Critical Style," *boundary 2*, (Spring 1980), 8(3):259–283.

3. See my "Prophetic Criticism: Oscar Wilde and His Post-Modern Heirs," *Contemporary Literature*, (Summer 1984), 25(2):250–259.

4. See my "The Genius of Technique" in *Tragic Knowledge: Yeats's Autobiography and Hermeneutics* (New York: Columbia University Press, 1981), pp. 81–114.

5. See, especially, my "The Unsummoned Image: T. S. Eliot's Unclassic Criticism," *boundary 2* (Fall 1980), 9(1): 91–124.

6. See my "The Prophet of Our Laughter: Friedrich Nietzsche As—Educator?" in "Why Nietzsche Now?" *boundary 2* (Spring/Fall 1981), 9(3)10(1):1–18. This is a special double issue which I edited on Nietzsche's influence in modern culture.

7. See my "The Spirit of Levity: Nietzsche's Influence?" the introduction to a forthcoming collection of critical essays on Nietzsche and modern culture which I edited for Indiana University Press.

8. Friedrich Nietzsche, *The Gay Science*, Walter Kaufmann, trans. and ed. (New York: Vintage, 1974), pp. 271–272.

9. Walter Pater, "Apollo in Picarady" in *Miscellaneous Studies* (London: Macmillan, 1910), pp. 143–144.

2. The Temptations of the Scholar: Walter Pater's Imaginary Portraits

1. Walter Pater, *Plato and Platonism* (London: Macmillan, 1910, p. 60; W. B. Yeats, *Autobiography* (New York: Collier, 1965), p. 201. See J. Hillis Miller "Walter Pater, A Partial Portrait," *Daedelus* (Winter 1976), 24:97–113; see also Perry Meisel, *The Absent Father: Virginia Woolf and Walter Pater* (New Haven: Yale University Press, 1980). And Gerald Monsman, *Walter Pater's Art of Autobiography* (New Haven: Yale University Press, 1981). Harold Bloom has been the most aggressive of Pater's champions among contemporary critics. But perhaps

the most useful of recent studies are those included in Philip Dodd's collection of essays by various Paterians, *Walter Pater: An Imaginative Sense of Fact* (London: Frank Cuss, 1981); see especially R. M. Seiler's "Walter Pater Studies: 1970–1980" and Gerald Monsman's "On Reading Pater." For Oscar Wilde's remarks, see "Mr. Pater's Last Volume," *The Artist As Critic*, Richard Ellmann, ed. (New York: Vintage, 1968), pp. 229–236.

2. *Selected Prose of T. S. Eliot*, Frank Kermode, ed., (New York: Harcourt Brace Jovanovich, 1975), pp. 37–44, 68–76. Eliot's general critical position and his specific views of Pater are not so clear-cut as perhaps my summary make them seem. The ambiguities, ironies, and ambivalences of Eliot's critical prose need more study that it has so far provoked. Nevertheless, my summary is consistent with Eliot's apparent intentions, and with the view of Eliot enshrined in the critical tradition after him, a tradition that owes more to Pater than its more notable members are willing to admit.

3. See Joseph Frank, "Spatial Form in Modern Literature," in *The Widening Gyre: Crisis and Mastery in Modern Literature* (Bloomington: Indiana University Press, 1963), pp. 3–104.

4. Eliot, *Selected Prose*, pp. 38–39.

5. Jacques Derrida, *Of Grammatology*, G. Spivak, ed. (Baltimore: Johns Hopkins University Press, 1977), p. 158.

6. T. S. Eliot, "Arnold and Pater," in *Selected Essays* (New York: Harcourt Brace Jovanovich, 1964), pp. 389, and 391.

7. Harold Bloom, "Walter Pater: The Intoxication of Belatedness," in *Figures of Capable Imagination* (New York: Seabury Press, 1976), p. 19.

8. *Ibid.*, p. 27.

9. *Ibid.*, p. 38.

10. Walter Pater, "The Child in the House," in *Miscellaneous Studies* (London: Macmillan, 1910), pp. 172, and 196.

11. The two best studies of the romance genre in English are Eugene Vinaver's *The Rise of Romance* (New York: Oxford University Press, 1971) and Northrop Frye's *Anatomy of Criticism* (Princeton: Princeton University Press, 1971), pp. 186– 223. See also Frye, *The Secular Scripture* (Cambridge: Harvard University Press, 1976) for his most recent thinking on the structure of romance. My point in using the phrase "the romance of interpretation" is to suggest that literary criticism is the current form of what Frye calls the "wish-fulfillment dream" that a ruling group of our time projects for itself.

12. Paul Ricoeur, *History and Truth*, Charles A. Kelbley, trans. and ed. (Evanston, Ill: Northwestern University Press, 1965), p. 37.

13. Paul Ricoeur, *The Rule of Metaphor*, Robert Czerny et al., trans. (Toronto: University of Toronto Press, 1977), p. 303.

14. Paul Ricoeur, *The Conflict of Interpretations*, Don Ihde, ed. (Evanston, Ill: Northwesten University Press, 1974), p. 489.

15. Walter Pater, "The Bacchanals of Euripides," in *Greek Studies* (London: Macmillan, 1910), p. 64.

16. For the last named essay, see *Selected Writings of Walter Pater* Harold Bloom, ed. (New York: Signet, 1974).

17. Walter Pater, *The Renaissance: Studies in Art and Poetry* (London: Macmillan, 1910), pp. 231–232.

18. *Miscellaneous Studies*, p. 249.

19. Published originally in 1873 as *Studies in the History of the Renaissance*, and subsequently revised and retitled. The edition quoted from is the 1910 London edition.

20. Pater, *Renaissance*, p. 104.

21. William Wordsworth, *The Prelude: A Parallel Text*, J. C. Maxwell, ed. (Baltimore: Penguin, 1971), pp. 51–55.

22. Pater, *Selected Writings*, p. 192.

23. See Mario Praz, *The Romantic Agony* (London: Oxford University Press, 1933), pp. 23ff. For a detailed discussion of Shelley's poem in this context of the femme fatale.

24. Paul Ricoeur, *Interpretation Theory: Discourse and the Surplus of Meaning* (Fort Worth: Texas Christian University Press, 1976), p. 94.

25. Oscar Wilde, *The Artist As Critic*, pp. 366–367.

26. Pater, *Selected Writings*, p. 194.

27. Michel Foucault, *The Archaeology of Knowledge*, A. M. Smith, trans. (New York: Harper and Row, 1976) offers by far the most influential thinking in this regard.

28. Charles Harrold and William Templeton, eds., *English Prose of the Victorian Era* (New York: Oxford University Press, 1938), pp. 1706–1707. Although Newman's work is slightly before Pater's first published essays, it is for all intents and purposes practically adjacent, especially since Pater, an Oxford man, was strongly influenced by the controversies provoked by the Tractarians. See U. G. Knoepflmacher, *Religious Humanism and the Victorian Novel* (Princeton: Princeton University Press, 1965) for the best study of this side of Pater's work.

29. Pater, *Miscellaneous Studies*, pp. 175, 188, 194.

30. Pater, *The Renaissance*, pp. 199–200.

31. Walter Pater, "Wordsworth," in *Appreciations* (London: Macmillan, 1910), p. 63. Pater is here quoting Wordsworth himself from *The Prelude*.

32. Pater, *The Renaissance*, pp. 119–120.

33. *Ibid.*, pp. 120. See also Walter Pater, *Plato and Platonism* (London: Macmillan, 1910), p. 158, for Pater's assertion concerning the effects of learning on the appreciation of the forms of the world.

34. Pater, *The Renaissance*, p. 102.

35. *Ibid.*, p. 218.

36. *Ibid.*, p. 227.

37. *Ibid.*, pp. 124–125.

38. *Ibid.*, p. 99.

39. *Ibid.*, pp. 26–27.

40. Pater, "Postscript (Romanticism)," *Selected Writings*, p. 209.

41. Walter Pater, *Marius the Epicurean*, 2 vols. (London: Macmillan, 1910), pp. 55–91 for Pater's retelling of the myth. Pater makes it the basis of his presentation of Marius' "imaginative love" of all things literary.

42. Ricoeur, *Interpretation Theory*, p. 95.

43. Pater, *Marius*, 2:224.

44. *Ibid.*, pp. 62, 65, 67, 71.

45. See Paul Valéry, *An Anthology*, James R. Lawler, ed. (Princeton: Princeton University Press, 1977), p. 65. For further discussion of Valéry on this matter, see my "The Irony of Being Metaphorical" *boundary 2* (Winter 1980, 8 (2):329–348.

46. Pater, *Marius*, 2:171.

47. *Ibid.*, pp. 27–28.

48. Walter Pater, *Gaston de Latour: An Unfinished Romance* (London: Macmillan, 1910.

49. *Ibid.*, pp. 42–43. The purity with which Pater renders both the heights and depths of the visionary experience is unmatched by any of his Romantic precursors. Only the stark, almost totally blank desertion of Samuel Beckett's visions from *Molloy* can equal the sober intensity here.

50. Walter Pater, *Imaginary Portraits* (London: Macmillan, 1910), pp. 152–153.

51. Iain Fletcher, *Walter Pater* (London: Longmans, Green, 1959), p. 5. Despite the increase of interest in Pater, this remains the single best study. See Pater, *The Renaissance*, p. 135.

52. Ricoeur, *The Rule of Metaphor*, p. 308.

53. Pater, *Plato*, p. 11.

54. *Ibid.*, pp. 142–43. See also Pater, *Appreciations*, pp. 13–14, where Pater discusses "the freedom earned by the master of style."

55. Pater, *The Renaissance*, p. 4.

56. Martin Heidegger, *Early Greek Thinking*, David Krell and Frank Capuzzi, rans. (New York: Harper and Row, 1975), p. 101; Pater, *The Renaissance*, pp. xii–xiii. Actually, of course, Pater sufferred his fatal heart attack and died shortly thereafter in the arms of his sister, leaving as he did so his essay on Pascal suspended in midsentence.

3. The Genius of Irony: Nietzsche in Bloom

1. Harold Bloom, "The Anxiety of Influence: Coleridge" in *Figures of Capable Imagination* (New York: Seabury, 1976).

2. Harold Bloom, "Lying Against Time" in *Agon* (New York: Oxford University Press, 1982), pp. 59–60.

3. Harold Bloom, *The Breaking of the Vessels* (Chicago: University of Chicago Press, 1982), 3–4.

4. *Ibid.*, p. 45.

5. *Ibid.*, p. 82.

6. James Joyce, *Dubliners: Text, Criticism, Notes*, Robert Scholes and A. Walton Litz, eds. (New York: Penguin, 1968), p. 40.

7. Don Gifford, *Notes for Joyce* (New York: E. P. Dutton, 1967), p. 37.

8. Joyce, *Dubliners*, p. 41.

9. Joyce, *Dubliners*, p. 470. The allusions in the story to St. Margaret Mary Alacoque suggest that Eveline sees Frank largely in terms of a redeemer figure.

10. *Ibid.*, pp. 38, 37, 39.

11. Harold Bloom, *The Anxiety of Influence* (New York: Oxford, 1973), p. 117.

12. Friedrich Nietzsche, *On the Genealogy of Morals,* Walter Kaufmann and R. J. Hollingdale, trans. (New York: Vintage, 1967), pp. 77–78.

13. Bloom, *Anxiety,* p. 89.

14. *Ibid.*, pp. 162–163.

15. Friedrich Nietzsche, *Ecce Homo,* Walter Kaufman, trans. (New York: Vintage, 1967), p. 335.

16. *Ibid.*, p. 327.

17. My point is perhaps most succinctly put by Oscar Wilde in his brilliant dialogue "The Decay of Lying" in *The Artist as Critic,* Richard Ellmann, ed. (New York: Vintage, 1969), p. 307: "Paradox though it may seem—and paradoxes are always dangerous things—it is none-the-less true that Life imitates art far more than Art imitates life." For Nietzsche's only attitude on this Quixote Syndrome, see Walter Kaufmann, *Nietzsche: Philosopher, Psychologist, Anti-Christ* (Princeton: Princeton University Press, 1967), p. 72.

18. Percy Bysshe Shelley, "A Defence of Poetry," *The Norton Anthology of English Literature,* vol. 11, M. H. Abrams et al., eds. (New York: Norton, 1979), p. 787. See also p. 785: "all the great historians . . . make copious and ample amends for their subjection to facts, by filling the interstices of their subjects with living images."

19. Longinus, "On the Sublime: The Greek Text Edited After the Paris Manuscript, W. Rhys Roberts, ed. (Cambridge: Cambridge University Press, 1935), p. 67.

20. Friedrich Nietzsche, *The Gay Science,* Walter Kaufmann, trans. (New York: Vintage, 1974), p. 110.

21. *Ibid.*, p. 254.

22. Nietzsche, *Ecce Homo,* pp. 308–309.

23. See Patrich Bridgewater, *Nietzsche in Anglo-Saxony* (Leicester, Eng.: Leicester University Press, 1972), pp. 149–162, for a discussion of the Nietzsche phenomemnon in America earlier in the century.

24. See David P. Allison, "Destruction/Deconstruction in the Text of Nietzsche," *boundary 2* (Fall 1979), 8(1):197–222; and David Cousens Hoy, "Forgetting the Text: Derrida's Critique of Heidegger," *boundary 2* (Fall 1979), 8(1):223–236.

25. Jacques Derrida, *Spurs: Nietzsche's Styles,* Barbara Harlow, trans. (Chicago: University of Chicago Press, 1979), p. 139.

26. See my "The Irony of Being Metaphorical," *boundary 2* (Winter 1980) for further discussion.

27. Harold Bloom *Yeats* (New York: Oxford University Press, 1970), p. 81 and *The Anxiety of Influence* (New York: Oxford University Press, 1973), p. 85.

28. Bloom, *The Anxiety of Influence,* p. 107.

29. Harold Bloom, *A Map of Misreading* (New York: Oxford University Press, 1975), p. 31.

30. Harold Bloom, *Figures of Capable Imagination* (New York: Seabury, 1976), p. 29.

31. Bloom, *The Anxiety of Influence*, p. 8.
32. Bloom, *A Map of Misreading*, p. 5.
33. Harold Bloom, *Kabbalah and Criticism* (New York: Seabury, 1975), p. 120.
34. Harold Bloom, *Poetry and Repression: Revisionism from Blake to Stevens* (New Haven: Yale University Press, 1976), pp. 113, 292, 234.
35. See Bloom, "Lying Against Time," in *Agon*.
36. Harold Bloom, *The Flight to Lucifer: A Gnostic Fantasy* (New York: Farrar, Straus and Giroux, 1979), p. 193.
37. Bloom *Yeats*, p. 405.
38. Friedrich Nietzsche, *Thus Spoke Zarathustra*, R. J. Hollingdale, trans. (New York: Penguin), p. 178.
39. Bloom, *A Map of Misreading*, pp. 28–29.
40. Northrop Frye, *An Anatomy of Criticism* (Princeton: Princeton University Press, 1957), p. 186.
41. Immanuel Kant, *Critique of Pure Reason*, F. Max Muller, trans. (Garden City, N.Y.: Doubleday, 1966), pp. 385–386.
42. Bloom, *Poetry and Regression*, p. 292.
43. James Joyce, *Ulysses* (New York: Random House, 1961), p. 731.

4. Afterwords: Geoffrey Hartman on the Critic's Desire for Representation

1. Friedrich Nietzsche, *The Gay Science*, Walter Kaufman, trans. (New York: Vintage, 1974), p. 232. The entire aphorism (no. 290) sounds the major theme of the fourth and final book of this 1882 edition, characterizing the cultivation of a unique personal style as a transformation of a wild piece of nature into a sublime, almost English kind of garden. When Nietzsche reprinted *The Gay Science* in 1887, adding a fifth book which, among other things, seriously questions all aesthetic justification of existence in the light of his arguments from *The Genealogy of Morals* (1887), the emphasis of the entire volume shifts and *The Gay Science* is forcibly transformed into a document of Nietzsche's later philosophy.
2. Ironically enough, the phrase "the one thing needful" comes from Luke 10:40, and refers to Christ's injunction to Martha not to be anxious over domestic duties (her sister Mary having neglected these to listen to the Master's teachings), because "only one thing is needful": to learn the truth of everlasting life and to believe it.
3. Friedrich Nietzsche, *On the Genealogy of Morals*, Walter Kaufmann, trans. (New York: Vintage, 1967), p. 97.
4. Stanley Corngold, "Mann as a Reader of Nietzsche," *boundary 2* (Fall 1980), 9(1):32.
5. James Joyce, *Dubliners: Text, Criticism, Notes*, Robert Scholes and A. Walton Litz, eds. (New York: Penguin, 1968), p. 31.
6. Joyce, *Dubliners*, p. 35.
7. See my essay "The Romance of Interpretation: A Postmodern Critical Style," *boundary 2* (Spring 1980), 8(3):259–283 for a more detailed discussion of this issue.

8. See Paul Bove's "Variations on Authority: Some Deconstructive Transformations of the New Criticism," in Jonathan Arac and Wallace Martin, eds., *The Yale Critics, 1970–1980*, pp. 3–14 (Minneapolis: University of Minnesota Press, 1983) for a brilliant discussion of this question.

9. Denis Donoghue, "The Critic as Moses?" *New York Times Book Review*, November 1980, p. 32.

10. *Ibid.*, p. 32.

11. Michael Sprinker, "Aesthetic Criticism," in Arac and Martin, eds. *The Yale Critics, 1970–1980*, pp. 43–65.

12. Sprinker, pp. 61–62.

13. Geoffrey Hartman, *The Unmediated Vision* (New York: Harcourt Brace, 1954), p. 124.

14. Geoffrey H. Hartman, ed., *Psychoanalysis and the Question of the Text* (Baltimore: Johns Hopkins University Press, 1978), p. lx.

15. *Ibid.*, p. 95.

16. "Preface" to *Lyrical Ballads* in *Criticism: The Major Texts*, W. J. Bate, ed. (New York: Harcourt Brace, 1952), p. 337.

17. Geoffrey Hartman, *Beyond Formalism* (New Haven: Yale University Press, 1970), p. x.

18. *Ibid.*,

19. William Wordsworth, *The Excursion*, 4, *The Poetical Works*, 5 vols., Ernest de Selincourt and Helen Darbishire, eds. (Oxford: Oxford University Press, Clarendon Press, 1940–1949), p. 755.

20. As quoted in Geoffrey Hartman, *The Fate of Reading* (Chicago: University of Chicago Press, 1975), pp. 246–247.

21. Hartman, *Beyond Formalism*, p. 25.

22. Or, at least according to Hartman's view of Frye, *Ibid.*, pp. 42–60.

23. *Ibid.*, p. x.

24. *Ibid.*, p. 368.

25. Hartman, *The Fate of Reading*, p. 10.

26. Earlier in the essay (*ibid.*, pp. 38–39) Hartman spoke of the text-psyche relationship, as pictured by Richards, in precisely these terms of the mother-child nurturing experience.

27. *The Anxiety of Influence* (New York: Oxford University Press, 1973), p. 78.

28. "Byzantium" *The Collected Poems of W. B. Yeats* (New York: Macmillan, 1966), p. 244.

29. "Aesthetic Poetry," *Selected Writings of Walter Pater*, Harold Bloom ed. (New York: New American Library, 1974), p. 190.

30. Pater, *Selected Writings*, p. 107.

31. Hartman, *The Fate of Reading*, p. 39.

32. *Ibid.*, p. 26.

33. Yeats, *Collected Poems*, p. 191.

34. Hartman, *The Fate of Reading*, pp. 49–50.

35. *Ibid.*, p. 69.

36. Frank Lentricchia, "Derrida, History, and Intellectuals," *Salmagundi* (Fall 1980), 7(3):287.

37. Yeats, "High Talk," *Collected Poems,* p. 331.

38. For a discussion of Said's work, *Orientalism,* see my essay "The Romance of Interpretation," (see note 7 above) and for a discussion of Foucault's work in this vein, in particular, *Discipline and Punish,* see Paul Bove's "The End of Humanism: Michel Foucault and the Power of Disciplines," in *Intellectuals in Power: A Genealogy of Critical Humanism* (New York: Columbia University Press, 1985).

39. "Monsieur Texte: On Jacques Derrida, His *Glas,*" *The Georgia Review* (Winter 1975) 29:765.

40. *Romanticism: Vistas, Instances, Continuities* Geoffrey Hartman and David Thorburn, eds., (Ithaca, N.Y.: Cornell University Press, 1973), p. 42.

41. *Ibid.,* p. 55.

42. Hartman, *Beyond Formalism,* p. 359.

43. Hartman, *Romanticism,* p. 40.

44. Harold Bloom, *The Flight to Lucifer: A Gnostic Fantasy* (New York: Farrar, Strauss and Giroux, 1979), p. 235.

45. Hartman, *Psychoanalysis and the Question of the Text,* p. x.

46. *Ibid.*

47. *Ibid.,* p. xi.

48. Hartman, *The Fate of Reading,* p. 260.

49. Hartman, *Psychoanalysis and the Question of the Text,* p. 86.

50. Geoffrey Hartman, *Criticism in the Wilderness: The Study of Literature Today* (New Haven: Yale University Press, 1980), p. 20.

51. See especially, "Centaur: On the Psychology of the Critic," in Hartman, *Criticism in the Wilderness,* pp. 214–225.

52. Yeats, *Collected Poems,* pp. 211–212.

53. *The Autobiography of W. B. Yeats* (New York: Collier, 1966), p. 128.

54. Yeats, *Collected Poems,* pp. 213, 185.

55. Friedrich Nietzsche, *The Will to Power,* Walter Kaufmann and R. J. Hollingdale, trans. (New York: Random House, 1967), pp. 250–251.

56. Hazard Adams, ed., *The Statesman's Manual* in *Critical Theory Since Plato* (New York: Harcourt Brace Jovanovich, 1971), p. 467.

57. Wallace Stevens, *The Palm at the End of the Mind: Selected Poems and Two Plays,* Holly Stevens, ed. (New York: Knopf, 1971), p. 185. The title of Wallace Stevens' poem is "Of Bright & Blue Birds & The Gala Sun."

58. Northrop Frye, *Anatomy of Criticism* (Princeton: Princeton University Press, 1957), p. 193; Harold Bloom, *A Map of Misreading* (New York: Oxford University Press, 1975), p. 4.

59. Nietzsche, *The Will to Power,* p. 469.

60. Nietzsche, *The Will To Power,* p. 521; Ronald Hayman, *Nietzsche: A Critical Life* (New York: Oxford University Press, 1980), p. 336.

61. Geoffrey Hartman, *Saving the Text: Literature/Derrida/Philosophy* (Baltimore: Johns Hopkins University Press, 1981). Hereafter all references to this book (abbreviated as *ST*) will be given in the text with appropriate page numbers.

62. Nietzsche, *Thus Spoke Zarathustra,* R. J. Hollingdale, Trans. (New York: Penquin, 1969), p. 89.

63. "The Solitary Reaper" in *Selected Poems and Prefaces of William Words-worth,* Jack Stillinger, ed. (Boston: Houghton Mifflin, 1965), pp. 367–368.

5. Against Nature: On Northrop Frye and Critical Romance

Note on epigraph: As quoted from Blake's *Jerusalem* in Northrop Frye, *Fearful Symmetry: A Study of William Blake* (Princeton: Princeton University Press, 1947), p. 247; and *Anatomy of Criticism* (Princeton: Princeton University Press, 1957), p. 98.

1. *The Marriage of Heaven and Hell* in *The Poems of William Blake,* W. H. Stevenson, ed. (London: Longman, 1971), p. 111.

2. Northrop Frye, *Creation and Recreation* (Toronto: University of Toronto Press), p. 6.

3. Like Emerson, all that is not "me" is categorized as "nature." As the revisionary psychoanalysis of Jacques Lacan and Edward W. Said's recent social critiques of Western imperialism both demonstrate, the "other" as defined by our culture tends to assume the characteristics of the feminine, again as defined by our culture. Rather than prisoners, ethnic or racial minorities, or homosex-uals as the typical "others" which our society rejects, women, it seems, are the models of the excluded and alienated. I am also indebted in part for this insight in this chapter to Linda Cullum of Temple University.

4. Northrop Frye, *The Critical Path: An Essay on the Social Context of Literary Criticism* (Bloomington: Indiana University Press, 1971), p. 68.

5. Northrop Frye, *The Educated Imagination* (Bloomington: Indiana University Press, 1964), p. 56.

6. The phrase "the total body" of a writer's works recurs throughout Frye, but first appears in the citation given.

7. The influence of Robert Graves' *The White Goddess* on Frye is always as considerable as that of Spengler's *The Decline of the West* and Yeats' *A Vision.* The most helpful study of Frye's labyrinth is Robert D. Denham's *Northrop Frye and Critical Method* (University Park and London: Pennsylvania State University Press, 1978). Professor Denham's *Northrop Frye: An Enumerative Bibliography* (Metuchen, N.J.: Scarecrow Press, 1974) and his Introduction to *Northrop Frye on Culture and Literature: A Collection of Review Essays,* Robert Denham, ed. (Chicago: University of Chicago Press, 1978) also have been extremely helpful. Even though my conclusions about Frye differ radically from his, I must ac-knowledge my indebtedness to his important work.

8. Blake, in *Jerusalem,* provides Frye with the paradigm of this antithesis.

9. Northrop Frye, *The Return to Eden: Five Essays on Milton's Epic* (Toronto: University of Toronto Press, 1965), p. 50.

10. *Ibid.,* p. 51.

11. Frye, *Fearful Symmetry,* p. 247.

12. *Ibid.,* p. 47.

13. Northrop Frye, *The Stubborn Structure: Essays On Criticism and Society* (Ithaca, N.Y.: Cornell University Press, 1970), p. 240.

14. Northrop Frye, *The Fools of Time: Studies in Shakespearean Tragedy* (Toronto: University of Toronto Press, 1967), p. 38.

15. *Ibid.,* p. 90.

16. *Ibid.,* p. 39.

17. Northrop Frye, *Spiritus Mundi* (Bloomington: Indiana University Press, 1976), pp. 103–104.

18. Frye, *Fearful Symmetry,* p. 8.

19. Frye, *Fearful Symmetry,* pp. 139–140.

20. See also, Northrop Frye, *The Myth of Deliverance* (Toronto: University of Toronto Press, 1983). Frye applies his theory of comedy to Shakespeare's so-called "problem-plays." An expansion of psychic energy is the net-result of visionary deliverance.

21. Northrop Frye, *The Great Code: The Bible and Literature* (New York: Harcourt Brace Jovanovich, 1982), p. 141.

22. Northrop Frye, *T. S. Eliot,* 2d ed. (New York: Capricorn Books, 1963, 1972), p. 41. Frye is quoting Eliot here from the latter's essay on John Marston in T. S. Eliot, *Selected Essays* (London: Faber, 1932), p. 232.

23. Northrop Frye, *The Well-Tempered Critic* (Bloomington: Indiana University Press, 1963), pp. 44–45.

24. See "Forming Fours," in Robert Denham, ed., *Northrop Frye on Culture and Literature,* p. 122 (Chicago: University of Chicago Press, 1978). This is Frye's review of C. G. Jung's *Two Essays in Analytic Psychology* and *Psychology and Alchemy* that originally appeared in *The Hudson Review* (Winter 1953).

25. See Frye, *Creation and Recreation,* p. 19 et passim.

26. See the preface to *The Great Code* as an example of the continuation of this notion in Frye's career: "A Scholar (especially) in an area not his own feels like a knight errant who finds himself in the middle of a tournament and has unaccountably left his lance at home" (p. xix). For one source of this figure for the scholar, see Matthew Arnold, preface to *Essays in Criticism:* First Series, Sister Thomas Marion Horton, ed. (Chicago and London: University of Chicago Press, 1968), p. 7.

27. Northrop Frye, *A Study of English Romanticism* (New York: Random House, 1968), p. 121.

28. My point is that certain kinds of male figures represent, like Dionysus and his avatars, Nature; they are her "champions," so to speak.

29. Frye, *Fearful Symmetry,* pp. 247–248.

30. Frye, *The Stubborn Structure,* p. 88.

31. Northrop Frye, *Anatomy of Criticism,* (Princeton: Princeton University Press, 1957), p. 119.

32. Robert D. Denham's discussion in *Northrop Frye and Critical Method* has been particularly helpful in clarifying all this.

33. Kafka represents the negative image or demonic parody of Frye's visionary quest.

34. Frye, *Anatomy of Criticism,* p. 321.

35. Frye, *The Stubborn Structure,* pp. 88–89.

36. I am thinking of Eliot's praise of "the mechanism of sensibility" which Donne possesses in "The Metaphysical Poets," enabling him to feel his thought as immediately as the odor of a rose and so unify his disparate experience;

similarly, I am thinking of Arnold's injunction in "The Function of Criticism at the Present Time" for poetry to be a criticism of life and so be united with, if still critical of, one's age; and finally, I am thinking of Coleridge's discussion of the Imagination in chapters 13 and 14 of *Biographia Literaria,* in which the unification of experience, of vision and reality, is asserted to be the creation of the secondary imagination. Of Wordsworth, more will be said shortly.

37. Frye, *The Great Code,* pp. 192–193.

38. *Ibid.,* p. 198.

39. That is to say, Frye's role, to an entire generation of scholar-critics, is that of the seducer.

40. Frye, *The Stubborn Structure,* p. 21.

41. See Fredric Jameson, *The Political Unconscious: Narrative as Socially Symbolic Act* (Ithaca, N.Y.: Cornell University Press, 1981).

42. Frye, *Anatomy of Criticism,* p. 187.

43. See Northrop Frye, *The Secular Scripture: A Study of the Structure of Romance* (Cambridge: Harvard University Press, 1976), p. 27 et passim.

44. Frye, *Anatomy of Criticism,* p. 186.

45. Harold Bloom, *A Map of Misreading,* (New York: Oxford University Press, 1975), p. 21.

46. See Frye, *The Secular Scripture,* p. 124.

47. Frye, *Anatomy of Criticism,* pp. 63–65.

48. *Ibid.,* pp. 118–119.

49. Frye's debt to Arnold's "The Study of Poetry" is most apparent here.

50. Frye, *Anatomy of Criticism,* pp. 345–346.

51. *Ibid.,* p. 354.

52. Frye, *The Well-Tempered Critic,* pp. 155–156.

53. Frye, *The Return to Eden,* p. 31.

54. Frye, *A Study of English Romanticism,* p. 109.

55. Frye, *The Critical Path,* p. 32.

56. *Ibid.,* p. 177.

57. Northrop Frye, *A Natural Perspective: The Development of Shakespearean Comedy and Romance* (New York: Columbia University Press, 1965), p. 159.

58. Murray Krieger, "Northrop Frye and Contemporary Criticism: Ariel and the Spirit of Gravity," in Murray Krieger, ed., *Northrop Frye in Modern Criticism,* pp. 6–21 (New York: Columbia University Press, 1966); Geoffrey Hartman, "Ghostlier Demarcations: The Sweet Science of Northrop Frye" in Krieger, ed., *Northrop Frye in Modern Criticism* and in Hartman's *Beyond Formalism,* pp. 23–29 (New Haven: Yale University Press, 1970); A. Walton Litz "Literary Criticism," in David Hoffman, ed., *Harvard Guide to Contemporary American Writing* (Cambridge: Harvard University Press, 1979); Frank Lentricchia, *After the New Criticism* (Chicago: University of Chicago Press, 1979); see also my reviews of Lentricchia's *After the New Criticism* and Wayne C. Booth's *Critical Understanding* (Chicago: University of Chicago Press, 1978) in *Contemporary Literature* (Winter 1982), 23:105–113.

59. Hoffman, *Harvard Guide,* pp. 65, 66.

60. Lentricchia, *After the New Criticism,* p. 26.

61. Frye, *Spiritus Mundi*, p. 11. Frye in his preface to *Spiritus Mundi*, p. x, calls this response to Fletcher the keystone to this book. Since it serves to disarm his rebellious heirs, it is no wonder that it appears so important to Frye.

62. Frye, *Spiritus Mundi*, p. 122.

63. See W. B. Yeats, *Essays and Introductions* (New York: Collier Books, 1961). Yeats' essay appears to have influenced several influential critics: Frye, Bloom, Hartman, Miller.

64. See my essay, "The Irony of Being Metaphorical," *boundary 2* (Winter 1980) 8(2):329–348, for a discussion of this topic.

65. See especially, J. Hillis Miller, *The Poets of Reality* (Cambridge: Harvard University Press, 1965).

66. Frye, *Fearful Symmetry*, p. 428.

67. W. B. Yeats, *Collected Poems* (New York: Macmillan, 1956), p. 204.

68. Frye, *The Great Code*, pp. 232–233.

69. Frye, *The Stubborn Structure*, pp. 5–6.

70. "The Acceptance of Innocence," a review of Samuel Putnam's new English translation of *Don Quixote*, in *The Canadian Forum* (December 1949) as reprinted in *Northrop Frye on Culture and Literature*, p. 163.

71. See Frye's fourth essay in *Anatomy of Criticism*.

72. Frye, *Anatomy of Criticism*, p. 309.

73. Jameson, *The Political Unconscious*, p. 74.

74. *Ibid.*, pp. 73, 75; see also my review of Jameson, "The Ideology of Romance," *Contemporary Literature* (Summer 1982), 23:381–389.

76. What Jameson does in his reading of Conrad's *Lord Jim* is to posit an unwitting antithesis between the novelistic insights and the romantic form, which corresponds, in Jameson's view, to Marx's self-conscious characterization, from *The German Ideology*, of the blind work of ideology in the work of German Romantic intellectuals. My objection to this procedure is that it subsumes Conrad to Jameson's view of Marx, i.e., it permits Jameson to "totalize" and appropriate Conrad in a way that grants the critic the superior role.

77. See my "The Ideology of Romance," pp. 382–383 for a fuller discussion.

78. Jameson would object to this revisionary reading of his text by saying I have done to him what I claim he does to Conrad. I would answer that there is no escape from this revisionary process.

79. Yeats, "The Circus Animals' Desertion," *Collected Poems*, p. 336.

80. Friedrich Nietzsche, *Twilight of the Idols* and *The Anti-Christ*, R. J. Hollingdale, trans. (New York: Penguin, 1968), p. 141.

81. Friedrich Nietzsche, *On the Genealogy of Morals* and *Ecce Homo*, Walter Kaufmann, trans. (New York: Vintage), p. 355.

82. Nietzsche, *Anti-Christ*, p. 186.

83. *Ibid.*, *The Anti-Christ*, p. 147.

84. Nietzsche, *The Twilight of the Idols*, pp. 40–41. Jacques Derrida in *Spurs: Nietzsche's Styles* (Chicago: University of Chicago Press, 1978) discusses Heidegger's reading of this passage in (Heidegger's *Nietzsche* vol. 1: *The Will to Power as Art*, David Farrel Krell, trans. (New York: Harper and Row, 1979). Derrida's point is that Heidegger fails to comment on Nietzsche's statement that with

Christianity truth was conceived in essentially feminine terms. I read Derrida's comment on Heidegger's lack of commentary here as an insight into the revisionary process of reading/writing by means of which one writer revises another writer. By inventing an attractive defect, privation, lacuna or absence, the later writer "womanizes" the earlier writer—an insight Nietzsche explicitly recognizes by naming his nemesis, Christianity, a woman. Such are the ways of the patriarchal tradition in post-Romantic writing. Or so it seems.

85. Frye, *Fables of Identity: Studies in Poetic Mythology* (New York: Harcourt, Brace, 1963), pp. 166–167.

86. Frye, *The Great Code*, pp. 175–176.

87. *Ibid.*, p. 88.

88. That is, it is an argument between competing visionary conceptions and the prophets of those visions.

89. The phrase appears in Frye, *Anatomy of Criticism*, p. 10.

90. Friedrich Nietzsche, *Daybreak*, R. J. Hollingdale, trans. (Cambridge: Cambridge University Press, 1982), pp. 14–15.

96. Frye, *The Great Code*, p. 137.

97. Frye, *Anatomy of Criticism*, p. 140.

93. Frye, *The Secular Scripture*, pp. 156–157.

94. Frye, *Anatomy of Criticism*, p. 97.

95. *Ibid.*, p. 98.

6. Paul de Man: Nietzsche's Teacher

1. Friedrich Nietzsche, *The Portable Nietzsche* Walter Kaufman, ed. and trans. (New York: Penguin, 1954, 1976), p. 175.

2. *Ibid.*, p. 179.

3. For a fuller discussion of such self-born mockery in Nietzsche, see my *Tragic Knowledge: Yeats's Autobiography and Hermeneutics* (New York: Columbia University Press, 1981), chapter one.

4. Nietzsche, *The Portable Nietzsche*, p. 131.

5. Stanley Corngold, "Error in Paul de Man," *Critical Inquiry* (Spring 1982), 8(3):489–507.

6. Three of de Man's most severe critics in recent years have been Gerald Graff, *Literature Against Itself* (Chicago: University of Chicago Press, 1979), Frank Lentricchia, *After the New Criticism* (Chicago: University of Chicago Press, 1980), and Edward W. Said, *The World, the Text, and the Critic* (Cambridge: Harvard University Press, 1983). For a discussion of de Man's deconstructive reading style, see Jonathan Culler, *On Deconstruction* (Ithaca, N.Y.: Cornell University Press, 1983).

7. See Lentricchia' chapter on de Man, "The Rhetoric of Authority" in *After the New Criticism* for the best discussion of these "phases" in de Man's career.

8. Corngold and de Man—on his response—argue over the literal version and semantic resonance of the following phrases from Nietzsche's notebooks: "wo etwas verfehlt werden *kenn,* wo der Irrthurn *stattfindet,*" (as quoted in Corngold, "Error in Paul de Man," p. 506). Corngold translates it as "Intelligence can exist

only in a world *in which something can go amiss, in which error takes place*—a world of consciousness" (p. 505). De Man translates the passage in *Allegories of Reading* (New Haven: Yale University Press, 1979), p. 102, as "Intelligence can only exist in a world *in which mistakes occur, in which error reigns*—a world of consciousness." In his response to Corngold in *Critical Inquiry* (Spring 1983), 9(2):509–514, de Man then translates the passage even more literally than his former student does as "The mention of intelligence *can only occur* in a realm *where something can be missed* (as one misses a target or a train), where (the) *error takes place*—in the realm of consciousness." I have placed the phrases in dispute in italics, for the convenience of philologically-minded readers.

9. Corngold, "Error in Paul de Man," p. 507.

10. *Allegories of Reading* (New Haven: Yale University Press, 1979), p. ix.

11. Corngold, "Error in Paul de Man," p. 507.

12. "A Letter from Paul de Man," *Critical Inquiry* (Spring 1982), 8(3):510.

13. For the best analysis of this strain in de Man, see Jonathan Arac's "Aesthetics, Rhetoric, History: Reading Nietzsche with Henry James," *boundary 2* (Spring/Fall 1981), 9(3)/10(2):437–454, especially pp. 444–448.

14. For de Man's meditation on masks and lies, see "Rhetoric of Tropes (Nietzsche)," in *Allegories of Reading*, pp. 103–118.

15. Paul de Man, *Blindness and Insight: Essays in the Rhetoric of Contemporary Criticism* (New York: Oxford University Press, 1971), p. 21.

16. De Man's most systematic statement of this position occurs in "The Epistemology of Metaphor," *Critical Inquiry*, 5:(1978), 13–30. See also Paul de Man "The Resistance to Theory," *Yale French Studies*, (Winter 1982), 63:3–20.

17. De Man, *Allegories of Reading*, p. 115.

18. De Man, *Blindness and Insight*, pp. 79–80.

19. *Ibid.*, p. ix.

20. *Ibid.*, p. 97.

21. Paul de Man, "The Rhetoric of Temporality," in Charles Singleton, *Interpretation: Theory and Practice* (Baltimore: Johns Hopkins University Press, 1969), p. 190.

22. De Man, *Blindness and Insight*, p. 97.

23. *Ibid.*, p. 98.

24. *Ibid.*, pp. 100–101.

25. See, De Man, "Lyric and Modernity," in *Blindness and Insight*, pp. 166–186, especially, pp. 170–173 on Yeats and pp. 184–186 on Baudelaire and Mallarmé. Paul de Man, at the opening of "Shelley Disfigured" especially refers to Yeats' "The Statues" as "a fine poem about history and form." Quoted in Bloom et al., *Deconstruction and Criticism* (New York: Seabury, 1979), p. 41. This remark, which contrasts sharply with Harold Bloom's sharp dismissal of the poem in *Yeats* (New York: Oxford, 1979), pp. 441–444 surely strikes a curiously antithetical note.

26. De Man, *Blindness and Insight*, p. 18.

27. *Ibid.*, p. 161.

28. Paul de Man, "Intentional Structure of the Romantic Image," in Harold Bloom, ed., *Romanticism and Consciousness*, pp. 76–77.

29. See, de Man, "Excuses" on Rousseau's *Confessions* in *Allegories of Reading*, especially pp. 300–301.

30. For a discussion of Romantic irony, see Anne Mellors, *English Romantic Irony* (Cambridge: Harvard University Press, 1981). For the daemonic conception of divinity, see Hans Jonas, *The Gnostic Religion* (Boston: Beacon Press, 1963), especially "The Two Gods," pp. 141–143.

31. De Man, *Allegories of Reading*, pp. 101–102.

32. De Man's argument on Nietzsche's *Birth of Tragedy* in "Genesis and Genealogy" in *Allegories of Reading* (pp. 79–102) is that even as Nietzsche criticizes the structure of Euripidean tragedy for its opening and closing invocations of a god, its highly rhetorical, even oratorical speeches, and its hysterical passions, his own text indulges in the very things he condemns. Such self-betraying irony, de Man argues, subverts Nietzsche's more polemical pronouncements on Wagner as the "re-birth" of the tragic spirit in the decadent modern world. In addition, Nietzsche's text ironically deconstructs itself, making it in fact closer to the self-destroying passions that possess the Greek tragic heroes than it would appear to be.

33. Jonathan Arac, "To Regress From The Rigor of Shelley: Figures of History in American Deconstructive Criticism," *boundary 2* (Spring 1980), 8(3):251–253.

34. De Man, "Shelley Disfigured," p. 68.

35. *Ibid.*, p. 68.

36. *Ibid.*, p. 69.

37. *Ibid.*, p. 66.

38. *Ibid.*, p. 41.

39. Nietzsche was, as an adolescent, an avid reader of Shelley. In the "Prologue" to *Thus Spoke Zarathustra*, he may be recalling the scene in "The Triumph of Life" where the Shelleyan narrator, after breaking off a branch from a tree, sees blood flow from the wound and discovers that what he supposed was a tree is actually Rousseau. Shelley, of course, is recalling in this scene Dante's famous discovery of Statius, Virgil's poetic master, also "buried," as it were, in a true shape of a tree.

40. De Man, *Blindness and Insight*, pp. 139–140: "instead of having Rousseau deconstruct his critics, we have Derrida deconstructing a pseudo-Rousseau by means of insights that could have been gained from the "real" Rousseau. The pattern is too interesting not to be deliberate."

41. De Man, "Shelley Disfigured," p. 64.

42. Harold Bloom, ed. *The Selected Poetry and Prose of Shelley* (New York: New American Library), p. 373. The lines come from "The Triumph of Life."

Index

Frye, Northrop (*Continued*)
169–71, 173–74, 187–88, 201–4; *Creation and Recreation*, 147, 149; *The Critical Path*, 148; "Criticism, Visible and Invisible," 160, 162–66; *The Educated Imagination*, 148–49; "Expanding Eyes," 182; *Fearful Symmetry: A Study of William Blake*, 152–55, 171, 183; *The Fools of Time*, 151; *The Great Code: The Bible and Literature*, 155–58, 167–68, 171, 184–85, 197–98, 246*n*26; "The Instruments of Mental Production," 186–87; *The Myth of Deliverance*, 246*n*20; *The Return to Eden*, 149–50; "The Search for Acceptable Words," 181; *The Secular Scripture*, 171, 202–3; *Spiritus Mundi*, 248*n*61; *The Stubborn Structure*, 150–51; *A Study of English Romanticism*, 158–60; *The Well-Tempered Critic*, 175

Gnosticism: in Bloom, 58–59, 61–62, 64, 82–84; in de Man, 224, 228; in Frye, 177, 202–3

Hartman, Geoffrey, 2, 93–145; and aesthetic humanism, 123, 127–28; on Bloom's *Anxiety of Influence* and family romance, 113–14; on Derrida, 115–16, 136–37; on Derrida and deconstruction, 140; on Frye, 180; on Frye's recovery of romance, 108; on Genet, 139; hermeneutics of indeterminacy, 125–27, 130; on New Criticism, 120; and Pater, 107; on Pater, 142; on I. A. Richards, 110, 243*n*26; on representation of the sublime, 121–22; romance, 101–4, 106, 109, 133, 138; and the romance of interpretation, 143; and the romantic poets, 105; Michael Sprinker on Hartman, 99–100; and style, 110–15, 117–21; on Paul Valery, 107–8; on Yeats' "Leda and the Swan," 125–27
——works: *Beyond Formalism*, 105; *Criticism in the Wilderness: The Study of Literature Today*, 98, 121–28; *The Fate of Reading*, 100; *Psychoanalysis and the Question of the Text*, 103, 119–20; "Reflections on Romanticism in France," 117; *Saving the Text*, 132, 135–37,

139–44; "Toward Literary History," 118; *The Unmediated Vision*, 102
Irony: in de Man, 235; in Nietzsche as a destructive influence, 68; genius of irony in Joyce's "Eveline," 66–67; romantic irony in Bloom, 62; *see also* Revisionism, irony of

Jameson, Frederic: on Frye in *The Political Unconscious*, 188–89; and the romance of interpretation, 190, 248*n*78; 248*n*76
Joyce, James: "Araby," 94–98; "Eveline" and the genius of irony, 64–67, 240*n*9

Lacan, Jacques: on the "Other," 245*n*3
Lentriccia, Frank: on Frye, 180–81
Litz, A. Walton: on Frye, 179–80
Longinus: "On the Sublime," 72

Newman, John Henry: *The Development of Christian Doctrine* and the "warfare of ideas," 127–28, 239*n*28
Nietzsche, Frederic, 6–8; his ascetic ideal, 69–70, 94; and Bloom, 67; his influence on Bloom, 82–83; Stanley Corngold and de Man on, 249–50*n*6; de Man on, 229–31; Epicurus, 74–76; "eternal recurrence," 85; and Frye, 201–3; Frye on, 198; and the irony of revision, 95; "parables of the demon," 71–72; ideology of romance, 97; and the romance of interpretation, 96, 134, 194–95; and Shelley, 251*n*39; on style and the "one thing needful," 93–94, 242*n*2; Zarathustra, 85, 87, 90, 205, 207
——works: *The Anti-Christ*, 190–93, 195–96; *The Birth of Tragedy*, 93; *Daybreak*, 200; *The Gay Science*, 7, 74–76, 93, 242*n*1; *On the Geneology of Morals*, 68–69, 94; *Thus Spoke Zarathustra*, 75–76, 84–86, 206; "Of the Vision and the Riddle" in *Zarathustra*, 84–86; *The Will to Power*, 133

Pater, Walter, 1, 9–53; on the aesthetic critic, 29–36; Eliot on Pater's aesthetic ideal, 15; on Goethe, 33; the House Beautiful, 35; on *La Giaconda*, 35; on Leonardo, 24–26; on the *Last Supper*,